Enter Through the Narrow Gate

It's All or Nothing

By
Danny Clifford

Copyright © 2021 Danny Clifford

All rights reserved

Published by:

Danny and Michelle Clifford

This book's written content may be reproduced and used to advance the Gospel message about Jesus of Nazareth, as being the only way to enter the Kingdom of Heaven.

The author guarantees all written contents are original and do not infringe upon the legal rights of any other person or work.

ISBN Universal: 978-0-9972888-6-5

Book Edited by: **Frank Kresen** and **Olorunlowu Darasimi**
Email: olorunlowudarasimi@gmail.com

Formatted by: **Brenda Van Niekerk**
brendavniekerk@hotmail.com

Cover Design by **Olorunlowu Abraham**
Cover Formatted by: **Brenda Van Niekerk**
brendavniekerk@hotmail.com

COPYRIGHT STATEMENT

All pictures from, "LUMO Project," are used with the permission from the Licensing & LUMO Coordinator, and were paid for by Heart and Soul Ministry.

These Images can be used in educational presentations, blogs, social media, with attribution to: http://www.LumoProjet.com

These images are not licensed for re-use in video, publishing, or other media and cannot be sold under any circumstances or used in any format for commercial gain. As the LUMO project produces its own publishing, photos cannot be licensed to other clients outside of FreeBibleimages.org.

You cannot redistribute this set of images online but you can create a link to the relevant page on FreeBibleimages.org to allow others to download these images under the same terms of download.

Downloaded pictures can be used in the retelling of Bible stories and narrative that are faithful to the Biblical account. They are not to be used in any context where the accompanying message is undermining the Christian faith and gospel. Last updated: January 5, 2016

TABLE OF CONTENT

EDITORS REVIEW 1
BOOK REVIEWS 2
DEDICATION 4
FORWORD 5
CHAPTER 1 4
    GOD'S PERFECT CREATION 9
CHAPTER 2 9
    WHAT HAPPENED IN EDEN 17
CHAPTER 3 27
    ABRAHAM'S PROMISE 29
    A SHADOW OF WHAT'S TO COME 29
CHAPTER 4 40
    PREPARE THE WAY 45
CHAPTER 5 60
    WHO IS GOD? WHO IS JESUS? 65
    WHAT ARE THEIR ROLES? 65
CHAPTER 6 69
    JESUS' MINISTRY 79
CHAPTER 7 104
    VALIDATING THE FATHER'S WILL 104
CHAPTER 8 119
    REPENTANCE 119
    GOD'S FIRST R-GATE OF SALVATION 119
CHAPTER 9 130
    RECONCILIATION 135

GOD'S SECOND R-GATE OF SALVATION 135
CHAPTER 10 143
    REDEMPTION 147
    GOD'S THIRD R-GATE OF SALVATION 147
CHAPTER 11 161
    REBIRTH 163
    GOD'S FOURTH R-GATE OF SALVATION 163
CHAPTER 12 172
    REGENERATION 175
    GOD'S FIFTH R-GATE OF SALVATION 175
CHAPTER 13 175
    DON YOUR ARMOR 193
CHAPTER 14 206
    WHY PRAY? 211
    DO MY PRAYERS REALLY MATTER? 211
CHAPTER 15 211
    HOW TO PRAY 217
CHAPTER 16 217
    THE MEASUREMENT OF FAITH IS HOPE 223
CHAPTER 17 223
    CAN I USE YOUR BOAT? 233
CHAPTER 18 243
    REWARDS - DEAD OR ALIVE? 245
CHAPTER 19 258
    THE CONDITION OF TODAY'S CHURCH 261
MY PRAYER FOR THIS BOOK 277
ABOUT THE AUTHOR 261

EDITORS REVIEW

I am a Christian Editor who has edited countless Christian books. But out of all these books, this is the first book that made me stop and question my relationship with God. I had to stop as I read through the book to work on myself spiritually and move closer to Him (God) whom I had previously reduced His importance in my life.

Enter through the Narrow Gate is an amazing, spirit driven, direct and factual book that will help direct you in the things of the Lord, encourage you to build your relationship with Him, and help you understand God more in His never ending attempt to move closer to us.

This book is direct and doesn't hide the facts that need to be to addressed by every Christian who has made up his/her mind to move closer to God and get to Heaven to reign with Him.

I have read countless books that hide the basic and most important facts that need to be known by each Christian who want to please God with his/her life, but this book is different. It is factual, direct and truth filled, backed up with Bible Verses to solidify the point that all the contents are true and they reveal what God has always wanted from every one that has accepted Him, for you to allow Jesus to be Lord over your life.

It is filled with truth and not judgmental. It directs one's path to the way and will of God, to help us build a beautiful relationship with Him and maintain it always. I'm confident that as you read through this book, you will realized I wasn't exaggerating, it is the truth. Read and enjoy this amazing work of God through Danny Clifford!

Editor

Olorunlowu Darasimi

BOOK REVIEWS

The central theme in the book is to "Enter through the narrow gate." The wide gate is the "easy" way, resting on one's laurels, seeking prosperity, and not willing to make any sacrifices. *"But small is the gate and narrow the road that leads to life, and only a few find it."* Matthew 7:13-14) Many Christian's assurance of salvation and spending eternity with God in heaven is a delusion.

Jesus intends for His words to jar us from complacency, to consider the genuineness of our commitment and relationship to Him. To enter the narrow gate of God's kingdom we must be willing to embrace by repentance both persecution and the ethics of the kingdom taught by Jesus in the Sermon on the Mount.

The heart of the book reveals the "Five R" gates of God's perfect plan of Salvation that each person must enter to receive salvation and establish a loving and obedient relationship with God, by becoming a believer and follower of Christ Jesus.

The illustrations in this book are beautiful, sometimes startlingly, and exquisite in detail. They add to and perfectly complement the patient and insightful interpretations of the various Scripture passages that convey the essential messages in *"Enter through the Narrow Gate."*

Editor

Frank Kresen

I love how the book quickly shifts the reader to the beginning of God's timeline, starting with Creation, then the fall of humanity, followed by an Eternal Covenant.

As Jesus is introduced and His ministry begins, He teaches to the masses. Signs, miracles, and wonders, are noted. As His ministry comes to an end, so does His life.

But what follows could be considered as scandalous as his radical teachings. A plan of salvation for the repentant sinner, regardless of how well or how wicked they lived their life. Eternal life for anyone who accepts Jesus as their Lord and Savior.

The consequences of compromising the True Gospel Message of Jesus Christ is, society has more influence on Christ's Church today, than the Christian Church effects and impacts the world.

The author ends the book with an accurate description of man's fleshly ministries and inventions that have invaded the majority of Christian Church's today, resulting in a perverted gospel message of prosperity, and messages designed to gain popularity with society and make you feel good because they do not mention sin, repentance, or hell, from the pulpit.

Our faith in Christ Jesus allows us to become obedient and willing servants, making it possible to carry this beautiful yet simple message of hope and salvation to a world that needs it more than ever. I strongly recommend this book for all Christians.

Michael Adcock

DEDICATION

Prophet of God, Daniel Senga, President and founder of JARME, International Revival of Portland, Maine. If God had not brought Prophet Daniel Senga from Kinshasa, Congo in Central Africa, to Portland, Maine, this book may never have been written. His prayers, edification, corrections, and Godly example have influenced me in my walk with Jesus.

The teachings in this book were taught to me by Prophet Senga and have inspired the writing of this book. I thank God from my heart for allowing Prophet Daniel Senga to be my spiritual mentor, Pastor, and friend.

Prophet Senga has recently written and published a new book **"Conditioned,"** from Amazon Books; (https://www.amazon.com/Last-Believer-Escaping-Conditioned-World/dp/0998186023). This book is a must read for Christians. Buy and read his new book,

Michelle, my beautiful wife and best friend, whose dedicated support, encouragement, and many hours of prayer, were instrumental in birthing this book. Thank you, sweetheart for your help in the clarity of the book's message and publishing this mighty work of God. You're God's daughter, a Lady of Honor, and a powerful prophetic servant in God's ministry. I love you forever.

Special Tribute to my Christian brothers in Pakistan. Ackram, Asher, Azazal, and Rocky, for your dedication to being true disciple's working diligently to spread the Gospel of Jesus, while being oppressed and persecuted in Islamic Pakistan.

When I visited with you in 2019, many souls gave their life to Jesus Christ, because of your special efforts and prayers. May God bless you, your families, and those you pray for, as you advance the Kingdom of Heaven in Pakistan.

FORWORD

As a young boy, whenever my parents gave me instructions or told me to something, I always asked "Why?" I had to know why.

Long ago, I remember my mom telling me, "Don't touch the red glowing area on top of the stove." I asked "Why?" She answered, "**Because I said so.**"

But her answer didn't satisfy my curiosity. Why couldn't I touch the top of the stove? I had to know why. So, one day I touched the glowing red top of the stove. Ouch! That hurt! I experienced why.

Knowing why can be a great motivating force. And, not knowing why may be a de-motivating factor, causing us pain, suffering, or even death.

When I was about six years old, my parents bought me a fishing pole and reel and took me fishing in the pond about two hundred feet behind our home. I loved fishing!

The next day I asked my mother if I could go fishing. She said, "No! Don't ever go to the pond alone. There must be an adult with you whenever you go to the pond. I asked why? Mom responded, you might slip and fall into the water and drown without an adult being with you. Do you understand?"

But her reasoning didn't satisfy my curiosity, so I told her "I took swimming lessons, and I know how to swim to safety. Why can't I go fishing?" She quickly answered, "**Because I said so.**"

While growing up, I heard the phrase, "Because I said so" so many times that I thought it was part of the answer to all my questions.

A few days later, my mother went shopping in Bangor, Maine about fifty miles away from our home in Lincoln. Mom left my older sister in charge to look after me. That afternoon, when I awoke from my nap, I thought, "I want to go fishing." So, I began to reason in my mind that if my mother knew how much I really enjoyed fishing, she would say yes

I could go without an adult. After all it was right behind my house and what harm could come to me fishing?

I convinced myself that no harm would come to me, and my mom wouldn't mind too much if I went fishing. So that afternoon I chose to disobey my mother's instructions. I snuck out the back door so my older sister wouldn't see me. I got my fishing pole off the back porch and went down to the pond behind our home.

There was a wooden wharf about 8 feet square floating out about ten feet off shore. It was anchored so it couldn't float away. The only way to get out onto the wharf was to walk on a thick wooden plank about fourteen feet long, two inches thick, and a foot wide. As I walked on the plank, it slowly bounced up and down with each of my steps until I made it to the wharf.

The water was about ten feet deep where the wharf was. As I stepped closer to the edge of the wharf to put my hook in the water, suddenly my feet slipped, and I immediately landed in the deep water and went under. When I came up to the surface, I was close to the wooden wharf. I tried to reach the top of the wharf, but my arm was too short to reach it.

I sank down under the water again, taking water into my mouth instead of air. I splashed around making my way back to the surface and I reached with all my strength to reach the wharf. But my fingers and arm were too short, so I began to sink down under the water. The last thing I remember seeing, was my fingers stretching to reach the slippery wooden dock. I missed my mark, I couldn't save myself. With my eyes still opened, I began to sink down underwater, with my arms reaching upwards.

The next thing I remember is opening my eyes in the hospital and feeling my mother's arms tight round my neck holding me close to her cheek. Her warm tears were running the side of my face, as she pressed her face to mine. I could hear her whispering saying, "Thank-you God for saving my son's life. My mind flashed back to her instructions: "Never go fishing without an adult, because if you do, you might die."

Right then, I learned why it was important to obey my parents. I understood from my experience, that if I disobeyed them, I could suffer consequences. I also learned that **knowing why** is a great motivating force in our lives. And, **not knowing why** is a disheartening factor that may cause us sickness, injury, or even death. Not knowing why may cause us to disobey divine instructions, resulting in our being enemies of God and separated from Him for all eternity.

Author,

Danny Clifford

CHAPTER 1

God's Perfect Creation

Here, in Genesis, we begin the most exciting and fulfilling journey imaginable as the Holy Bible, brings to light some of God's personality character traits, while clearly explaining His structured plan of creation and describing the responsibility and authority He gave to the human race when He created us.

God who is Spirit, said, *"Let Us make man in Our image, according to Our likeness; let them have dominion over the fishes of the sea, over the birds in the air, and over the cattle, over all the earth and over every creeping thing that creeps on the earth." So God created man in His own image; in the image of God He created him; male and female He created them*. (Genesis 1:26-27)

Adam was created in God's likeness, not a physical likeness because God has no physical body. But spiritually created in God's image holy, righteous, moral, and perfect in God's likeness. God created us fully equipped with the physical and spiritual senses we need to communicate and walk with Him.

Go created mankind a **spirit** being with a **body** of flesh that was holy, righteous, and pure, without sin. We were also created with an **eternal soul** to live forever and **a free will** to choose what we wanted.

The purpose of man's **spirit** is to communicate with God's Spirit, and in turn communicate what God's Holy Spirit says to our soul.

Our **body** of flesh contains the spirit and soul of man as long as the body remains alive. Our mind is part of our body and functions only in the physical realm. Our body of flesh is sensitive to the things of the flesh and natural physical surroundings. For example, sight, hearing, smell, touch, and taste.

The body sends information regarding the senses, emotions, desires, and needs, to the mind. The mind gathers information and articulates to the soul what the body wants. Initially, at creation, every thought function that went through Adam and Eve's mind was holy, righteous, and pure. It was all good, because no evil existed in humanity at that time.

Our **soul,** also known as the **heart of man**, is confined in the body. The soul of man is the real me and you; our personalities, likes, dislikes, and attitudes. The Soul of Man, is the decision-making part of us humans. The soul decides either to go with what man's spirit which is from God, communicates to the soul, or the soul could decide to go with what the body communicates, through the mind, to it. This process of decision making we refer to as our **free will**.

One of the most important traits God created in humanity is the ability to **freely choose** to accept and be obedient to God's will for us, or to reject God's will and do what we want to do.

God created us with an **independent will** so we could chose to love and obey Him or reject Him. A **free will** independent of God's Will. Humans beings are free to choose, to say, and do what we desire to do.

CHAPTER 1 - GOD'S PERFECT CREATION

We are not robots or puppets on a string who do whatever God tells us. Humans really are in charge and responsible for making their own choice.

God knew humans could not have a loving relationship with Him unless we have a free and independent will to decide for ourselves to accept and obey Him or reject Him in disobedience.

No matter what we decide to believe, God must honor what we choose, even when it goes against His Will, and structure of creation. God cannot go against His Own Word, therefore, God must honor our choices.

Though God is sovereign and all powerful, Scripture clearly tells us that He limited Himself, concerning the affairs of earth, to working through human beings. God has restricted Himself to working through human beings, to accomplish His Will on earth. God did this, even at the cost of becoming a human being. This is the story woven through-out God's Word. God needs human beings to ask for His Kingdom to come, and for His Will to be done, here on earth as it is in Heaven.

Without question, humans were forever to be God's link to authority and activity on earth. God chose from the time of creation to accomplish His will on the earth through humans, not independently of them.

What was God's intentions?

God's intentions are specific and clear. Initially, God gave Adam, Eve, and their descendants, dominion and authority over the entire Earth and all creation. *"Be fruitful and increase in number; fill the earth and subdue it. Rule over the fish in the sea and the birds in the sky and over every living creature that moves on the ground."* (Genesis 1:28)

Whatever God intended for Adam and Eve, He intended for the entire human race. The Bible says, *"When I consider your heavens, the work of your fingers, the moon and the stars, which you have set in place, what is mankind that you are mindful of them, human beings that you care for them?*

You have made them a little lower than the angels and crowned them with glory and honor. You made them rulers over the works of your hands; you put everything under their feet: all flocks and herds, and the animals of the wild, the birds in the sky, and the fish in the sea, all that swim the paths of the seas." (Psalms 8:3-8)

God loved Adam and Eve so much, that He gave them the dominion and authority over all earth's creation. Adam, and his future descendants, were to be God's managers of the earth. God's governor, representing God's Will on earth. The Bible confirms this by telling us, *"The highest heavens belong to the LORD, but the earth he has given to man"* (Psalms 115:16)

God didn't give ownership of the earth to man, But He did assign the authority and responsibility of governing His Will, on planet Earth, to humanity. We were created to represent God here on earth.

The Garden

God had planted a garden in the east, in Eden and in the garden, *"The Lord God made all kinds of trees grow out of the ground, trees that were pleasing to the eye and good for food. In the middle of the garden were the tree of life and the tree of the knowledge of good and evil."* (Genesis 2:8-9)

So, God took Adam and put him in the Garden of Eden to work in it and take care of it. God told Adam, You are free to eat from any tree in the garden; *but you must not eat from the tree of the knowledge of good and evil, for when you eat of it you will surely die.* (Genesis 2: 16-17)

God brought all the living creatures to the man to see what he would name them. So, Adam gave names to all the livestock, all the birds, and all the wild animals. When he had finished, naming all of them, God saw Adam had no suitable helper to help him.

We really can't imagine what it was like to be the first and only person on earth. It is one thing to be lonely, but to be the only human being on earth. Adam had no parents, and no other human to talk to. He had to learn to be a human all by himself.

God said, *"It is not good for the man to be alone. I will make a helper who is just right for him*." God caused Adam (the Hebrew name for man) to fall into a deep sleep and took a rib from his body and made the female species of humanity. Then, God brought her to the Adam.

Adam was pleased with his help-mate and said, *"At last!" "This one is bone from my bone, and flesh from my flesh! She will be called woman, because she was taken from man." That is why a man leaves his father and mother and is united to his wife, and they become one flesh."* (Genesis 2: 23-24)

God wanted a family of sons and daughters who could personally relate to Him, and He to them. The Bible says, *"Has not the LORD made them one? In flesh and spirit, they are His. And why one? Because He was seeking godly offspring."* (Malachi 2:15)

So He created Adam and Eve with the ability to reproduce spiritual beings, in exactly their likeness. Godly offspring to represent Himself on earth. The dictionary definitions define representation as: "a person to speak and act with the authority on the part of another; to be a substitute or agent for;" A representative is one who re-presents the will of another. A delegate usually being invested with the authority of the principal.

Re-presenting God is no small task. When the Bible says that mankind is the image and glory of God, It is telling us God was recognized in humans. (Reference I Corinthians 11:7)

In the first two chapters of Genesis, the Bible discloses God's deepest desire which is to relate to and fellowship with the people He created, and they with Him. God made us in His image so human beings could accurately represent God and His Will here on Earth.

Adam represented God's Will on earth. Adam was God's governor assigned to manage God's Will. The earth was under Adam's charge, he was the guardian and watchman. How things went on planet Earth, for the better or worse, depended on Adam and his descendants. Think about this for a moment. If the earth remained a paradise, it would be because of mankind. If things became messed up, it would be because of people. If the serpent ever gained control, it would be because of humankind.

Life was really good in the Garden of Eden. Adam and Eve chose to be obedient to God and followed the instructions He gave them. God's Holy Spirit dwelled in their bodies. Their body, mind, and soul were pure, knowing only God's goodness. No sickness, no disease, no physical aliment's, it was a magnificent relationship as God walked and communed with them in the cool of the day. *"Adam and his wife were both naked, and they felt no shame."* (Genesis 2)

God had created hundreds of fruit trees for mankind to eat from, and told Adam that only the fruit from the "Tree of Knowledge of Good and Evil" was off limits to humanity. God instructed Adam, before Eve was created from Adam, *"You are free to eat from any tree in the garden; but you must not eat from the tree of the knowledge of good and evil, for when you eat from it you will certainly die."* (Genesis 2:16-17)

In my imagination, I visualize one of Adams first conversations with his delightful new companion must have been about the rules of the garden.

God did not want robots who simply did what He wanted them to do. God wanted Adam and Eve to obey His structure of creation out of their love and trust for Him. This one restriction was not a difficult test. It was a simple test of their love, obedience, and trust in God.

God wants us to love Him and obey Him because we trust Him. True love requires a choice! If God had not allowed mankind the ability to choose **to do, "good,"** or **reject, "good,"** we would be serving God out of obligation, not choice.

God did not prevent or physically restrain in any way Adam and Eve from eating the fruit from the forbidden tree. They had access to the tree and the freedom to eat the forbidden fruit, if they chose to do so. However, there was a serious consequence for disobeying The Lord's instruction. He told Adam, *"**You will surely die.**"*

God put His very life and Spirit into us. He communed with us; we were His children, and **He was our Father**. Adam had a direct relationship with God that no human being has ever experienced except, Jesus Christ.

God's Creation was good, perfect in every way.

CHAPTER 2

What Happened In Eden

Before we learn the truth about what happened in Eden, we need to learn about another part of God's creation, the Heavenly angels.

The Bibles teaches us that God created the angels as spiritual beings. They were created holy, righteous, intelligent, having diverse spiritual shapes, and sizes, with names, and different responsibilities. They lived with God in the height of Heaven, performing worship and enjoying being around God and all His glory.

God put one of the powerful Cherub angels into an exalted position right over the throne of the universe and named him **Lucifer**.

Prophet Ezekiel tells us, this message came to me from the LORD, "Son of man, sing this funeral song for the king of Tyre. Give him this message from the Sovereign LORD. *You were the model of perfection, full of wisdom and exquisite in beauty. You were in Eden, the garden of God."*

"Your clothing was adorned with every precious stone—red carnelian, pale-green peridot, white moonstone, blue-green beryl, onyx, green jasper, blue lapis lazuli, turquoise, and emerald—all beautifully crafted for you and set in the finest gold. They were given to you on the day you were created."

"I ordained and anointed you as the mighty angelic guardian."

"You had access to the holy mountain of God and walked among the stones of fire. You were blameless in all you did from the day you were created until the day evil was found in you."

"Your rich commerce led you to violence, and you sinned. So I banished you in disgrace from the mountain of God. I expelled you, O mighty guardian, from your place among the stones of fire."

"Your heart was filled with pride because of all your beauty. Your wisdom was corrupted by your love of splendor. So I threw you to the ground and exposed you to the curious gaze of kings."

"You defiled your sanctuaries with your many sins and your dishonest trade. So I brought fire out from within you, and it consumed you. I reduced you to ashes on the ground in the sight of all who were watching."

"All who knew you are appalled at your fate. You have come to terrible end and you will exist no more." (Ezekiel 28:12-19)

Lucifer was created as the model of perfection, full of wisdom and exquisite in beauty. He was adorned with every precious stone beautifully crafted and set in the finest gold, given to him on the day God created him.

God ordained and anointed him as the mighty angelic guardian. He had access to God's holy mountain, and he walked among the stones of fire. Lucifer was holy, righteous, and good. He was blameless in all that he did, until **evil was found in Lucifer.**

"How you are fallen from heaven, O Lucifer, son of the morning! How you are cut down to the ground, you who weakened the nations! For you have said in your heart: 'I will ascend into heaven, I will exalt my throne above the stars of God; I will also sit on the mount of the congregation.

On the farthest sides of the north; I will ascend above the heights of the clouds, I will be like the Most High.' Yet you shall be brought down to Sheol, to the lowest depths of the Pit. (Isaiah 14:12-15)

Lucifer's pride caused him to devise a plan in his heart to assault God's throne above the stars of God.

- I will ascend to the heavens;
- I will raise my throne above the stars of God;
- I will sit enthroned on the mount of assembly, on the utmost heights of Mount Zaphon;
- I will ascend above the tops of the clouds;
- I will make myself like the Most High.

Pride overcame Lucifer. His plan was to lead one-third of Heaven's angelic being who sided with him in an all-out assault on the throne of God and rule everything by forcibly taking control of **God's Throne.**

It is vitally important for you to know and understand that **God is Holy**. And, **it is impossible** for evil (Lucifer and his evil angelic forces) to coexist at the same time and or in the same place with God.

Lucifer and his host of angels who followed him became enemies of God. There was no room for them in Heaven any longer. War broke out in heaven. Archangel Michael and his angels went to battle with Lucifer, also known as The Red Dragon, and his angels. Lucifer and his evil forces were defeated.

So Lucifer and the evil unclean angels, who supported him in his rebellion against God, were literally ejected from God's throne with all the quickness and power of lightning. They were cast down to planet Earth. They were confined and restrained to planet Earth and the atmospheric Heaven around Earth, by the command of God's Word.

Lucifer and his forces of evil spirits (unclean angels) were now enemies **of God** and **eternally separated** from God, **forever**.

When Lucifer was cast out of heaven to Earth, he was never again called Lucifer. He became the seducer, the deceiver of all humanity. His name changed. That age-old serpent became known by several other names, including the Serpent, Satan, meaning the Accuser, the Evil one," the "Wicked one," and "the Devil.

What Happened in Eden?

Satan entered the Garden of Eden in the guise of a serpent, the craftiest of all the animals God created. The serpent approached Eve and asked, *"Did God really say, 'You must not eat from any tree in the garden?"*

Eve told the serpent, *"We may eat fruit from the trees in the garden, but God did say, "You must not eat fruit from the tree that is in the middle of the garden, and you must not touch it, or you will die."* (Genesis 3:1-3)

Satan quickly contradicted God's instructions by saying, *"You will not certainly die."* Then, he planted a seed of doubt when he told Eve, *"For God knows that when you eat from it, your eyes will be opened, and you will be like God, knowing good and evil."* (Genesis 3:4-5)

Satan implied that God was strict, stingy, and holding back something nice from them. The serpent assured Eve that the forbidden fruit was good to eat and, when they ate it, they would be like God, knowing good and evil. Instead of trusting and obeying God, Eve focused on the one thing God had forbidden them to have. She listened to Satan's deceiving lie and after listening, she choose to reject God's instructions regarding eating the forbidden fruit and believe Satan's enticing deceptive lie.

"Eve looked at the fruit and saw that the fruit of the tree was good for

food and pleasing to the eye, and also desirable for gaining wisdom. She took some and ate it. She also gave some to her husband, who was with her, and he ate it." (Genesis 3:6)

When Eve presented the forbidden fruit to Adam who was close by, Adam didn't reject the fruit. He didn't remind Eve of God's command, *"not to eat the fruit from the tree of knowledge of good and evil."* Instead, Adam listened to Eve, and willingly and knowingly chose to rebel and disobey God, by eating the forbidden fruit.

Spiritual Death

Adam and Eve did not die physically when they ate the forbidden fruit. However, they suffered a far worse consequence. Humanity gained the knowledge of good and evil that Satan promised, but it wasn't at all what he had told them. Adam and Eve died a spiritual death when they disobeyed God's command.

When Adam ate the forbidden fruit, Satan's rebellious evil nature entered the heart of mankind and God's relationship with the entire human race was shattered.

Because God is incapable of coexisting with evil, God had no choice but to remove His Holy Spirit from dwelling in Adam and Eve's bodies.

In God's absence — evil entered and was birthed in the hearts of Adam and Eve. From that moment till now — evil has manifested itself in all human beings. The results left humanity spiritual dead to God.

In God's absence, evil existed.

Perhaps this illustration of light and darkness will help you better understand **good** and **evil**. If a person were to ask me "Does darkness exist?" My answer would likely be "yes." But, this is incorrect. The truth is darkness can only exist in the absence of light. If there is no light present, then darkness exists. However, where light exists there is no darkness. In the sun's absence, darkness exists. But when the sun comes around, darkness flees, it does not exist.

In a similar way, evil can exist only in the absence of God! **Where God's presence is, there is no evil**. When we choose to reject God and His Goodness, whatever we choose to do is evil, because it lacks God.

So, God who is good, created us with the ability to accept and believe in Him and his precepts of creation, or, to reject Him. However, once we reject God and His goodness, **whatever we choose to do outside of God is evil**.

God loves us more than we can imagine. But He could not stop or interfere with Eve's decision to believe Satan lie. He must have been deeply disappointed when Adam choose to reject goodness and choose to do evil. God had to honor what they chose. It is the blueprint by which God created creation, and God will never go against His own Word and concepts of creation.

How did we become "Sons and Daughters of the Wicked One?

The Bible says, *"When Adam sinned, sin entered the world. Adam's sin brought death, so death spread to everyone, for everyone sinned,"* (Romans 5:12). This means, since Adam and Eve's fall from God's grace in the Garden of Eden, every human being born (exception Jesus Christ the off spring of the Holy Spirit) **was** born, **is** born, and **will be** born as a spiritual **Child of the "Wicked One."**

Because of sin, Satan became the spiritual head over of the human race when Adam choose to disobey—and rebel against God's Word instructing Adam, *"You are free to eat from any tree in the garden; but you must not eat from the tree of the knowledge of good and evil, for when you eat from it you will certainly die,"* (Genesis 2:16-17). The moment Adam acted and ate the forbidden fruit—he gave the dominion God had given to humanity — to Satan.

It is very important for us to understand the dominion, and when I say dominion I mean the authority, that God gave to Adam and Eve to reign and rule over His creation on earth.

The authority God gave the human race was so all-inclusive that when Adam and Eve chose Satan's evil – over God and His goodness, this rebellious evil act caused the spiritual headship of the entire human race to shift from God our Creator to — Satan, a powerful created spirit cherubim created by God, who had rebelled against God and become God's enemy.

This is why Jesus referred to Satan as the *"ruler of the world"* on three different occasions, (John 12:31, 14:30, and 16:11) during His ministry on earth.

Disciple John told us, *"The whole world lies under the sway of the wicked one." We have become enslaved in a sinful nature.* (I John 5:19)

Apostle Paul, speaking of the spiritual power of sin, said, *"I know that nothing good lives in me, that is, in my sinful nature. For I have the desire to do what is good, but I cannot carry it out" …"For the sinful nature desires what is contrary to the Spirit, and the Spirit what is contrary to the sinful nature. They are in conflict with each other, so that you do not do what you want."* (Romans 7:18 and Galatians 5:17)

The consequences of Eve's decision to believe Satan's lie, and Adam's willingness to listen to Eve instead of obeying God's instructions, are, every human baby born from the seed of a man, was, is, and will be, born with a rebellious human nature.

1. - Born separated from God.

2. - Born enemies of God.

3. Born physically alive – but spiritually **dead to God**.

4. - Born under the spiritual headship of Satan. Born as spiritual Children **of the "Wicked one**, the Devil."

How does Adam's Sin affect human beings today?

God has no authority to intervene or intercede in our lives unless we ask God – and give Him permission to do something in our lives.

Spiritual warfare between Good (God) and evil (Satan) began on earth when Satan lied to Eve and stole God's prize creation. God's Holy Spirit was removed from Adam, Eve, and their descendants, leaving a spiritual void that was filled with Satan's rebellious sinful nature. Satan; the Devil became our spiritual father.

Today, billions of human beings are under the influence of evil spirits, drugs, alcohol, pornography, immoral sexual desires, television, food, work, sports, and the list goes on and on.

Satan has millions more of us chained and bound by sicknesses, diseases, and illnesses, because the motives of our heart are evil and sinful, opposed to God's goodness. We are born slaves to sin, chained to Satan's principalities, dominions, powers, and evil strongholds.

CHAPTER 2 - WHAT HAPPENED IN EDEN

Imagine for a moment what God must have felt when Adam and Eve sinned. Maybe you can feel a small portion of the love, hurtful pain, and compassion God must have felt, after creating everything in the Heavens and on earth. After creating mankind and after God gave Adam and Eve complete authority to represent Him on earth, Humanity was the Apple of God's eye. God loved us so much. Then one day, Adam and Eve rejected God and all God's goodness and believed Satan's lie.

Picture yourself as the parent of a 10-year-old son and a 9-year-old daughter whom you have raised from birth and love dearly. You enjoy playing with them, teaching and sharing all your goodness with them. You're preparing and planning for their future. You love them so much.

You trained them in the ways of your creation. There was only one thing that you told them not to do. You told them never to go with a stranger on foot or get into a vehicle with a stranger, no matter what the stranger said or did. You lovingly explained, if they rejected your instructions and disobeyed you, they would surely die!

Then one day, you watch from a distance as your two children are walking alongside a road when a strange vehicle slows down and stops right beside your children. They stop walking and turn facing the vehicle. They appear to be listening to someone in the vehicle. You want to interfere, but you can't because you promised your children you would not interfere in their affairs unless they asked you to. You wait for them to yell to you.

After a few seconds, you see the vehicle's back door open, and your daughter gets into the back seat. Your heart jumps as you watch. You hope your son chooses to scream for you, so you can help them. If he would just cry out for help, you could intervene and make things good, but he doesn't yell for your help, he just stands there watching.

After a few seconds your daughter appears from the back seat and walks towards her brother and offers him some food to eat. He accepts and begins to eat the food as they both get into the back seat of the car. The door closes, and the vehicle makes a U-turn and speeds away in the opposite direction from you.

Your heart is broken. All the love you gave them, all the goodness you taught them, all the time you spent with them, walking, talking, sharing, and planning their life are shattered. It's gone. You were a good parent. Of all the hundreds of things that you gave them to use and do, there was only one thing you instructed them not to do: Never go with a stranger on foot or in a vehicle, no matter what they say, or do, or promise, because when they do, they will die!

Your children focused their attention on listening and believing what someone else told them, instead of what you told them. They chose to do what they wanted to do, what their minds and emotions told them to do. They disobeyed your instructions.

All you ever wanted from them was to love you, trust you and obey you. You could have forced them to obey you by building a fence around them which would have prevented them from leaving your presence. But you knew that **true love requires choice**.

They had no knowledge of the evil that would come to them. They didn't think through the consequences of rejecting your instructions and believing in someone else's lying words. Only now do they realize it cost them their innocence, their separation from you, and their eternal human life. They disobeyed you, and it changed what you prepared and intended for them when you conceived and birthed them.

Let me ask you this question: If you were in God's position and you had created the Earth for your children to rule and reign, and now they were under the spiritual control of an evil sibling you had created years earlier; wouldn't you do all that you could do to get your children back?

Well, this is exactly what God did. God sent His one and only Begotten Son, Jesus, from eternity to earth two thousand years ago, to provide a **way** and a **right** for all human beings to choose to become Children of God instead of remaining, "**Children of the Wicked One**."

If Adam and Eve had eaten the fruit from "the Tree of Life" with the rebellious sinful nature in them, there would be no means for reconciling the human race back to God. So, God quickly removed Adam and Eve from the Garden of Eden, before they could eat from "the Tree of Life"

God said, "*The man has now become like one of us, knowing good and evil. He must not be allowed to reach out his hand and take also from the tree of life and eat, and live forever.*" (Genesis 3:22)

After Adam and Eve were escorted from the Garden of Eden, for the next one thousand years, the spiritual condition of mankind deteriorated.

The Lord saw how great the wickedness of the human race had become on the earth and that every inclination of the thoughts of the human heart was only evil all the time. So the Lord said, "I will wipe from the face of the earth the human race I have created and with them the animals, the birds and the creatures that move along the ground, for I regret that I have made them." (Genesis 6: 5-7)

Then, Noah was born. Noah found favor in the eyes of the LORD. So, God gave Noah the instructions for building an ark, how to supply the ark with food and animals, and told Noah His plans for destroying all mankind. So Noah did everything exactly as God had commanded him. (Genesis chapter 6).

When the flood finished and the ground had dried, God said to Noah, *"Leave the boat, all of you, you and your wife, and your sons and their wives. Release all the animals, the birds, the livestock, and the small animals that scurry along the ground so they can be fruitful and multiply throughout the earth."* (Genesis 8:15-17)

So when Noah, his wife, and his sons and their wives left the ark, *"God blessed Noah and his three sons saying "Be fruitful and multiply. Fill the earth."* (Genesis 9:1)

Then Noah built an altar to the LORD, and there he sacrificed as burnt offerings; the animals and birds that had been approved for that purpose. And the LORD was pleased with the aroma of the sacrifice and said to Himself, *"I will never again curse the ground because of the human race, even though everything they think or imagine is bent toward evil from childhood.* (Genesis 8:20- 22)

About 292 years after the flood, while Noah was still alive, Abram was born as a tenth-generation grandson to Noah, through the bloodline of Noah's son Shem.

Noah lived for the first 58 years of Abraham's life, and then three hundred and fifty years after the flood, Noah died at the age of 950 years old. (Reference; Genesis Chapters 8-11)

Five-thousand years ago, the history of a family's blood lines, the culture, and legends, were passed down through the generations by storytelling.

Abraham would have been told about his relatives Noah, Methuselah, and Enoch and their faith, obedience, and relationship with God. And, Abraham would have passed his history down to Isaac and Ismael as well.

CHAPTER 3

Abraham's Promise

A Shadow of What's To Come

Abraham is one of the greatest examples in the Prophetic Holy Bible for Christians to read and learn from in developing their intimate relationship with God. In fact, Abraham plays a prominent role and example of faith in Christianity, Islam, and Judaism.

Whenever I read about the many blessing that God promised those who love and obey Him, I often think about Abraham and how he listened, obeyed, and learned to trust in God for everything. Because he leaned on God for all things in life, God blessed Abraham and used him, throughout his lifetime, as an example for us to trust in God, and grow our relationship with Him.

What makes Abraham such a great example?

The answer is; God put Abraham through many, struggles, life-threatening situations, trials, and a very special test. One of the most difficult test God gave any human being was to Abraham. God asked Abraham to sacrifice his son Isaac, the son that God had promised Abraham's descendants would come from.

And through it all, Abraham believed and obeyed, he learned to trust in God, which caused his relationship with God to mature and grow. Abraham's faith in God allowed him to live his life from one circumstance and experience to the next, simply by depending totally on God.

Abraham developed a relationship with God that was so strong—that God showed Abraham His mysterious plan of salvation for the all peoples of the earth. Jesus told us, "*Your father Abraham rejoiced to see My day, and he saw it and was glad.*" (John 8:56)

God revealed to Abraham how he would bless the peoples of the earth through Abraham and his descendants. It all began with promises that God made to Abram. God made three promises to Abram early in their relationship:

5. "*I will bless those who bless you, and I will curse him who curses you; and in you, **all the families of the earth shall be blessed**.*" (Genesis 12:3)

6. Later on when God visited Abraham to tell him about Sodom, the LORD said, "*Shall I hide from Abraham what I am doing, since Abraham shall surely become a great and mighty nation, and **all the nations of the earth shall be blessed in him***? (Genesis 18:18)

7. God said to Abraham, "*Look as far as you can see in every direction, north and south, east and west. I am giving all this land, as far as you can see, to you and your descendants as a permanent*

possession." (Genesis 13:14-15 NLT)

8. God's third promise to Abram was Descendants. *And I will give you so many descendants that, like the dust of the earth, they cannot be counted! Go and walk through the land in every direction, for I am giving it to you."* (Genesis 13:17)

Ten years passed by and God had not fulfilled His promises to Abram. "The Lord spoke to Abram in a vision and said to him, *"Do not be afraid, Abraham, for I will protect you, and your reward will be great."* But Abraham replied, *"O Sovereign Lord, what good are all your blessings when I don't even have a son? Since you've given me no children, Eliezer of Damascus, a servant in my household, will inherit all my wealth. You have given me no descendants of my own, so one of my servants will be my heir."*

Then the Lord said to him, *"No, your servant will not be your heir, for you will have a son of your own who will be your heir."* Then the Lord took Abraham outside and said to him, *"Look up into the sky and count the stars if you can. That's how many descendants you will have!"* And Abraham believed the Lord, and the Lord counted him as righteous because of his faith. (Genesis 15:1-6)

The LORD told him, *"I am the LORD who brought you out of Ur of the Chaldeans to give you this land as your possession."* But Abram replied, *"O Sovereign LORD, how can I be sure that I will actually possess it?"* The LORD told him, *"Bring me a three-year-old heifer, a three-year-old female goat, a three-year-old ram, a turtledove, and a young pigeon."*

So Abram presented all these to him and killed them. Then he cut each animal down the middle and laid the halves side by side; he did not however, cut the birds in half. Some vultures swooped down to eat the carcasses, but Abram chased them away.

As the sun was going down, Abram fell into a deep sleep, and a terrifying darkness came down over him. Then the LORD said to Abram, *"You can be sure that your descendants will be strangers in a foreign land, where they will be oppressed as slaves for 400 years. But I will punish the nation that enslaves them, and in the end they will come away with great wealth.*

As for you, you will die in peace and be buried at a ripe old age. After four generations, your descendants will return here to this land, for the sins of the Amorites do not yet warrant their destruction."

After the sun went down and darkness fell, Abram saw a smoking firepot and a flaming torch pass between the halves of the carcasses. So the LORD made a covenant with Abram that day and said, *"I have given this land to your descendants, all the way from the border of Egypt to the great Euphrates River."* (Genesis 15:8-18)

God's Covenant with Abram was serious business. God was selecting what would become **the smallest and weakest nation of people on earth** to become His priest and examples for the entire world to follow. This was an incredible promise from God, and a huge responsibility for Abram.

Why did God send this strange vision to Abram?

I believe God's passing through the sacrifice Abram had prepared for Him, was a visible sign and assurance to Abram that the Covenant God just made with him was real. Gods plan to develop a nation of peoples he would call His own began with this vision revealed to Abram.

Sarai tried to help God fulfil His promise to Abram

During their marriage, Sarai had not been able to bear any children for her husband, Abram. So after living in Canaan for ten years, Abram's wife Sarai, took her Egyptian slave Hagar and gave her to Abram to be his substitute wife. Sarai thought she would build a family using Hagar.

In Abram's day, a married woman who could not have children was shamed by her peers and was often required to give a female servant to her husband in order to produce heirs. The children born to the substitute wife were considered to be the children of the wife.

It was common practice and appropriate during Abram's time for a husband to accept his wife's maid-servant as a substitute wife. So, Abram accepted his wife's servant, Hagar as a substitute wife which was according to the ways of the Chaldeans culture.

Did Abram's accepting Hagar as a substitute wife, show a lack of faith?

During Abram's lifetime, it was a family requirement commonly practiced to marry within the family so as not to have interracial marriages and mixed cultures with differing beliefs and gods.

Sarai was selected as Abram's wife because she was a half-sister to Abram. Sarai had the same father as Abram, but a different mother. She was also a descendant of Shem. When God promised Abram children, Sarai was Abram's wife, they were one. Abram's promise from God was also Sarai's promise.

So when Sarai tried to help God achieve his promise of children for her husband Abram, she was acting on man's traditions and ways. A son from a descendant of Ham (Ishmael) was Sarai's plan – but not part of God's plan.

God's plan for Abram's children was different than Sarai's and Abram's plan. God speaking through His Prophet Isaiah tells us, *"For my thoughts are not your thoughts, neither are your ways my ways," declares the LORD. "As the heavens are higher than the earth, so are my ways higher than your ways and my thoughts than your thoughts. "For my thoughts are not your thoughts neither are your ways my ways," declares the LORD.* (Isaiah 55:8-9)

Abram agreed with Sarai's proposal, to sleep the Egyptian maid servant Hagar. So Sarai took Hagar and gave her to Abram as a substitute wife. Hagar, being an obedient servant, submitted to her mistress's request. Abram had sexual relations with the Egyptian maid-servant and she became pregnant. But when Hagar knew she was pregnant, she began to treat her mistress, Sarai, with contempt.

Then Sarai said to Abram, *"This is all your fault! I put my servant into your arms, but now that she's pregnant, she treats me with contempt. The Lord will show who's wrong; you or me!"* Abram replied, *"Look, she is your servant, so deal with her as you see fit."* (Genesis Chapter 16)

Hagar Runs Away Pregnant with Abrams Child

The angel of the Lord found Hagar beside a spring of water in the wilderness, along the road to Shur and said to her, *"Hagar, Sarai's servant, where have you come from, and where are you going?" "I'm running away from my mistress, Sarai,"* she replied. The angel of the Lord said to her, *"Return to your mistress, and submit to her authority."*

Then he added, *"I will give you more descendants than you can count." "You are now pregnant and will give birth to a son. You are to name him Ishmael (which means 'God hears'), for the Lord has heard your cry of distress. This son of yours will be a wild man, as untamed as a wild donkey! He will raise his fist against everyone, and everyone will be against him. Yes, he will live in open hostility against all his relatives."* (Genesis 16:8-12)

So, Hagar gave Abram a son, and Abram named him Ishmael. Abram was eighty-six years old when Ishmael was born.

Thirteen years later, *"When Abraham was ninety-nine years old, the Lord went to him and said, "I am El-Shaddai — God Almighty. Serve me faithfully and live a blameless life. I will make a covenant with you, by which I will guarantee to give you countless descendants." At this, Abram fell face down to the ground.* (Genesis 17:1-3)

"I will make you the father of a multitude of nations! **I am changing your name.** *It will no longer be Abram. Instead, you will be called* **Abraham***, for you will be the father of many nations. I will make you extremely fruitful. Your descendants will become many nations, and kings will be among them! I will confirm my covenant with you and your descendants after you, from generation to generation."* (Genesis 17:4-7)

The Everlasting Covenant God made with Abraham is;

CHAPTER 3 - ABRAHAM'S PROMISE - A SHADOW OF WHAT'S TO COME

9. "I will always be your God, and the God of your descendants after you. And I will give the entire land of Canaan, where you now live, as a foreigner, to you and your descendants. It will be their possession forever, and I will be their God." (Genesis 17:7-8)

10. *"Regarding Sarai your wife, her name will no longer be Sarai. From now on her name will be **Sarah**."* "And, I will bless her and give **you a son from her**! Yes, I will bless her richly, and she will become the mother of many nations. Kings of nations will be among her descendants." (Genesis 17:16).

11. Then Abraham bowed down to the ground, but he laughed to himself in disbelief. How could I become a father at the age of 100? He thought. And how can Sarah have a baby when she is ninety years old? So, Abraham said to God, "**May Ishmael live under your special blessing!**" (Genesis 17:16-18)

12. But God replied, "**No**, Sarah your wife, will give birth to a son for you. You will name him **Isaac**, and I will confirm my covenant with him and **his descendants as an everlasting covenant**." (Genesis 17:19)

13. "As for Ishmael, I will bless him also, just as you have asked. I will make him extremely fruitful and multiply his descendants. He will become the father of twelve princes, and I will make him a great nation." (Genesis 17:20)

14. "But **my covenant will be confirmed with Isaac**, who will be born to you and Sarah about this time next year." (Genesis 17:21)

Abraham must have been stunned when God said, "I will bless her and give you a son from her! Yes, I will bless her richly, and she will become the mother of many nations".

Imagine what was going through Abraham's mind. For 13 years, Abraham thought God had already fulfilled his promise of a son when Ismael was born. But when God told Abraham, "I will confirm my covenant with **Isaac and his descendants** as an everlasting covenant."

God is telling Abraham your first son Ismael, who was birthed by Sarai's Egyptian servant Hagar, was not the son I promised you.

But Isaac, your wife Sarah's first son, **is the legitimate son**, the heir to my promised Covenant that I promised you.

It's as if Ismael was an illegitimate child. God would bless Ismael because of His promises to Abraham, but Isaac was the son whom God would confirm His Covenant with.

Terms and Responsibilities of God's Covenant with Abraham and his Descendants.

- *"Your responsibility is to obey the terms of the covenant. This is the covenant that you and your descendants must keep: Each male among you must be circumcised. You must cut off the flesh of your foreskin as a sign of the covenant between me and you. From generation to generation, every male child must be circumcised on the eighth day after his birth."*

- *"This applies not only to members of your family but also to the servants born in your household and the foreign-born servants whom you have purchased. All must be circumcised. Your bodies will bear the mark of my everlasting covenant. Any male who fails to be circumcised will be cut off from the covenant family for breaking the covenant."* (Genesis 17:9-14)

On that very day, Abraham took his son, Ishmael, and every male in his household, including those born there and those he had bought. Then he circumcised them, cutting off their foreskins just as God had told him. Abraham was ninety-nine years old when he was circumcised, and Ishmael, his son was thirteen. (Genesis 17:23-25)

Hagar and Ishmael were Sent Away

Sarah's pregnancy and Isaac's birth must have had a devastating

CHAPTER 3 - ABRAHAM'S PROMISE - A SHADOW OF WHAT'S TO COME

impact on Ismael. For 13 years he had been treated as Abraham's son and heir. But when Isaac was born, the future became uncertain because Isaac was the son of Sarah and Abraham, and Ismael was the son of a slave woman and Abraham.

When Isaac was weaned, *Abraham prepared a huge feast to celebrate the occasion. But Sarah saw Ishmael and her Egyptian servant; Hagar making fun of her son, Isaac. So, she demanded Abraham, "Get rid of that slave woman and her son. He is not going to share the inheritance with my son, Isaac. I won't have it!"*

Abraham was very upset. But God told Abraham, *"Do not be upset over the boy and your servant. Do whatever Sarah tells you, for Isaac is the son through whom your descendants will be counted. But I will also make a nation of the descendants of Hagar's son because he is your son, too."*

Abraham got up early the next morning, prepared food and a container of water and strapped them on Hagar's shoulders. Then he sent her away with their son Ismael. She wandered aimlessly in the wilderness of Beersheba until the water was gone. Then, she put the boy in the shade of a bush and sat down by herself about a hundred yards away. "I don't want to watch the boy die," she said, as she burst into tears.

But God heard the boy crying, and the angel of God called to Hagar from heaven, *"Hagar, what's wrong? Do not be afraid! God has heard the boy crying as he lies there. Go to him and comfort him, for I will make a great nation from his descendants."*

Then God opened Hagar's eyes, and she saw a well full of water. She quickly filled her water container and gave the boy a drink.

And God was with the boy as he grew up in the wilderness. He became a skillful archer and he settled in the wilderness of Paran. His mother arranged for him to marry a woman from the land of Egypt. (Genesis 21:8-21)

There is one promise that we haven't discussed yet and that is the promise God made to Abram when He said, "***All peoples on earth will be blessed through you.**" (Genesis 12:3).

When God changed Abram's name to Abraham, God promised this same promise again using his new name, "*Abraham will surely become a great and powerful nation, and **all nations on earth will be blessed through him**.*" (Genesis 18:18)

So, what is this promised blessing God spoke to Abraham?

God revealed the answer through an amazing teaching and revelation, in which God tested Abraham's faith and obedience like few men have ever been tested.

God instructed Abraham to sacrifice Isaac, the covenant son. The son God promised Sarah and Abraham that kings and many nations would come from.

The year was about 2050 BC, and God says to Abraham, *"Take your son, your only son, yes, Isaac, whom you love so much and go to the land of Moriah. Go and sacrifice him as a burnt offering on one of the mountains, which I will show you."* (Genesis 22:2)

What if this was you. What would you do? How would I respond to God's request?

Why did God ask Abraham to sacrifice his covenant son? Some nations were practicing human sacrifice, but God condemned this as a terrible sin. God did not want Isaac to die, but God did want Abraham to sacrifice Isaac in his heart.

God was testing Abraham's love and obedience. God needed to be assured that Abraham loved Him, more than he loved the promise that He gave Abraham,

What was Abraham's response to God's Request?

CHAPTER 3 - ABRAHAM'S PROMISE - A SHADOW OF WHAT'S TO COME

Abraham could have tried negotiating with God. He could have said, "No way." He could have said to God, "Why not Ishmael?" He could have even asked God for some time to think about it. But Abraham didn't dwell on God's request for a few days while he thought it over.

Instead, Abraham obeyed quickly. *"The next morning, Abraham got up early. He saddled his donkey and took two of his servants with him, along with his son, Isaac. Then he chopped wood for a fire for a burnt offering and set out for the place God had told him about."* (Genesis 22:3)

Abraham began a journey of about 60 miles that resulted in one of the greatest acts of obedience and faith in all recorded human history. His mission was to sacrifice his only son, whom he loved, on Mount Moriah.

Over the years, Abraham's loving and obedient relationship with God had matured to the point where Abraham's faith was pleasing to God. Abraham knew when God promised something, He always delivered on His promises. God never failed Abraham! So, in Abraham's heart he knew nothing was impossible for God!

Imagine being in Abraham's scandals for the next few minutes. You have been walking for two days trying to control your thoughts and emotions.

Headed for the mountain God said he would show you. The mountain where God asked you to sacrifice your son Isaac. The son God promised as your heir. The son you love immensely.

Some of us would be thinking, "I waited years for God's promise of land and descendants. Now, God wants me to give up my son Isaac, whom I love dearly, as a sacrifice. I already did that with Ishmael. If I sacrifice Isaac, what about my descendants, the land that God promised them, kings, and nations?"

On the third day of Abraham's journey, he looked up and saw the place in the distance. "Stay here with the donkey," Abraham told the servants. "The boy and I will travel a little farther. We will worship there, and then we will come right back." (Genesis 22:4-5).

So, Abraham placed the wood for the burnt offering on Isaac's shoulders, while he carried the fire and the knife. As the two of them walked on together, Isaac turned to Abraham and said, "Father?" "Yes, my son?" Abraham replied. "We have the fire and the wood," the boy said, "but where is the sheep for the burnt offering?" "God will provide a sheep for the burnt offering, my son," Abraham answered. And they both walked on together. (Genesis 22:6-8).

When they reached the place God had told him about, Abraham built an altar there and arranged the wood on it. He bound his son Isaac and laid him on top of the wood. Then he reached out his hand and took the knife to slay his son.

But the angel of the Lord called out to him from heaven, *"Abraham! Abraham!" "Yes," "Here I am," he replied. "Do not lay a hand on the boy," he said. "Do not do anything to him. Now I know that you fear*

CHAPTER 3 - ABRAHAM'S PROMISE - A SHADOW OF WHAT'S TO COME

God, because you have not withheld from me your son, your only son."

Abraham looked up and there in a thicket he saw a ram caught by its horns. He went over and took the ram and sacrificed it as a burnt offering instead of his son. (Genesis 22:9-13).

God was so pleased with Abraham that, *"The angel of the* L<small>ORD</small> *called to Abraham from heaven a second time and said, "I swear by myself, declares the* L<small>ORD</small>, *that <u>because you have done this and have not withheld your son, your only son</u>, I will surely bless you and make your descendants as numerous as the stars in the sky and as the sand on the seashore. Your descendants will take possession of the cities of their enemies,* **and through your offspring all nations on earth will be blessed, because you have obeyed me**." (Genesis 22:15-18).

The story of Abraham and Isaac truly is a shadow of what was to come. I don't know where or when God showed Abraham, *"The Day of The Lord."* It may have been when God told him to go to the land of Moriah. (Genesis 22:2). Or, it may have been when Abraham looked afar off and saw that mountain. Maybe this is when God showed him, *"the Day of the Lord."* (Genesis 22:4)

It could have happened when *"Abraham lifted his eyes and looked, and there was a ram caught in a thicket by his horns."* Perhaps this is when Abraham saw, "the Day of the Lord." (Genesis 22:13).

No matter when or where, and what version or translation of the Holy Bible you may read, Jesus said, *"Your father Abraham rejoiced at the thought of seeing my day;* ***he saw it and was glad.****"* (John 8:56)

I believe Abraham saw and fully understood the parallel between the ram offered on the altar as a substitute for Isaac, and Christ offered on the Cross as a substitute for us. Because Abraham obeyed God and was willing to give up his Covenant son Isaac — God gave up His Only Begotten Son, Jesus, to fulfil the First Promise he made to Abraham.

1. *"**All the families on earth will be blessed through you**."* (Genesis 12:3)

2. *"Shall I hide from Abraham what I am doing, since Abraham shall surely become a great and mighty nation, and all the nations of the earth shall be blessed in him?"* (Genesis 18:18)

When Adam and Eve disobeyed God, He removed His Holy Spirit from dwelling in our human body, because evil was in the hearts of mankind.

But, when Abraham obeyed God by offering to give up his son Isaac, "This is what the LORD says: *Because you have obeyed me and have not withheld even your son, your only son, I swear by my own name that I will certainly bless you. I will multiply your descendants beyond number, like the stars in the sky and the sand on the seashore. Your descendants will conquer the cities of their enemies. And through your descendants all the nations of the earth will be blessed—all because you have obeyed me."* (Genesis 22:16-18)

So, what is the Promised Blessing for All the Families of the earth?

Apostle Paul tells us, *"I was chosen to explain to everyone[c] this mysterious plan that God, the Creator of all things, had kept secret from the beginning."* (Ephesians 3:9)

As you read what I have written, you will understand my insight into this plan regarding Christ. God did not reveal it to previous generations, but now by his Spirit he has revealed it to his holy apostles and prophets.

And this is God's plan: *Both Gentiles and Jews who believe the Good News share equally in the riches inherited by God's children. Both are part of the same body, and both enjoy the promise of blessings because they belong to Christ Jesus.* (Ephesians 3:4-6)

*The mystery that has been kept hidden for ages and generations, but is now disclosed to the Lord's people. To them God has chosen to make known among the Gentiles the glorious riches of this mystery, **which is Christ in you, the hope of glory**.* (Colossians 1:26-27)

But when the fullness of the time had come, God sent forth His Son, born of a woman, born under the law, to redeem those who were under the law, that we might receive the adoption as sons. (Galatians 4:4-5)

Christ redeemed us from the curse of the law by becoming a curse for us, for it is written: "Cursed is everyone who is hung on a pole." He redeemed us in order that the blessing given to Abraham might come to the Gentiles through Christ Jesus, so that by faith we might receive the promise of the Spirit." (Galatians 3:13-14)

For you are all sons of God through faith in Christ Jesus. For as many of you as were baptized into Christ have put on Christ. There is neither Jew nor Greek, there is neither slave nor free, there is neither male nor female; for you are all one in Christ Jesus. And if you are Christ's, then you are Abraham's seed, and heirs according to the promise. (Galatians 3:26-29)

And because you are sons, **God has sent forth the Spirit of His Son into your hearts,** *crying out, "Abba, Father!" Therefore you are no longer a slave but a son, and if a son, then* **an heir of God through Christ**. (Galatians 4:6-7)

CHAPTER 4

Prepare the Way

Below is a historical timeline from Prophet Malachi's birth to John the Baptist birth.

- 435 B C – One of the seven wonders of the ancient world, A 43 foot Statue of Zeus made of gold, bronze, ivory, and ebony, was completed by Phidias. It was located at the sanctuary of Olympia, Greece, and erected in the Temple of Zeus.
- 430 B C – Malachi became a prophet of God.
- 390 B C – Aramaic language began to replace Hebrew as the Jewish language.
- 330 B C – Alexander the Great defeated the Persian Empire.
- 255 B C – The Hebrew Old testament Bible was translated into Greek and called the Septuagint. 70 to 72 Jewish scholars reportedly took part in the translation process. The scholars worked on it from (285-247 B.C.).
- 215 B C – Great Wall of China was built.
- 146 B C, the Greeks were finally defeated at the Battle of Corinth, by the Roman Empire. Rome completely destroyed and plundered the city of Corinth as an example to other Greek cities. From this point on Greece was ruled by Rome.
- 100 B C – Julius Caesar was Born
- 46 B C – Julius Caesar became dictator for life, then was assassinated two years later.
- 37 B C – "Herod the Great," was appointed King of Judea by the Romans.
- 30 B C – Cleopatra and her lover Marc Antony, both died by suicide.

- 25 B C – Virgin Mary, mother of Jesus, was born.
- 6 /5 B C – John the Baptist and Jesus were born

Malachi, the last book in the Old Testament, was the last of a long succession of prophets that had preceded him for hundreds of years. But after Malachi died, God didn't speak to the Children of Israel. It was like the heavens closed up. Not a single divine spokesman from God appeared before the Children of Israel for over four-hundred-years.

With the flip of a page in our English Bibles, we go from the Old Testament into the New Testament and John the Baptist and Jesus appeared on the scene in Palestine (formerly the Promised Land of Canaan).

The world that Jesus is about to be born into, bears little resemblance to the one we're leaving behind in Malachi's time. This is a time in history where the entire civilized world was relatively peaceful under Roman Rule. Traveling was easy and news spread quickly.

Aramaic had replaced Hebrew as the common language spoken and Greek was the universal written language throughout Palestine and the entire Mediterrian area. Israel and the rest of the known world at that time, were ruled by the Roman Empire.

Just as Christianity today is divided into different groups such as Baptist, Catholics, Lutherans, Methodists, Pentecostals, and non-denominational evangelical churches. Two thousand years ago, the Jewish religion also had distinct groups that influenced and controlled the Jewish religious behavior and the political issues of the day. They were the Pharisees, the Sadducees, and the Scribes (who were also called Teachers of the Law.

These three groups made up the Jewish ruling council called the **Sanhedrin**. Only a small minority of people actually belonged to these groups, but their strong influence on Jewish society was undeniable. However, there existed well-define differences in each of these groups.

The Pharisees were the largest of the groups, consisting of about six thousand members out of a total population of about one million people in Palestine, during Jesus time. The Pharisees saw themselves as a separate group of people. They were above the common people and saw that the common folk kept to the religious laws. The Pharisees claimed Mosaic authority for their interpretation of Jewish Laws. They were a strict group of religious Jews who advocated the obedience to the most-minute parts of the Jewish law and traditions.

They believed the Law was twofold, consisting of the Written Law and the Oral Law (the teachings of the prophets and the oral traditions of the Jewish people). Their main theological beliefs were angels and spirits, providence, prayer, necessity of faith, good works, the last judgment, the Messiah, and the immortality of the soul. The Pharisees ended up rejecting Jesus' claim to be the Messiah because; Jesus did not follow all their traditions and because Jesus associated with notoriously wicked people.

The Sadducees were a wealthy, upper class, Jewish priestly party, who rejected the authority of the Bible beyond the five books of Moses. They represented the authority of the priestly sanctions and privileges established since the days of Solomon.

They believed the Temple could be used as a place to transact and profit from business. The Sadducees and the Pharisees were the two major parties of the Jewish Sanhedrin. However, the Sadducees did not believe in resurrection, and they rejected the notion of spirits or angels. Whereas, the Pharisees believed in the resurrection and acknowledged spirits and angels.

The Scribes were called Teachers of the Law. They had knowledge of the law and could interpret and regulate Jewish laws, but they did not interfere with or assume any role in the guidance of the people. They were interpreters of the Law of Moses, who emphasized the traditions of the Law. Many teachers of the Law were Pharisees and it is presumed that some scribes were also Pharisees.

The Scribes could draft legal document such as contracts for marriage, divorce, loans, inheritance, mortgages, the sale of land, and the like.

As Christ Jesus comes on the scene, the Jews are unwilling subjects and slaves of the Roman Empire and had been for about 70 years. Roman oppression consisted of heavy taxation, confiscation, verbal and physical intimidations, physically beatings, sexual assaults, and crucifixions. Israel has been without a Prophet of God for over four hundred years

There was a growing anticipation that a great prophet or the Messiah, mentioned in the Old Testament, would come soon. (Reference Luke 3:15)

The Messiah the Jews were expecting was a mighty and powerful king who would physically come and set the children of Israel free, establish his kingdom as powerful and far reaching as King David's, and then, rule and judge the evil nations and peoples that had mistreated, abused, enslaved, and killed the Jews for so many years.

These are but two of many Old Testament prophecies of the Messiah to come.

- *"Therefore the Lord Himself will give you a sign: Behold, a virgin will be with child and bear a son, and she will call His name Immanuel.* (Isaiah 7:14)

- *"Rejoice greatly, Daughter Zion! Shout, Daughter Jerusalem! See, your king comes to you righteous and victorious, lowly and riding on a donkey, on a colt, the foal of a d*onkey. (Zechariah 9:9)

Looking back, it's crystal clear that God brought about the perfect sitting politically and religiously for the work of His Son. The Bible says, *"But when the set time had fully come, God sent his Son, born of a woman, born under the law, to redeem those under the law, that we might receive adoption to Sonship."* (Galatians 4:4-5)

Finally God's silence ends.

CHAPTER 4 - PREPARE THE WAY

It began just as prophet Malachi had written four-hundred years earlier, "*I will send my messenger, who will prepare the way before me. Then suddenly the Lord you are seeking will come to his temple; the messenger of the covenant, whom you desire, will come," says the LORD Almighty.* (Malachi 3:1-2)

About a year before Jesus was born, there was a Jewish priest named Zechariah. He and his wife Elizabeth were righteous in God's eyes, careful to obey all of the Lord's commandments and regulations. They had no children because Elizabeth was unable to conceive, and they were both very old.

One day, Zechariah was serving God in the Temple. While Zechariah was inside the Holy Place burning the incense, a great crowd stood outside, praying.

Suddenly, "an angel of the Lord" appeared to him, standing to the right of the incense altar. Zechariah was shaken and overwhelmed with fear when he saw him. But the angel said, "*Don't be afraid, Zechariah! God has heard your prayer. Your wife, Elizabeth, will give you a son, and you are to name him John. You will have great joy and gladness, and many will rejoice at his birth, for he will be great in the eyes of the*

Lord. He must never touch wine or other alcoholic drinks. ***He will be filled with the Holy Spirit, even before his birth****. And he will turn many Israelites to the Lord their God.*

He will be a man with the spirit and power of Elijah. He will prepare the people for the coming of the Lord. He will turn the hearts of the fathers to their children, and he will cause those who are rebellious to accept the wisdom of the godly."

Zechariah asked the angel, *"How can I be sure this will happen? I'm an old man now, and my wife is also well along in years."*

Then the angel said, *"**I am Gabriel**! I stand in the very presence of God. It was he who sent me to bring you this good news! But now, since you didn't believe what I said, you will be silent and unable to speak until the child is born. For my words will certainly be fulfilled at the proper time."*

Meanwhile, the people were waiting for Zechariah to come out of the sanctuary, wondering why he was taking so long. When he finally did come out, he couldn't speak to them. Then they realized from his gestures and his silence that he must have seen a vision in the sanctuary.

When Zechariah's week of service in the Temple was over, he returned home. Soon afterward his wife, Elizabeth, became pregnant and went into seclusion for five months. *"How kind the Lord is!"* she exclaimed. *"He has taken away my disgrace of having no children."* (Luke 1:8, 11-25)

Angel Gabriel visits Virgin Mary

In the sixth month of Elizabeth's pregnancy, God sent angel Gabriel to Nazareth, a village in Galilee, to a virgin named Mary. She was engaged to be married to a man named Joseph, a descendant of King David. Gabriel appeared to her and said, *"Greetings, favored woman! The Lord is with you!"* Confused and disturbed, Mary tried to think what the angel could mean.

CHAPTER 4 - PREPARE THE WAY

Don't be afraid, Mary," the angel told her, *"for you have found favor with God! "You will conceive and give birth to a son, and you will name him Jesus. He will be very great and will be called the Son of the Most High. The Lord God will give him the throne of his ancestor David. And he will reign over Israel forever; his Kingdom will never end!"*

Mary asked the angel, *"But how can this happen? I am a virgin."* The angel replied, *"The Holy Spirit will come upon you, and the power of the Most High will overshadow you. So, the baby to be born will be holy, and he will be called the Son of God. What's more, your relative Elizabeth has become pregnant in her old age! People used to say she was barren, but she has conceived a son and is now in her sixth month. For the word of God will never fail.*

Mary fully understood what God was asking of her to do. She knew she was favored by God to be asked, she also knew who the Child inside her was, and would become.

So, Mary responded to Gabriel, "I am the Lord's servant. May everything you have said about me come true." And then the angel left her. (Luke 1:26-38).

Mary who was a virgin and pledged to marry Joseph when Gabriel visited her. But before Joseph took Mary as his wife and had sexual relations with her, Mary already became pregnant with child.

Imagine for a moment being Mary as she explains her pregnancy to Joseph. Joseph must have been bewildered by Mary's description of who had caused her pregnancy and her attitude toward the child inside her. Joseph had never had sexual relations with Mary, therefore, he knew the child she was carrying was not his. Joseph must have been bewildered to believe Mary had done anything wrong, and he must have found it even more challenging to believe that the Father of the child Mary was carrying was *God*.

For a woman, not to be a virgin on the wedding night was a disgrace and shameful to her and her entire family and was grounds for voiding the marriage, and possible death. Now, visualize being in Joseph's situation.

Two thousand years ago, a Jewish marriage involved three basic steps:

1. Firstly, the two families agreed to the union.

2. A public announcement was made. At this point the couple was "pledged." This was similar to today's engagement of a couple except in Jesus's time, the "pledge" (engagement) could only be broken through death or divorce (even though sexual relations were not yet permitted).

3. The couple were married, and then, they began to live together.

Because Mary and Joseph were engaged, Mary's apparent unfaithfulness carried a severe social stigma. According to Jewish civil law, Joseph had the right to divorce Mary, and the Jewish authorities could have had her stoned to death. (Reference; Deuteronomy 22:23-24).

This was the situation and conditions that Joseph pondered. So, Joseph decided he had to break off the engagement quietly, because he did not want to publicly discredit and shame Mary. He loved her, but her pregnancy was disgraceful to him.

An angel of the Lord visited Joseph

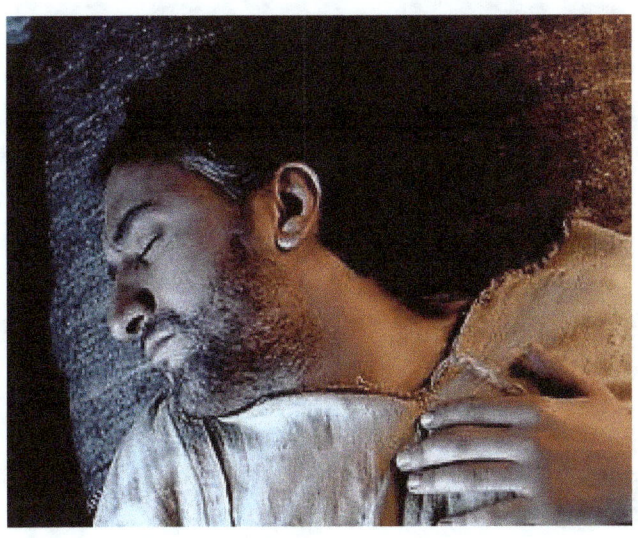

As Joseph considered the situation, an angel of the Lord appeared to him in a dream and said, "*Joseph, son of David, do not be afraid to take Mary as your wife. For the child within her was conceived by the Holy Spirit. And she will have a son, and you are to **name him, "Jesus**," for he will save his people from their sins.*" (Read Matthew 1:18-27)

When Joseph woke up, he did as the angel commanded him and took Mary as his wife, but he did not have sexual relations with her, until after Mary gave birth to Jesus.

A few days later, Mary hurried to the hill country of Judea, to the town where Zechariah lived. She entered the house and greeted Elizabeth. At the sound of Mary's greeting, Elizabeth's child leaped within her, and Elizabeth was filled with the Holy Spirit.

Elizabeth gave a glad cry and exclaimed to Mary, "God has blessed you above all women, and your child is blessed. *Why am I so honored, that the mother of my Lord should visit me? When I heard your greeting, the baby in my womb jumped for joy. You are blessed because you believed that the Lord would do what he said.*" (Luke 1:26-45)

The Birth of John the Baptist

When it was time for Elizabeth's baby to be born, she gave birth to a son. When the baby was eight days old, they all came for the circumcision ceremony. They wanted to name him Zechariah, after his father. But Elizabeth said, "No! His name is John!"

"What?" they exclaimed. "There is no one in all your family by that name." So, they used gestures to ask the baby's father what he wanted to name him. He motioned for a writing tablet, and to everyone's surprise, he wrote "**His name is John**." Instantly Zechariah could speak again, and he began praising God.

John grew up and became strong in spirit. And he lived in the wilderness until he began his public ministry to Israel. (Luke 1:57, 59-64, and verse 80.).

The Birth of Jesus

World history tells us that Caesar Augustus had become the leader of Rome when his great uncle, Julius Caesar, was murdered as a result of a conspiracy by many Roman senators. The same senate voted Caesar Augustus the first Roman Emperor.

The Bible says it was the Roman Emperor Augustus who decreed that a census should be taken throughout the Roman Empire. Word of the decree from Rome reached Nazareth, in Israel, when Mary was late in her pregnancy with Jesus.

Joseph was a blood descendant of King David, so to follow Jewish custom, he had to return to his ancestors' birthplace, which was Bethlehem, about ninety miles from Nazareth, to register for the collection of taxes. (Reference Luke 1:1-5)

When they arrived in Bethlehem, Joseph went to check at the inn for a place to stay. The inn was like a reception room at a private house or a public shelter. The town was crowded, and Joseph found no rooms for Mary. But someone was kind and offered them a place to stay in an animal manger near their home.

A manger was an area under the main home or near the home, where the lambs and goats were fed and able to bed down and were protected from wild animals and robbers. In the Old Testament, a manger is where the Passover lambs that were selected for sacrifice were kept for four days, prior to being sacrificed to God, before twilight on Passover eve.

Mary gave birth to her firstborn son, baby Jesus in an animal manger. She wrapped baby Jesus in rags and strips of cloth and laid him in an animal's feed crib with hay to keep him warm.

That night the most majestic baby announcement the world has ever known took place. Shepherds were in the fields nearby, guarding their flocks of sheep.

Suddenly, the angel was joined by a vast host of others; the armies of heaven, praising God and saying, "Glory to God in highest Heaven, and peace on earth to those with whom God is pleased." The Savior, yes, the Messiah, the Lord has been born today in Bethlehem, the city of David! And you will recognize him by this sign: You will find a baby wrapped snugly in strips of cloth, lying in a manger." (Luke 2:8-12)

CHAPTER 4 - PREPARE THE WAY

Seven Hundred Years before John the Baptist and Jesus were born, Prophet Isaiah prophesied of someone's coming who would be preparing the way for the Lord. He said, *"The voice of one crying in the wilderness. "Prepare the way of the LORD; Make straight in the desert a highway for our God. Every valley shall be exalted and every mountain and hill brought low. The crooked places shall be made straight and the rough places smooth. The glory of the LORD shall be revealed, and all flesh shall see it together. For the mouth of the LORD has spoken."* (Isaiah 40:3-5).

"Prepare" means "clear the way." Clear the obstacles away. In Prophet Isaiah's day, there were few roads, so the custom of sending representatives ahead to "prepare the way" for the visit of a monarch was customary practice. When a king traveled, or a majestic ruler was coming from a distant land to visit their area, the people in that area would build roads so that the royal chariot would not have to travel over rough terrain or get stuck in the mud.

"Highway" represents the hearts of the people who must be spiritually prepared by repentance for God's glory to be revealed on earth.

2000 years ago, whenever a high-ranking Roman official traveled, he was always preceded by a messenger, called a herald, who would have arrived in town ahead of the important person to announce that someone of prominence would soon arrive. So, when John the Baptist came on the scene in Israel, the Bible says, "a message from God came to John son of Zechariah, who was living in the wilderness. Then John went from place to place on both sides of the Jordan River, preaching that people should be baptized to show that they had repented of their sins and turned to God to be forgiven." (Luke 3:2-3).

People from Jerusalem, Judea, and all over the Jordan Valley went out into the wilderness to see and hear John's message. They were familiar with the Temple's rituals and processes for the forgiveness of sins, which involved a priest and an animal whose life and blood would be sacrificed on an altar. But when they arrived in the wilderness to see John, there was no animal to sacrifice, no altar, and no Temple priest.

Instead, they saw John, dressed in "clothing made of camel's hair, with a leather belt around his waist, preaching a message for them to repent of their sins from their heart, individually, and turn to God for forgiveness, because the kingdom of Heaven was near. John's message convicted them that true repentance required a "change of heart."

And this was his message: "*I baptize with water those who repent of their sins and turn to God. But someone is coming soon who is greater than I am, so much greater that I'm not worthy even to be his slave and carry his sandals. He will baptize you with the Holy Spirit and with fire.*" (Matthew (3:11).

Many identified with his message, confessed their sins, and were baptized by John in the Jordan River. They were baptized as an outward sign of their inward repentance. (Reference Matthew 3:1-2 and 5).

The Hebrew culture of baptism of water had existed for a long time. The Jews often baptized Gentiles (non-Jews) who had converted to Judaism. But to baptize a Jew as a sign of repentance was a radical departure from Jewish custom. John took a known Hebrew custom and gave it new meaning.

John's message was a big change for the Children of Israel, because John's message went against the attitudes and rituals of the Temple system and the doctrines of society, such as those of the Sadducees and Pharisees. In fact, John's baptism was not authorized by Jewish law. But

John was called to preach by God, armed with the Word of God, and "filled with the Holy Spirit, even before his birth." (Luke 1:15).

While John was preaching repentance and baptism, this heightened people of Israel's expectation and hope of the Messiah to come soon. John's message and its effect on the Jewish people stirred up the Levite Priests and Temple officials in Jerusalem. They wondered who John the Baptist was, so they traveled out into the countryside to ask John, "*Who are you?*" John told them, "I am not the Messiah." "*Well then, who are you?*" they asked. "Are you Elijah?" "No," he replied. "*Are you the Prophet we are expecting?*" "No." "*Then who are you? We need an answer for those who sent us. What do you have to say about yourself?*" (John 1:20-2).

John replied in the words of the prophet Isaiah: "*I am a voice shouting in the wilderness, 'Clear the way for the Lord's coming!'*" But the people asked again. "If you aren't the Messiah or Elijah or the Prophet, what right do you have to baptize?"

John told them, "*I baptize with water, but right here in the crowd is someone you do not recognize. Though his ministry follows mine, I'm not even worthy to be his slave and untie the straps of his sandal.*" This encounter took place in Bethany, an area east of the Jordan River, where John was baptizing. (John 1:25-28)

The next day, John saw Jesus coming toward him and said, "*Look! The Lamb of God who takes away the sin of the world!*

He is the one I was talking about when I said; 'A man is coming after me who is far greater than I am, for he existed long before me.' I did not recognize him as the Messiah, but I have been baptizing with water so that he might be revealed to Israel." (John 1:29-31 NLT).

Jesus had traveled from Galilee to the Jordan River to be baptized by John. But John tried to talk him out of it. "*I am the one who needs to be baptized by you,*" he said, "*so why are you coming to me?*"

But Jesus said, "*It should be done, for we must carry out all that God requires." So, John agreed to baptize him*. (Matthew 3:13-15)

After Jesus was baptized, when He came up immediately out of the water; "and behold, the heavens were opened, and he (John) saw the Spirit of God descending as a dove and lighting on Him (Jesus).

And behold, a voice from heaven said, "***This is My Beloved Son, in whom I am well-pleased and delighted!***" (Matthew 3:16-17 AMP Bible).

God, the Father used this occasion to testify with a heavenly voice that Jesus was His Beloved Son.

John the Baptist's Last Testimony

He has come from above and is greater than anyone else. We are of the earth, and we speak of earthly things, but he has come from heaven and is greater than anyone else. He testifies about what he has seen and heard, but how few believe what he tells them! Anyone who accepts his testimony can affirm that God is true. For he is sent by God. He speaks God's words, for God gives him the Spirit without limit.

The Father loves his Son and has put everything into his hands. And anyone who believes in God's Son has eternal life. Anyone who doesn't obey the Son will never experience eternal life but remains under God's angry judgment." (John 3:31-36).

One of the amazing teachings of Jesus ministry occurred when John the Baptist, who was in prison when he heard about the deeds of the Messiah Jesus. So, he sent his disciples to ask him, *"Are you the one who is to come, or should we expect someone else?"* (Matthew 11:2-3)

It appears John may have had some doubt about Jesus being the true Messiah. When the men came to Jesus, they said, *"John the Baptist sent us to you to ask, 'Are you the one who is to come, or should we expect someone else?'"*

At the time John was imprisoned, Jesus cured many who had diseases, sicknesses, and evil spirits, and had given sight to many who were blind. So, Jesus told John' messengers, *"Go back and report to John what you have seen and heard: The blind receive sight, the lame walks, those who have leprosy are cleansed, the deaf hears, the dead are raised, and the good news is proclaimed to the poor. Blessed is anyone who does not stumble on account of me."* (Luke 7:20-23)

What prompted John to ask Jesus, "Are you really the Messiah?"

John the Baptist had proclaimed *"Jesus is the Son of God"* and identified Jesus as the *"Messiah"* when he baptized him. Some think John was weakened by being in prison and facing death, and for this reason he lost some faith and doubted while under persecution.

But my personal speculation is; John assumed from what he was taught by the Old Testament scrolls and writings that the Messiah would come and establish His kingdom and then the Messiah would set up the judgment.

So, when John heard that Jesus was performing good deeds of healing, casting out demons, raising dead corpses to life, and performing many other miracles and still preaching the Good News of the Kingdom of Heaven, it may have confused John. It was not what John had expected. John didn't understand God's "Day of Grace" would last more than 2000 years. John didn't understand that it would be more than 2000 years before God would judge the world.

No matter what John's reasoning was, the Bible says *John sent his disciples to ask Jesus, "Are you the one that is to come, or should we expect someone else?"*

After John's disciples hear what Jesus told them, they left. When they left, Jesus told the multitudes there, *"Truly I tell you, among those born of women there has not risen anyone greater than John the Baptist; yet whoever is least in the kingdom of Heaven is greater than he."* (Matthew 11:11)

How Can Someone least in the Kingdom of Heaven, be greater than John the Baptist?

Today, you and I have the complete Holy Bible, we have the Holy Spirit of God available to teach us all things. Today, the least person in the kingdom of Heaven sees and understands the finished work of,

CHAPTER 4 - PREPARE THE WAY

"Messiah Jesus."

This is why the night before Jesus was crucified, He told his disciples, "*I no longer call you servants, because a servant does not know his master's business. Instead I have called you friends, for everything that I learned from my Father I have made known to you.*" (John 15:15)

Are you looking for a different kingdom of heaven than what Jesus taught? Is your expectation of the kingdom that Jesus ushered in is one of physical wealth and earthly riches, with little or no persecution, as you serve in the Kingdom of God? Are you asking Jesus, "Is this the kingdom that is to come, or should we expect another?"

John the Baptist prepared the people for the coming of the Lord Jesus. He preached that they should repent from their sins and turn to God for their forgiveness, because the kingdom of Heaven was near. Then, he baptized them in the Jordan River as an outward sign of their inward repentance, from their heart. John performed a water baptism.

John said, "*I baptize with water those who repent of their sins and turn to God. But someone is coming soon who is greater than I am so much greater that I'm not worthy even to be his slave and carry his sandals.*" "*He will baptize you with the Holy Spirit and with fire.*"

John the Baptist was a wild-looking man who had no power or position in the Jewish political system, but he spoke with almost irresistible authority. People were moved by his words because he spoke the truth, challenging them to turn from their wicked ways of sin and repent. The people responded by the hundreds. When the people repented, he baptized them as a symbol of their repentance. But even as the people crowded to him, he pointed to beyond himself, never forgetting his main role, which was **to prepare the way and announce the coming of the Savior.**

The words of truth that "John the Baptist" spoke, moved many to repentance, however it also provoked others to resistance and resentment. One of the men John provoked was King Herod. John condemned and challenged King Herod to admit his sin of marrying illegally Herodias, who was his brother's wife before Herod married her. When King Herod heard about this, he had John arrested for condemning him of this sin.

A short time after John's arrest and imprisonment, King Herod had John the Baptist killed. He was beheaded, and his head put on a platter and brought to King Herod's wife, Herodias. Herod and his wife were able to have John killed but they were not able to stop his message.

The One John had announced, was already on the move. John had accomplished his mission. What John the Baptist prepared, Jesus was now ready to fulfill.

CHAPTER 5

Who Is God? Who Is Jesus?

What Are Their Roles?

Who is God?

He's been described as everything from an impersonal life-force to a benevolent, personal, Almighty Creator.

He has been called by many names, including: "Zeus," "Jupiter," "Brahma," "Allah," "Ra," "Odin," "Ashur," "Izanagi," "Viracocha," "Ahura Mazda," and "the Great Spirit" to name just a few.

He's seen by some as "Mother Nature" and by others as "Father God." But who does God claim to be?

What has God revealed about Himself?

To begin with, nowhere in the Holy Bible, not even once, does God ever refer to Himself as "Mother" or "Mother Nature." Calling God

"Mother Nature" is totally unacceptable for anyone, but especially for a Christian.

Never is God referred to or called "Mother" by the prophets to whom He spoke. Calling God "Mother Nature" is comparable to calling your earthly father "Mom."

Whenever God refers to Himself in parental terms, in the Holy Scriptures, He always addresses Himself as "**Father**," never "Mother. "He calls Himself "a **Father to Israel**,"

In one instance, when His "children" were particularly disrespectful to Him, He said to them, *"A son honors his father, and a servant his master. If then I am the Father, where is My honor? And if I am a Master, where is My reverence?"* (Malachi 1:6)

His prophets acknowledged Him as Father by saying, "*You are our Father, we are the clay, and You are our potter; And all of us are the work of Your hand,*" (Isaiah 64:8).

In another scripture, "*Do we not all have one Father? Has not one God created us?*" (Malachi 2:1)

The Bible says, "***God is Spirit,*** *and those who worship Him must worship Him in spirit and truth.*" (John 4:24).

In the beginning God created the heavens and the earth. Now the earth was formless and empty, darkness was over the surface of the deep, and **the Spirit of God** *was hovering over the waters.* (Genesis 1:1-2).

Now the Lord is the Spirit, and where the Spirit of the Lord is, there is freedom. (II Corinthians 3:17).

"*The Spirit of God has made me; the breath of the Almighty gives me life.*" (Job 33:4)

God is called ***"Almighty"*** in virtually every book of the Old Testament, often dozens of times, because of His great unlimited authority and power.

The Scriptures also tells us that **God is all-knowing**, *"For whenever our heart condemns us, God is greater than our heart, and he knows everything."* (I John 3:20)

God is Divine, he is capable of being everywhere at the same time. It means his divine presence encompasses the whole of the universe. (Reference; Psalms 139:7-10).

Divinity is the quality of being God. Explaining "Who is God" is easy because you either believe The Holy Bible or you don't. The Bible is clear, it says what it means, and it means that it says.

The Children of Israel throughout the Old Testament believed **in only one God.**

Who is Jesus?

Undoubtedly, "Jesus of Nazareth," is the most controversial human being in the history of the world. What makes Him so divisive is people not knowing and understanding His role and relationship to the human race and with His Father, the Only True Most High God.

Old scrolls and geological historic findings about Jesus have caused some controversies and divisions among the world's cultures. But, the root cause of the world's divisiveness regarding Jesus, is **the Bible's New Testament documentation** of the **eyewitnesses** who observed Jesus healing people of diseases and illnesses, delivering people from demon possession, and raising dead bodies back to life in front of thousands of people. The Bible says, *"And there are also many other things that Jesus did, which if they were written one by one, I suppose that even the world itself could not contain the books that would be written."* Amen. (John 21:25)

So, it should not surprise you, to learn that the Holy Bible's New Testament writings, about Jesus, have been at the center of these controversies and divisions for over two thousand years.

In the Beginning at Creation God said,

*"Let **us** make mankind in **our** image, in **our** likeness, so that they may rule over the fish in the sea and the birds in the sky, over the livestock and all the wild animals, and over all the creatures that move along the ground."* (Genesis 1:26)

Who is God speaking to when He said, *"Let **us** make mankind in our image, in our likeness?"*

The New Testament Gospel of John is unique because John focuses on the nature of Christ (the deity of Jesus) as opposed to the historical accounts of Jesus' life as in Matthew, Mark, and Luke.

The theme throughout the Gospel of John is *Jesus **divine nature*** (deity) and, Jesus ***human nature.*** Jesus was a perfect human being. Within Jesus are two distinct natures: ***divine and perfect human.***

The book of John begins by revealing some astonishing information about who was with God at the beginning of creation. Disciple John tells us,

1. *"In the beginning was the Word, and **the Word was with God** and **the Word was God**.*

2. *He* [The Word] *was in the beginning with God.*

3. *All things were made through Him [the Word], and without Him nothing was made that was made.*

4. *In Him was life, and the life was the light of men."* (John 1:1-4)

Notice the word, "**Word**," is capitalized and used as a pronoun. John is clearly describing "the Word" as **a person.** He is also saying that whoever the Word is, was with God in the beginning, and that person (the Word) is God.

Then, Disciple John, introduces us to another witness. *"There was a man sent from God whose name was John* [John the Baptist]. *He came as a witness to testify concerning that light, so that through him all might believe.* (John 1:6-7)

CHAPTER 5 - WHO IS GOD? WHO IS JESUS? - WHAT ARE THEIR ROLES?

He [the Word the Light] *was in the world, and though the world was made through him, <u>the world did not recognize him</u>.*

He [the Word] came to that which was his own, <u>but his own did not receive him</u>.

*Yet to all who did receive him, <u>to those who believed in</u> **his name**, he gave <u>the right</u> to become children of God; children born not of natural descent, nor of human decision or a husband's will, <u>but born of God</u>.* (John 1:10-13)

So, who is the Word?

John the Baptist makes a shocking revelation when he tells us, *"And **the Word became flesh** and dwelt among us, and we beheld His glory, the glory as of the only begotten of the Father, full of grace and truth.* (John 1:14)

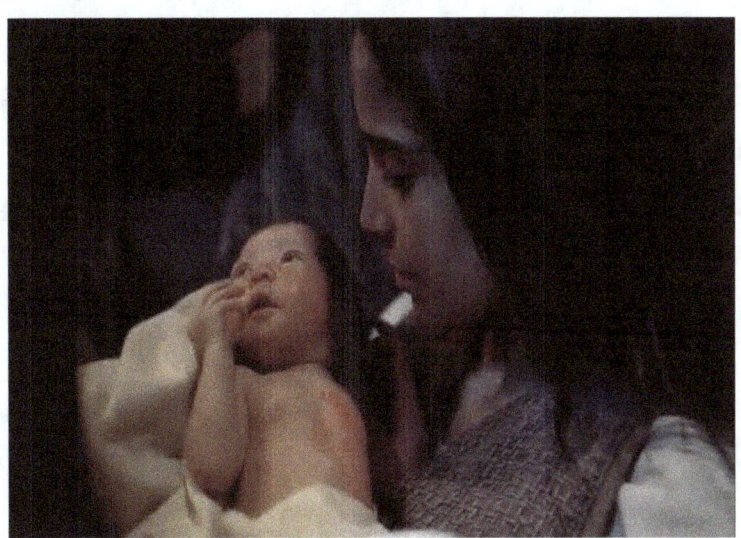

The Word is the one and only Son, Jesus Christ, who came from the Father, full of grace and truth. *"For the law was given through Moses, but **grace and truth came through Jesus Christ**."*

*No one has seen God at any time. The only begotten Son, who is in the bosom of the Father, **He has declared Him**.* (John1:17-18)

After reading this first chapter of John, it's very clear who God the Father was speaking to when He said, *"Let us make mankind in our image, in our likeness."* God was speaking to **His only begotten Son, Jesus**, [The Word] who *was in the beginning with Go*d.

[Jesus is the Word], all things were made through Him and without Him nothing was made that was made.

In Him [Jesus, the Word] was life, and the life was the light of men.

John the Baptist testifies, *"And I have seen and testified that this is the Son of God."* (John 1:34)

Jesus, the Son of God, *"is the image of the invisible God, the firstborn over all creation. For in him all things were created: things in heaven and on earth, visible and invisible, whether thrones or powers or rulers or authorities; all things have been created through him and for him. He is before all things, and in him all things hold together. For God was pleased to have all his fullness dwell in him. ... "For in Christ all the fullness of the Deity lives in bodily form."* (Colossians 1:15-19 and 2:9)

[God in these last days], *"has spoken to us by his Son, whom he appointed heir of all things, and through whom also he made the universe." "The Son is the radiance of God's glory and the exact representation of his being, sustaining all things by his powerful word.*

God, said this about His Son, Jesus. *"In the beginning, Lord, you laid the foundations of the earth, and the heavens are the work of your hands. "Sit at my right hand until I make your enemies a footstool for your feet"*? (Hebrews 1:2-3, 10, and 13)

[Today] we see Jesus, *who was made lower than the angels for a little while, now crowned with glory and honor because he suffered death, so that by the grace of God he might taste death for everyone.*

In bringing many sons and daughters to glory, it was fitting that

CHAPTER 5 - WHO IS GOD? WHO IS JESUS? - WHAT ARE THEIR ROLES?

God, for whom and through whom everything exists, should make the pioneer of their salvation perfect through what he suffered. Both the one who makes people holy and those who are made holy are of the same family.

Both the one who makes people holy and those who are made holy are of the same family. <u>So Jesus is not ashamed to call them brothers and sisters</u>. He says, *"I will declare your name to my brothers and sisters; in the assembly I will sing your praises."*

Since the children have flesh and blood, he too shared in their humanity so that by his death he might break the power of him who holds the power of death—that is, the devil— and free those who all their lives were held in slavery by their fear of death.

For this reason he had to be made like them, <u>fully human</u> in every way, in order that he might become a merciful and faithful high priest in service to God, and that he might make atonement for the sins of the people. (Hebrews 2:9-12 and 14-15, and 17)

Does the Bible tell us what role, if any, Jesus had with the saints in the Old Testament?

Yes, it does. One day, "While the Pharisees were gathered together, Jesus asked them, *"What do you think about the Christ? Whose Son is He?"* They said to Him, "The Son of David."

Jesus said to them, "How then does David in the Spirit call Him 'Lord,' saying: **'The Lord said to <u>my Lord</u>,** *"Sit at My right hand, Till I make your enemies your footstool?"*

"If David then calls Him 'Lord,' how is He his Son?" (Matthew 22:41-45)

Jesus was referring to the Old Testament scripture in Psalms 110:1, where David said, *"The Lord,* (God the Father) *said unto my Lord* (King David's Lord, Jesus), *sit at my right hand until I make thine enemies thy footstool. .* (Psalms 110:1). Jesus asked the Pharisees, *"If David then calls*

*Him **'Lord,'** how is He his Son?"*

In these two scriptures Jesus reveals, he not only pre-existed with God in the Old Testament, but King David was clearly saying **his LORD** and **the LORD of the Old Testament** – **is Jesus**.

Early in Jesus Ministry, He made a shocking statement to a Jewish crowd in Jerusalem saying, *"And the Father who sent me has Himself testified concerning me. **You have never heard His voice nor seen His form**."* (John 5:37).

Shortly after this, Jesus made a similar astonishing statement when He told a crowd, *"**No one has seen the Father** except the one who is from God; only he has seen the Father."* (John 6:46). Jesus was telling the Jews, that he, Jesus, came from God, His Father, and **only He had seen God.**

When Jesus proclaimed to be the Son of God, He contradicted one of the most treasured teachings of Jewish scripture that God is composed of strictly **one divine being**.

Today, it's easy for you to believe and understand the mystery that God is actually a family composed of **the Father**, His **Only Begotten Son**, and **God's Holy Spirit**.

However, 2000 years ago most Jews didn't understand, and many were offended to the point of being furious with rage, when Jesus told them, *"Your father Abraham rejoiced to see My day, and he saw it and was glad."* (John 8:56)

Since Abraham had lived and died nearly 2,000 years earlier, when Jesus made this statement, he gave them a bold clear clue to his identity and role. Jesus was telling them that He knew Abraham personally, and this offended the Jews greatly. In fact, they considered it blasphemy that a mere man, (as they viewed him) "not yet fifty years old," had the audacity to claim he had known their patriarch Abraham.

But what Jesus said next was even more shocking to them, because he revealed his role fully to them when he said, *"Most assuredly, I say to you before Abraham was, "I AM."*

CHAPTER 5 - WHO IS GOD? WHO IS JESUS? - WHAT ARE THEIR ROLES?

The title "**I Am**" is actually a <u>divine title of God</u>! And, The Jews knew when God appeared to Moses from the burning bush, he identified himself as "**I AM WHO I AM**" and "**I AM.**" (Reference; Exodus 3:14).

By saying **I Am**, Jesus claimed that he did not only pre-dated Abraham and knew him personally, but Jesus, by identifying him-self as "**I AM**," was telling Abraham's descendants that he had eternally existed in the Old Testament and was **the God of Abraham**, **Isaac, Jacob**, and **Moses**.

The moment Jesus referred to himself as, "**I Am**," the crowd surrounded him and *"they took up stones to throw at him; but he hid himself and went out of the temple,"* (Reference; John 8:56-59)

You see, when Jesus referred to himself as, "**I Am**" Jesus was also claiming to be the one who led Israel out of Egypt.

Jesus was also asserting to be the spiritual **Rock** for the Children of Israel, in the Old Testament, and He was. Apostle Paul confirms this when he wrote to the Christians in Corinth, *"all ate the same spiritual food, and all drank the same spiritual drink. For they drank of that spiritual* **Rock that followed them**, *and* <u>that **Rock** was Chris</u>*t*." (I Corinthians 10:3-4)

A Rock that followed them!!

I wonder if it was Jesus, who spoke this to Moses, *"And the* L<small>ORD</small> *said to Moses,* "*Behold, I come to you in the thick cloud, that the people may hear when I speak with you, and believe you forever."* (Exodus 19:9)

Could it have been Jesus ... speaking as the Angel of the Lord — who spoke to Abraham and said; "By Myself I have sworn, **says the L**<small>**ORD**</small>, because you have done this thing, and have not withheld your son, your only son — blessing I will bless you, and multiplying I will multiply your descendants as the stars of the heaven and as the sand which is on the seashore; and your descendants shall possess the gate of their enemies. In your seed all the nations of the earth shall be blessed, **because you have obeyed My voice**." (Genesis 22:15-18)

Jesus; the Perfect Divine Human Being

Every human baby conceived from the seed of man and birthed from the womb of woman contains the father's DNA, and the rebellious evil nature of their spiritual father, the Devil. But **Jesus was different**.

You see, Jesus, "the only begotten Son of God, was born with His Father's DNA and a divine, holy, and righteous human nature, pure in every way. Born without sin.

When Virgin Mary gave her permission to angel Gabriel by saying, *"I am the Lord's servant. May everything you have said about me come true."* God's Holy Spirit hovered over Virgin Mary and she conceived and nine months later, gave birth to the only perfect human being born from the womb of a woman.

The blood that flowing through Jesus veins was holy, righteous, and pure blood. However, he was one-hundred percent human being in every way.

He inherited all of His Fathers' attributes and qualities. He is fully God, **but only as, "God the Son."** Jesus, according to His own words is not to be considered as co-equal with God the Father. Jesus told us, *"For the Father is greater than I."* (John 14:28)

He is the image of the invisible God, the firstborn over all creation. For by Him all things were created that are in Heaven and that are on earth, visible and invisible, whether thrones or dominions or principalities or powers. All things were created through Him and for Him. And He is before all things, and in Him all things consist." (Colossians 1:15-17)

For the Scriptures say, *"God has put all things under his authority." (Of course, when it says "all things are under his authority," that does not include God himself, who gave Christ his authority.)* (I Corinthians

15:27 AMP)

The Author of Hebrews tells us, *"The Son is the radiance of God's glory and the exact representation of his being, sustaining all things by his powerful word.* (Hebrews 1:3).

"Seeing then that we have a great High Priest who has passed through the heavens, Jesus the Son of God, let us hold fast our confession." (Hebrews 4:14)

Jesus called himself, "**Son of Man,**" over one-hundred times in the four Gospel books of the New Testament. And, over 75 times the term, "**Son of God**," is used in describing Jesus, in the same gospel books.

Jesus truly is both the "**Son of God**," and the "**Son of Man.**" Apostle Paul tells us, "***For in Christ all the fullness of the Deity lives in bodily form***," (Colossians 2:9).

Jesus reveals His Role with Humanity

"For I have come down from heaven not to do my will but to do the will of Him who sent me. "For my Father's will is that everyone who looks to the Son and believes in him shall have eternal life, and I will raise them up at the last day." (John 6:38-40)

*"In this, the love of God was manifested toward us that God has sent His only begotten Son into the world that we might live through Hi*m. (I John 4:9)

The author of Hebrews tells us, *"God, for whom and through whom everything was made, chose to bring many children into glory. And it was only right that He should make Jesus, through his suffering, a perfect leader, fit to bring them into their salvation." "So now Jesus and the ones he makes holy have the same Father. That is why Jesus is not ashamed to call them his brothers and sisters."* (Hebrews 2:10-11)

"Since the children have flesh and blood, he too shared in their humanity so that by his death he might break the power of him who holds the power of death (the devil) and free those who all their lives were

held in slavery by their fear of death. (Hebrews 2:14-15)

For this reason he had to be made like them, fully human in every way, in order that he might become a merciful and faithful high priest in service to God, and that he might make atonement for the sins of the people. Because he himself suffered when he was tempted, he was able to help those who were being tempted. (Hebrews 2:17-18)

Jesus created us, along with all of creation, and breathed into us the breath of life. He is the Savior of all peoples and all nations. Jesus is our Lord, our High Priest, and our Lawyer (advocate) before God the Father.

Jesus has been – and is – the **divine being** in the Family of God who serves as **the mouth of God** communicating **the will of the Father to human beings.**

The Holy Bible is God's Prophetic Word. It reveals what has been in God's mind from the beginning of time.

What is Jesus Role with His Father, God?

Jesus is always subordinate and obedient to "God the Father" who is "the source of all things." Jesus did not consider himself equal to His Father. They function together in total harmony and in one accord with Jesus being subordinate to His Father, God, and always obedient and submissive to His Father's will.

Jesus told us:

- *"I and the Father are one."* (John 10:30)
- *"Understand that the Father is in me, and I in the Father."* (John 10:38)
- *"Anyone who has seen me has seen the Father. How can you say, 'Show us the Father'? Don't you believe that I am in the Father, and that the Father is in me?"* (John 14:9-10)
- *"Believe me when I say that I am in the Father and the Father is in me."* (John 10:30)

- *"For the Father is greater than I."* (John 14:28)

How Does the Father, the Son and the Holy Spirit Function as One?

A few years ago, my spiritual mentor Prophet Daniel Senga asked me to attend a Pastors' conference hosted by one of the greatest Evangelist of our time, Evangelist Reinhard Bonnke. I asked Evangelist Bonnke, "How does God function as God the Father, Jesus the Son, and God's Holy Spirit?

Evangelist Bonnke said, "This is how I picture the, **Family of God** functioning:"

I. **God the Father** is – "the **Will of God.**"
II. **God the Son** is – the **Word of God**
III. **God's Holy Spirit** is – the **Power of God.**

And to help you understand How the Family of God functions, visualize:

1 - When "**God the Father**" Willed something;

2 - **God the Son** – [the Word] – **spoke it**. And, once *the Word* spoke the Father's Will;

3 - The **Holy Spirit of God**, the **Power of God** – performed what "**the Word" spoke**.

Thus the Father's Will is accomplished.

Jesus Loves You

Jesus wants you to know that he loves you immensely and wants you to enter into a relationship with God the Father, through Him. Jesus is telling you, "*I am the way, the truth, and the life. No one comes to the Father except through me*" (John 14:6)

"*I am the gate; whoever enters through me will be saved.*" (John 10:9)

"Behold, I stand at the door and knock. If anyone hears my voice and opens the door, I will come in to him and dine with him, and he with me." (Revelations 3:20)

It's time to get up, unlock your heart's door, and open it to Jesus. Listen to what He has to say before you reject Him. He loves you and will forgive you no matter what you have done.

"Salvation is found in no one else, for there is no other name under heaven given to mankind by which we must be saved." It is by the name of Jesus Christ of Nazareth that mankind is saved from Hell. (Reference Acts 4:10 and 12)

CHAPTER 6

Jesus' Ministry

Two-thousand years ago, the Jews were at conflict within themselves. They were worried about food for their families, what clothes to wear, what people thought of them, and how to improve their well-being. They were troubled about living under Roman rule and worried about their sons being successful, their daughters and wives being abused and taken advantage of by the Roman soldiers, who had no respect for them.

The Jews were accustomed to a political system where they were ruled by two distinct persons: A king ruling over their physical life, and the High Priest ruling their religious life. They knew the teachings of the prophets that were written in the scrolls of scriptures regarding a Messiah who would come and save them from the world.

Most of the Jewish people were expecting a Messiah to be like King David, only better. A physical leader who would come establish His earthly Kingdom and restore Israel's lost glory. They imagined their Messiah would defeat the Romans and free the Jewish people. Once Israel's freedom was established they assumed the Messiah would establish His kingdom of wealth and physical dominance here on earth. Then God's judgment would come upon the world because of how Israel had been mistreated for so long.

This was the culture setting in Israel when Jesus came on the scene. The Jews were expecting a Messiah, but not a Messiah who would be both – Israel's High Priest and their ruling king.

Jesus, the Minister of reconciliation, was sent by God the Father with authority to do the Father's will here on Earth. Jesus told us, *"Do you not believe that I am in the Father, and the Father in Me? The words that I speak to you I do not speak on my own authority; but the Father who dwells in me does the works."* (John 14:10)

"The time has come," he said. *"The kingdom of God has come near. Repent and believe the good news!"* Jesus was about thirty years old when he began his public ministry. (Mark 1:14-15 and Luke 3:23)

What Jesus did is tied inseparably to who He is. At the time Jesus began his ministry, much of the world was under the rule of the Roman Empire, including Israel. The city of Jerusalem was occupied with Roman soldiers because the Roman Governor lived there. Israel was enslaved, mistreated, and heavily taxed by the Romans.

Everywhere Jesus went, signs, wonders, and miracles followed him. People spoke well of him and were amazed by the gracious words that came from his lips. *"How can this be?"* they asked. *"Isn't this Joseph's son?"*

Here is a brief look at some of the Father's will that Jesus demonstrated and taught to His disciples. Imagine yourself being a disciple two thousand years ago as you walk and witness a tiny portion of what Jesus said and did.

A Demon testifies that Jesus is the Holy One of God

One Sabbath day, Jesus was teaching in the synagogue in the town of Capernaum, when a man possessed by a demon; an evil spirit cried out, shouting, *"Go away! Why are you interfering with us, Jesus of Nazareth? Have you come to destroy us? I know who you are the Holy One of God!"*

But Jesus reprimanded him. *"Be quiet! Come out of the man,"* he ordered. At that, the demon threw the man to the floor as the crowd watched; then it came out of him without hurting him further.

Amazed, the people exclaimed, "What authority and power this man's words possess! Even evil spirits obey him and they flee at his command!"

The news about Jesus spread through every village in the entire region. (Reference Luke 4:22-36)

Leprosy Is Healed by Jesus, Immediately.

In one of the villages, Jesus met a man with an advanced case of leprosy. When the man saw Jesus, he bowed with his face to the ground, begging to be healed. "*Lord*," he said, "*if you are willing, you can heal me and make me clean.*"

Jesus reached out and touched him. *I am willing,*" He said. "*Be healed*!" And instantly the leprosy disappeared.

Then Jesus instructed him not to tell anyone what had happened. But despite Jesus' instructions, the report of his power spread even faster, and vast crowds came to hear him preach and to be healed of their diseases. (Reference; Luke 5:12-15)

A Paralyzed Man Is Healed

One day Jesus was teaching, and Pharisees and teachers of the law had come from every village of Galilee and from Judea and Jerusalem. The power of the Lord was with Jesus to heal the sick.

"Some men came carrying a paralyzed man on a mat and tried to take him into the house to lay him before Jesus.

When they could not find a way to do this because of the crowd, they went up on the roof and lowered him on his mat through the tiles into the middle of the crowd, right in front of Jesus.

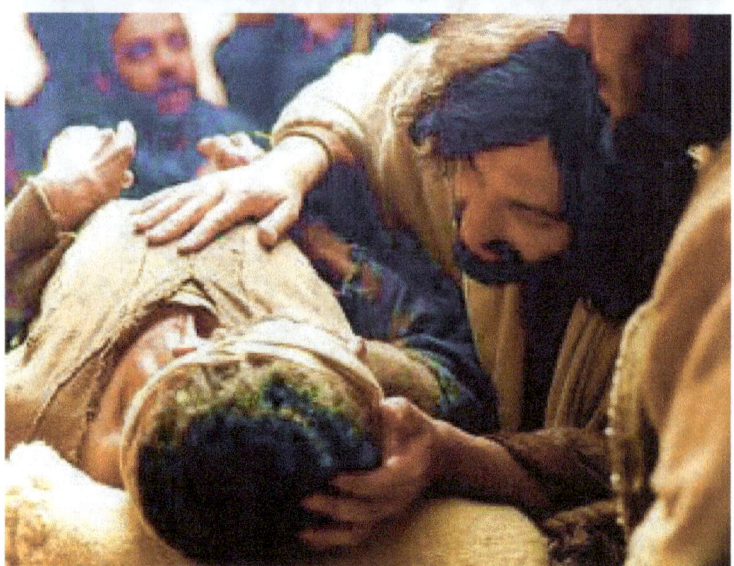

When Jesus saw their faith, he said, *"Friend, your sins are forgiven."*

But the Pharisees and teachers of religious law said to themselves, *"Who does he think he is? That's blasphemy! Only God can forgive sins!"*

Jesus knew what they were thinking and asked, *"Why are you thinking these things in your hearts? Which is easier: to say, 'Your sins are forgiven,' or to say, 'Get up and walk'? But I want you to know that the Son of Man has authority on earth to forgive sins."*

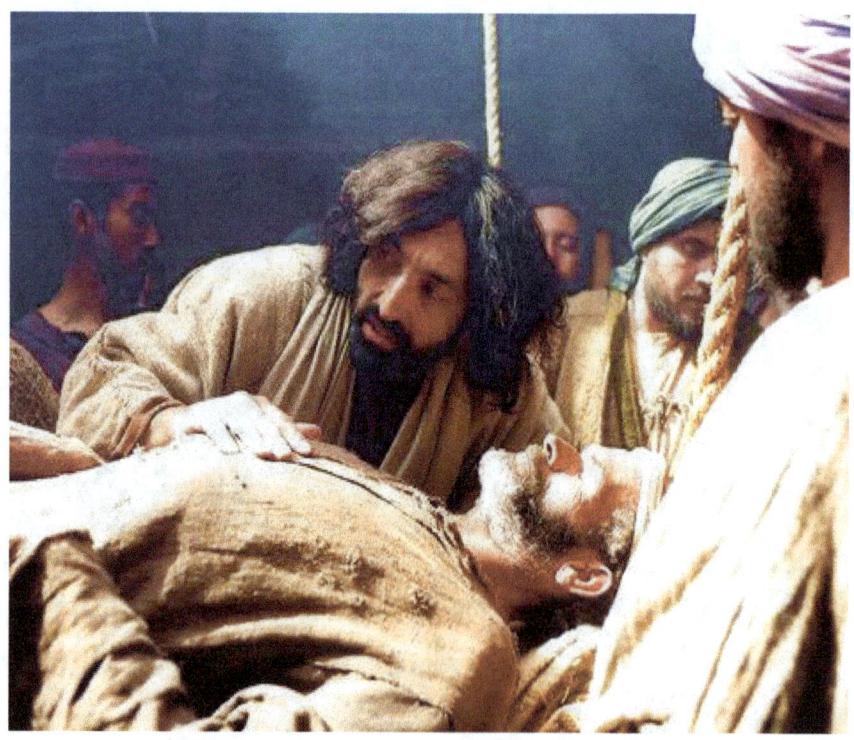

So, he said to the paralyzed man, *"I tell you, get up, take your mat and go home."*

Immediately he stood up in front of them, took what he had been lying on and went home praising God.

Everyone was amazed and gave praise to God. They were filled with awe and said, *"We have seen remarkable things today* (Luke 5:17-26)

A Demon Possessed Man Is Healed

When Jesus arrived by boat in Gerasenes which is across the lake from Galilee. As he stepped out of the boat and onto the shore the bible says "He was met by a demon-possessed man from the town. For a long time, this man had not worn clothes or lived in a house, but had lived in the tombs.

When he saw Jesus, he cried out and fell at his feet, shouting at the top of his voice, "*What do you want with me, Jesus, Son of the Most High God? I beg you, don't torture me!*" For Jesus had commanded the impure spirit to come out of the man.

ENTER THROUGH THE NARROW GATE - IT'S ALL OR NOTHING

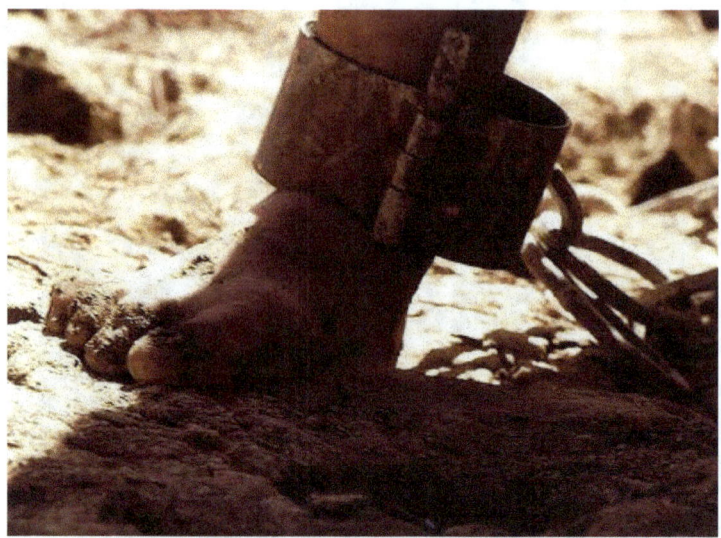

Many times, it had seized him, and though he was chained hand and foot and kept under guard, he had broken his chains and had been driven by the demon into solitary places.

Jesus asked him, "*What is your name*?" "*Legion*," he replied, because many demons had gone into him.

And they begged Jesus repeatedly not to order them to go into the Abyss.

CHAPTER 6 - REPENTANCE JESUS' MINISTRY

So, Jesus gave them permission to go into the pigs.

When the demons came out of the man, they went into the pigs, and the herd rushed down the steep bank into the lake and was drowned.

When those tending the pigs saw what had happened, they ran off and reported this in the town and countryside, and the people went out to see what had happened.

When they came to Jesus, they found the man from whom the demons had gone out, sitting at Jesus' feet, dressed and in his right mind; and they were afraid.

CHAPTER 6 - REPENTANCE JESUS' MINISTRY

Those who had seen it told the people how the demon-possessed man had been cured. Then all the people of the region of the Gerasenes asked Jesus to leave them, because they were overcome with fear. So, he got into the boat and left.

The man from whom the demons had gone out begged to go with him but Jesus sent him away saying, *"Return home and tell how much God has done for you."*

So, the man went away and told all over town how much Jesus had done for him. (Luke 8:27-39)

A Blind Man Shouts, "Son of David, Have Mercy on me." "Rabbi, I want to see."

On another occasion, as Jesus, his disciples, and a large crowd, were leaving the city of Jericho, "a blind man, Bartimaeus, was sitting by the roadside begging.

When he heard that is was Jesus of Nazareth, he began to shout,

"Jesus, Son of David, have mercy on me!

Many rebuked him and told him to be quiet, but he shouted all the more, *"Son of David, have mercy on me!"*

Jesus stopped and said, "*Call him.*"

So, they called to the blind man. *Cheer up! On your feet! He's calling you."* Throwing his cloak aside, he jumped to his feet and came to Jesus.

"*What do you want me to do for you*?" Jesus asked him.

The blind man said, *"Rabbi, I want to see."*

"*Go,*" said Jesus, "*your faith has healed you.*"

Immediately he received his sight and followed Jesus along the road. (Mark 10:46-52)

Jesus heals A Deaf Man with a Speech Impediment

Then they brought Jesus a deaf man with an impediment in his speech, and begged Him to put His hand on him. Jesus put his fingers in his ears, and spat and touched his tongue.

Then, looking up to heaven, He sighed, and said to him, "*Ephphatha*," that is, "*Be opened*."

Immediately his ears were opened, and the impediment of his tongue was loosed, and he spoke plainly. (Mark 7:32-35)

The waves, weather, and wind obeyed Jesus.

Jesus got into a boat and his disciples followed him. "Suddenly a furious storm came up on the lake so that the waves swept over the boat.

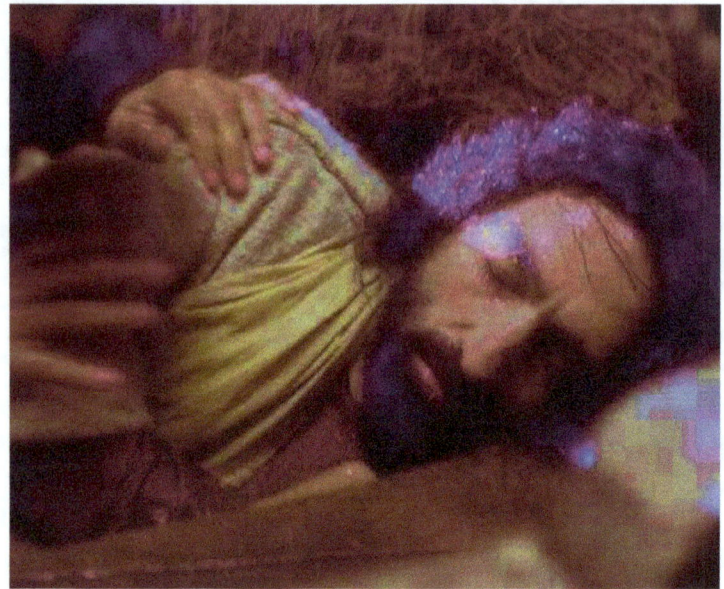

But Jesus was sleeping. The disciples went and woke him, saying *"Lord, save us! We're going to drown!"*

Then he got up and rebuked the winds and the waves, and it was completely calm.

CHAPTER 6 - REPENTANCE JESUS' MINISTRY

The men were amazed and asked, "*What kind of man is this? Even the winds and the waves obey him!*" (Matthew 8:24-27)

Even Death obeyed Jesus as a Dead Man Is Brought Back to Life

Jesus went to a town called Nain, and His disciples and a large crowd went along with Him. As He approached the town gate, a dead person was being carried out; the only son of his mother, and she was a widow. And a large crowd from the town was with her.

When the Lord saw her, His heart went out to her and He said "Don't cry."

Then He went up and touched the bier they were carrying him on and the bearers stood still.

He said, "*Young man, I say to you, get up!*"

The dead man sat up and began to talk, and Jesus gave him back to his mother.

They were all filled with awe and praised God. "*A great prophet has appeared among us,*" they said. "*God has come to help his people.*" This news about Jesus spread throughout Judea and the surrounding country. (Read Luke 7:11-17)

But the Children of Israel missed it; they didn't see it. They didn't hear it. They were spiritually blind and deaf, to who Jesus was. They were looking for a different type of king and kingdom. Instead of a king and a High Priest in one person, they were looking for their physical freedom, physical prosperity, and then the judgment. They expected the Messiah to set up His kingdom and rule like King David, and then the judgment to follow.

But the Messiah was first offered to the lost sheep of Israel in the person of a human being named "Jesus of Nazareth." "*He came to that which was his own, but his own did not receive him. Yet to all who receive him, to those who believe in his name, he gave them to become children of God; children born not of natural descent, nor of human decision or a husband's will, but born of God.* (John 1:11-13)

To this very day, many of the Children of Israel are still looking for their "Messiah." But, Messiah Jesus has already come, and His Good

News message was delivered first to the lost sheep of Israel, the Jews, and because of the hardness of their hearts, the Children of Israel rejected Jesus as "the Christ." (Reference; Matthew 11:16-19.)

This is but a few of the many miracles Jesus performed during his shorty ministry on earth. Jesus came to Earth to teach and demonstrate the Father's Will.

Jesus did many other things as well. If every one of them were written down, I suppose that even the whole world would not have room for the books that would be written. (John 21:25)

CHAPTER 7

Validating The Father's Will

No will goes into effect until the person who made the will has died. And, no one can receive benefits from "the will" unless they are named as a beneficiary in "the Will" and abide by the conditions of "the Will."

Since the downfall of humanity in the Garden of Eden, the Father's will has been for the reconciliation of the human race. In order for God to reconcile all peoples of all nations to himself, He needed several things to happen.

1. God needed a human being who was holy, righteous, perfect in every way, and willing to volunteer, be the sacrifice as a scape-goat for the entire human race. Taking on their death sentence in their place so they could become children of God once again.

2. Only a Worthy human Redeemer with holy, righteous, and pure blood, would appease God's wrath against sin and satisfy the death penalty God imposed on humanity, in the Garden of

Eden.

3. This Worthy Redeemer's Blood would be used to wash away the sins of all peoples – of all the nations on earth, who would believe in the Lords sacrifice and their sins.

4. The Redeemer's death would put into effect a Peace Treaty, allowing God to remove the separation and enemy status of humanity and allow us to be reconciled to Him, if they but believe in Jesus.

5. Once reconciled, we would establish a loving obedient relationship with God the Father **through Jesus, the Family Redeemer.**

If these conditions were meet, then God's wrath against sin, His forgiveness for sins, and His removal of sin, could be accomplished by sacrificing a perfect human being.

The conditions for God's plan to work in humanity are;

6. Human beings must turn away from their evil lifestyle,

7. Humble themselves

8. Believe in Jesus, and confesses their sins (repent).

If any human being does this, then God's Perfect Plan of Salvation will be put into effect. After that, God's Holy Spirit will come and dwell in our body, allowing God to become our Father and us to become His Children, free from the spiritual shackles of "Satan the Wicked one."

There was a man named Nicodemus, a Jewish religious leader who was a Pharisee. After dark one evening, he came to speak with Jesus. *"Rabbi,"* he said, *"we all know that God has sent you to teach us. Your miraculous signs are evidence that God is with you.* "Jesus replied, *"I tell you the truth, unless you are born again, you cannot see the Kingdom of God."*

"What do you mean?" exclaimed Nicodemus. *"How can an old man*

go back into his mother's womb and be born again?"

Jesus replied, *"I assure you, no one can enter the Kingdom of God without being born of water and the Spirit. Humans can reproduce only human life, but the Holy Spirit gives birth to spiritual life. So don't be surprised when I say, '**You must be born again**."* (John 3:3-7)

John the Baptist told us, *"But as many as received Him, to them He gave* **the right to become children of God***, to those who believe in His name:* (John 1:12)

The only thing that could appease God's wrath against sin and satisfy the death penalty God imposed on humanity was the blood of a perfect human being. A human-family redeemer who would volunteer to be sacrificed.

This human volunteer had to be a first-born male, perfect in every way; holy, righteous, and pure without any sin whatsoever. This is the only sacrifice God, the Father, would accept. But God couldn't find a perfect male human being that met these conditions, because all humans have sinned and fallen short of His glory. *For everyone has sinned; we all fall short of God's glorious standard.* (Romans 3:23)

God loves us so much that His Only Son, Jesus volunteered to leave His Father's throne in eternity, vacate all his splendor and glory to come to Earth, to be born as a human being with a divine spirit, to demonstrate the will His Father, God, to humanity.

Because God's children are human beings—made of flesh and blood—the Son also became flesh and blood. For only as a human being could he die, and only by dying could he break the power of the devil, who had the power of death. Only in this way could he set free all who have lived their lives as slaves to the fear of dying.

"Therefore, it was necessary for Jesus to be made in every respect like us, his brothers and sisters, so he could be our merciful and faithful High Priest before Father God. Then he could offer a sacrifice that would take away the sins of the people." (Hebrews 2:14-15, and 17)

CHAPTER 7 - VALIDATING THE FATHER'S WILL

Jesus stepped off his Father's throne and came from eternity to Earth. He told us, "For it is my Father's will that all who see his Son and believe in him should have eternal life. I will raise them up at the last day." (John 6: 40)

When Jesus was a young boy living in Nazareth, his step-father, Joseph, taught and raised him in the carpentry trade. When Jesus began his ministry, all the local people assumed Joseph was Jesus' blood father. So, they referred to Jesus as "son of Joseph," Sometimes they called him "the carpenter's son" or "Joseph's son."

Later on, as Jesus travelled away from the Nazareth region, he became known as "Jesus of Nazareth." Even the Temple Leaders and Priests knew Him as "Jesus of Nazareth." They didn't know Jesus was born in Bethlehem of Judea, where His ancestors, including King David, were born.

After Jesus had completed His Fathers work of teaching and demonstrating His Father's will for humanity, He willingly gave himself up as a ransom and took the death sentence for all mankind.

Jesus loves you and me so much that he volunteered to step out of heaven to take your and my death sentence that God the Father cursed the human race with, because of our mankind's sin in the Garden of Eden. Jesus came to earth knowing he was going to be crucified on our behalf, so that His Father, God, could forgive us of all our sin.

Today, *"In the case of a will, it is necessary to prove the death of the one who made it, because a will is in force only when somebody has died; it never takes effect while the one who made it is living."* (Hebrews 15:16-17).

Being crucified on a cross 2000 years ago was a curse. It was the lowest form of punishment for a human being at that time, and it was reserved for the lowest class of people.

As Jesus was nailed onto the cross and then hoisted up between heaven and earth, blood oozed from the multitude of open wounds on

His body. The blood flowed onto the cross and dripped onto the ground, as His body hung in shame.

All the horrific sins, sicknesses, diseases, addictions, and evil deeds of the entire world were heaped on Him while He hung on the cross.

As Jesus breathed out His last breath before giving up his spirit, He said *"It is finished."* At that moment, God's Will was put into effect on the Cross at Calvary. (Reference John 19:30)

When Jesus said, *"It is finished,"* Satan began his victory dance, thinking he had killed "the only begotten Son of God." He had tried several times to kill Jesus, but never could quite make it happen. Jesus always escaped.

Satan thought he was superior to Jesus on earth because he had the authority and dominion of the world. He had received it when he deceived Eve and Adam in the Garden of Eden. That was when Satan became the Prince of this World.

Now Satan was extremely happy he had finally achieved his dream. He thought Jesus was dead for good. Satan didn't have a clue that God the

CHAPTER 7 - VALIDATING THE FATHER'S WILL

Father had orchestrated this spectacular plan of sending His Only Son to Earth as a once-and-for-all-time atonement. A perfect sacrifice to pay in full the ransom that God had established for all humanity's sin.

Telestai is a Greek word that means to bring something to completion, to finalize something, as the word "finished" implies. Two thousand years ago, at the time Jesus was crucified, the word **Telestai** was also used on financial invoices and contracts where money was owed. It was written on or stamped on the document, meaning "the account has been paid in full.

So, when Jesus cried out, **"*IT IS FINISHED*"** and bowed his head and gave up His spirit, He was not declaring His life was over and finished. No way! He was stating that the authority of hell and death that Satan held over human souls was "finished."

The moment he breathed out his final breath, The Father's Will went into effect right before Satan's eyes and there was nothing he could do about it. That was when Satan realized he had made the biggest mistake since he'd led an all-out assault on God's throne in heaven and was cast down to earth.

Satan believed he had killed Jesus, but this was the worst mistake in Satan's existence. One he would never recover from because now he was condemned and his head-ship and stranglehold over the human race was under assault. Satan was in full retreat, trying to protect Hades.

Prior to Jesus' death, when human being died, their soul went to one of two locations in Hades. One location was called "Abraham's Bosom." Within shouting distance of Abraham's Bosom, but separated by a great abyss, was a second location reserved for the wicked. Even though the souls of the saints of old were comfortable in Abraham's Bosom, the Devil held them captive as he held the keys to death and the grave.

However, the righteous no longer are down under the earth's ground in Abraham's Bosom; they are with Jesus in Paradise. This change occurred when Jesus was resurrected from the dead.

When one of thieves, who was killed with Jesus at Calvary, asked, *"Jesus, remember me when you come into your kingdom."*

CHAPTER 7 - VALIDATING THE FATHER'S WILL

Jesus told him, *"Today, you will be with me in paradise."*(Luke 23:432-43)

After Jesus gave up his spirit and died, the spiritual battle became so violent that it manifested into the physical realm:

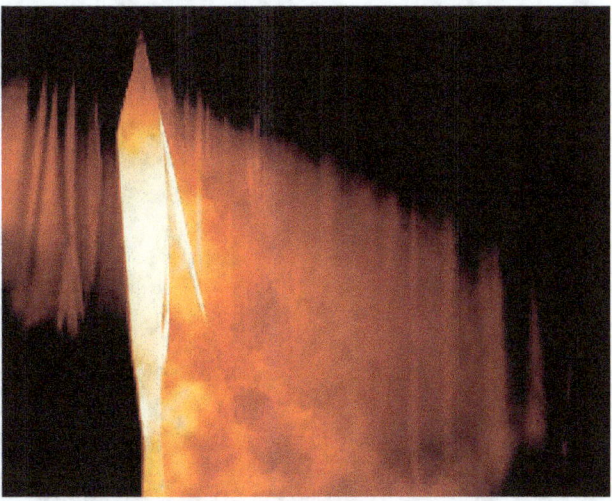

"The curtain of the temple was torn in two from top to bottom. The earth shook and the rocks split. The tombs broke open.

When the centurion and those with him who were guarding Jesus saw the earthquake and all that had happened, they were terrified, and exclaimed, *"Surely he was the Son of God!"* (Reference Mathew 27: 50-54)

CHAPTER 7 - VALIDATING THE FATHER'S WILL

They took his body off the cross and laid him in Joseph's tomb, but his soul went into the heart of the earth, Hades, for three days (Reference Matthew 12:40). But that's not where the story ends!

While in Hades, Jesus overpowered Satan on his home turf. He destroyed his strongholds, his principalities, and powers of darkness. He took from the Devil the authority he had stolen from Adam, disarming him of the head-ship over all people who would believe in him and make him Lord of their life.

When Jesus finished destroying the Devil's works in Hades, he took the keys of death and the grave away from the Devil. He told all the saints the "Good News" of His coming. Then He removed the locks and opened the gates of Hades, setting the righteous saints of old free.

Abraham, Isaac, Jacob, Samuel, and all the rest of the Old Testament faithful were ransomed from the power that Satan and Hades had over them, holding them prisoners of war. Jesus set them free. Then, Jesus came up out of Hades, He defeated death and the grave and brought the saints of old out of Hades with Him.

The Bible says, "*The bodies of many holy people who had died were raised to life. They came out of the tombs after Jesus' resurrection and went into the holy city and appeared too many people."* (Matthew 27:52-53)

Then three days later, Jesus dead body came back to life again. As he stepped out of the deaths tomb alive, He declared, *"I am the living one. I died, but look — I am alive forever and ever! And I hold the keys of death and Hades."* (Revelation 1:18)

No one on planet Earth had ever risen from the dead without a human being interceding to God, on behalf of the dead person.

The first and only one human to ever have done this was Jesus of Nazareth. By doing this, Jesus destroyed Satan's spiritual contract of his head-ship over the human race.

Jesus did not only rise from death to life, he also ascended into heaven

CHAPTER 7 - VALIDATING THE FATHER'S WILL

alive with his body, in front of dozens of eyes witnesses.

Wouldn't it be nice if you could start life all over again, as a Child of God?

YOU CAN! If you ask Jesus to come into your heart and save your soul right now, he will do it. The Bibles says, *"If you confess with your mouth the Lord Jesus and believe in your heart that God has raised Him from the dead, you will be saved. For with the heart one believes unto righteousness, and with the mouth confession is made unto salvation"*

"For whoever calls on the name of the Lord shall be saved." (Romans 10:9-10, and 13)

Remember if anyone does not have the Spirit of Christ, they do not belong to Christ. *"But if Christ is in you, then even though your body is subject to death because of sin, the Spirit gives life because of righteousness.*

And if the Spirit of him who raised Jesus from the dead is living in you, he who raised Christ from the dead will also give life to your mortal bodies because of his Spirit who lives in you." (Romans 8:10-12)

Jesus could have stopped it when they started beating him, but He didn't. He could have called down a host of angels when they were whipping the flesh off His back, but He didn't.

He could have commanded them to stop before they began to drive the nails into His hands and feet, but He didn't. Jesus went through it all, because God the Father loves us so very much and wants us to choose to have a loving, obedient relationship with Him, through His Son Jesus.

Jesus loves you so much that He left heaven, knowing He had to endure all the hateful punishment, pain, curses, and shameful death of crucifixion on a cross. All of it was for you and me.

He died for you. It's time to *"Repent and be baptized, every one of you, in the name of Jesus Christ for the forgiveness of your sins. And you will receive the gift of the Holy Spirit."* (Acts 2:38)

There is only one way for a human being to come to receive forgiveness and salvation from God. *"Salvation is found in no one else, for there is no other name under heaven given to mankind by which we must be saved."* (Acts 4:12)

If we choose to reject Jesus' offer and die without changing that decision, we will spend all eternity separated from God in anguish and torment in hell with Satan.

You may be contemplating suicide. You may be dependent on drugs,

CHAPTER 7 - VALIDATING THE FATHER'S WILL

pornography, alcohol, sexual immorality, food, or prescription drugs. No matter what you have done, no matter what Satan has you chained and addicted to, God will forgive you. All you need to do is choose to believe in Jesus as your Savior and confess your sins and mean it from your heart.

The moment, you believe in Jesus and ask God to forgive your sinful life, God sprinkles the holy righteous blood of Jesus on your heart. It's the blood of Jesus that separates and removes all the sins you have ever committed.

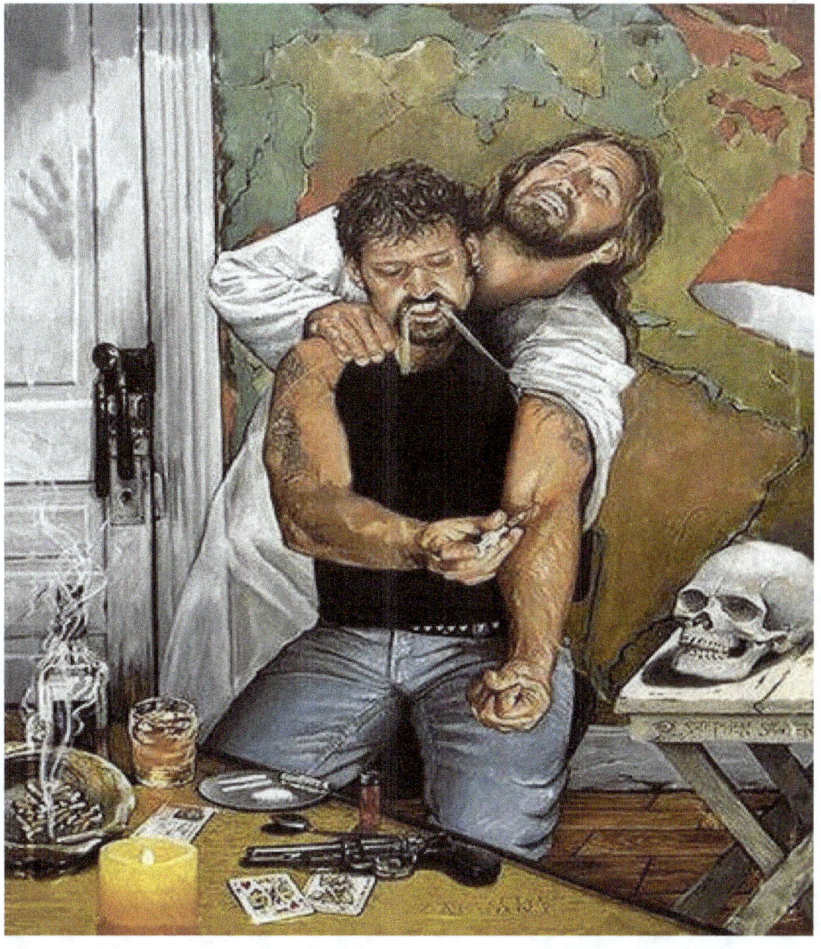

Instantly, you're set free from being a slave to Satan's bondage, addictions, and evil deadly life-style. Jesus Blood, Death, Resurrection, and His Ascending alive into heaven. Alive, was the price of your freedom from Satan. *So, if the Son sets you free, you will be free indeed."* (John 8:36)

Not only are you free, but you are born-again spiritually, in Christ Jesus as a Child of God with God's Holy Spirit indwelling in you. God the Father is your Daddy! All your addictions, the emptiness and lack of purpose in your life will be taken away and replaced with real peace, real joy, and real purpose for life as God's Holy Spirit takes up residence in your body.

Maybe you have never believed in Jesus. Or, perhaps you thought you were saved, but you fell back into sin, and now you're not sure if you're saved or not.

Jesus told us "*I am the gate; whoever enters through me will be saved. They will come in and go out, and find pasture.*" (John 10:9).

Open your heart's door to Jesus now.

CHAPTER 8

Repentance

God's First R-Gate of Salvation

It is extremely important for Christians to understand God's plan of salvation. If we can understand God's plan of salvation from His view and judgment, it will produce an abundant loving and obedient relationship of worshipping God forever!

The next five chapter's cover what God hears, sees, and does, when we choose to believe and accept Jesus as our Savior.

Try to put in sequence, from God's perspective, the following five R gates of Salvation. Again, this is what God sees, hears, and does.

- Rebirth
- Regeneration
- Reconciliation
- Repentance
- Redemption

The Five R Gates of Salvation are:

Repent – Repentance (humans must repent before God Almighty)

Reconcile - Reconciliation (when we repent—God reconciles to Him)

Redeem – Redemption (God redeems us in the blood of Jesus)

Rebirth - Born Again of God's Holy Spirit

Regeneration - Making disciples of all peoples of all nations.

We can never be reconciled to God with sin in us, because God is holy, sin and God will never co-exist. When we choose to believe and accept Jesus as our Savior and make him Master of our life, the first "R Gate" we must go through is *repentance.* True repentance brings change is us.

Before true reconciliation can take place between two differing people or parties, one of them must come to the realization that their belief, attitude, and actions were wicked, wrong, and sinful against the other person. The person who did the wrong will feel remorse, sorrow, and regret for their actions against the other party and these feelings will cause the person who did the wrong to feel the need **to confess and admit their sinful actions to the other person or party**. When heartfelt true repentance is asked for—then forgiveness can be granted.

Have you ever had someone hurt you spiritually or physically and then quickly tell you they were sorry they hurt you and ask you to forgive them? But their apology, attitude, and behavior didn't reflect sincerity. Their motive was only to continue benefiting from the relationship they had with you. They needed you, to do something for them.

Well, that's exactly what many of us do with God. We want something from God, so we tell Him we're sorry, but we really don't mean it in our heart. We tell God we give our life to Him to fulfilling an emotional commitment, but we have no intentions of honoring our commitment to **die to our old self**. At the first sign of strife and

CHAPTER 8 - REPENTANCE - GOD'S FIRST R-GATE OF SALVATION

hardship or sorrow, we crawl off the cross with our sinful nature still alive. We didn't die to our old sinful self.

We even promise God, "If you get me out of this mess, I'm yours. I'll do what you want me to do. I'll go where you want me to go." But we really don't mean it. We want God's goodness and the world's sinful pleasures, so we try to have a selfish affair with God, instead of surrendering and committing to loving relationship with Him.

The more we use God in this manner, the more accustomed to God's ways we become. This is a very dangerous situation for us, because this kind of adulteress affair puts us in a place where we have no fear of God. Our heart needs to be broken in order for us to sincerely repent of our sins.

God expects us to crucify our old lifestyle of sin on the cross with Jesus. Apostle Paul tells us, *"Those who belong to Christ Jesus have nailed the passions and desires of their sinful nature to his cross and crucified them there."* (Galatians 5:24)

In addition, God expects us to physically and spiritually surrender and exchange our old life for a new one. The Bibles says, *"Therefore, if anyone is in Christ, he is a new creation; old things have passed away; behold, all things have become new.* (II Corinthians 5:17)

When we hear the Good News Gospel Message about Jesus and the kingdom of heaven and we believe it in our heart, God's Holy Spirit woos and prepares us to do, what God wants from us.

We experience a deep pain of grief and sorrow for living a sinful lifestyle against God. The grief and regret is followed by an intense desire; a longing to urgently change our old life and turn away from it to face Jesus and live a new life for God. True repentance must take place in our heart, and we must speak the confession with our mouth in order for God to forgive us of our sins. **True repentance will always bring change in your life**, you'll become a new person.

In Old Testament Israel, there was a young teenage boy named David, who, armed with a few small stones and a slingshot, killed a giant of a man named Goliath. That same David became a great warrior and the King of Israel.

One of the greatest examples of repentance in the Bible occurred after King David had committed adultery with Bathsheba. One evening, King David got up from his bed and walked around on the roof of his house. From there he saw a very beautiful woman bathing. So, he sent someone to find out who she was. The messenger returned saying, "The woman is Bathsheba, the wife of Uriah the Hittite, a captain in your Army who is away at battle fighting the Amorites."

David sent messengers to bring Bathsheba to him. She came to him, and he had sexual relations with her. After a few weeks passed, Bathsheba realized she was pregnant so she sent word to David that she was expecting his child.

David devised a plan to bring Bathsheba's husband, Uriah, back from the battle, to visit and sleep with his wife, so everything would be fine when Bathsheba had her baby. This way, there would be no reason for Uriah to question his wife about who the father of the child was.

When Uriah returned from the battle, he reported directly to King David at the palace. David asked him how Joab and the army were getting along and how the war was progressing. Then he told Uriah, *"Go on home and relax."* David even sent a gift to Uriah after he had left the palace. But Uriah didn't go home. He slept that night at the palace entrance with the king's palace guard.

The next day, when David heard that Uriah had not gone home, he summoned him and asked, *"What's the matter? Why didn't you go home last night after being away for so long?"* Uriah replied, *"The Ark and the armies of Israel and Judah are living in tents, and Joab and my master's men are camping in the open fields. How could I go home to wine and dine and sleep with my wife? I swear that I would never do such a thing."*

David told him, *"Well, stay here today, and tomorrow you may return to the army."* So, Uriah stayed in Jerusalem that day and the next. Then

David invited him to dinner and got him drunk. But even then, he couldn't get Uriah to go home to sleep with his wife. Again, he slept at the palace entrance with the king's palace guard. David's plan had failed.

The next morning when David found out that Uriah had slept with the palace guards, he devised another plan and wrote out orders to Uriah's commander; Joab, that would put Uriah and his company in the fiercest part of the battle. David sealed the orders and gave them to Uriah to deliver to commander Joab.

When Joab received the written orders, he did what Kind David commanded. He put Uriah at a place in the battle where he knew the enemy's strongest defense was, and Uriah died in battle. Joab sent a messenger and told David, *"Some of your officers were killed in battle, including Uriah the Hittite."*

When Bathsheba heard that her husband was dead, she mourned for him. After the time of mourning was over, she became David's wife. (Reference; Samuel 11:1-24)

But God was displeased with David's sinful deeds. God sent Prophet Nathan to David to tell this story: "There were two men in a city. One man was rich, but the other man was poor. The rich man had lots of sheep and cattle. But the poor man had nothing except one little female lamb that he'd bought. The poor man fed the lamb, and the lamb grew up with this poor man and his children. The lamb ate from the poor man's food, drank from his cup, and slept on the poor man's chest. The lamb was like a daughter to the poor man.

"Then a traveler stopped to visit the rich man. The rich man wanted to give food to the guest, but he did not want to take any of his own sheep or cattle to feed the traveler. So, the rich man took the lamb from the poor man and cooked it for his visitor.

After hearing this, David became very angry with the rich man in the story. He said to Nathan, *"The man who did this should die! He must pay four times the price of the lamb because he did this terrible thing and because he had no mercy."*

Then Nathan told David, "**You are that man**! This is what the LORD, the God of Israel, says: *'I anointed you king of Israel and saved you from the power of Saul. I gave you your master's house and his wives and the kingdoms of Israel and Judah. And if that had not been enough, I would have given you much, much more. Why then have you despised the word of the LORD and done this horrible deed?*

For you have murdered Uriah the Hittite with the sword of the Ammonites and stolen his wife. From this time on, your family will live by the sword because you have despised me by taking Uriah's wife to be your own. Because of what you have done, I will cause your own household to rebel against you. I will give your wives to another man before your very eyes, and he will go to bed with them in public view. You did it secretly, but I will make this happen to you openly in the sight of all Israel.'" (II Samuel 12:7-12)

After hearing how terrible his sin was before God, David said to Nathan, "*I have sinned against the LORD.*" Nathan replied, "*The LORD has taken away your sin. You are not going to die. But because by doing this you have shown utter contempt for the LORD, the son born to you will die.*" (II Samuel 12:13-14)

David was under "The Law Covenant" (the Law of Moses). The penalty for adultery and murder required a death sentence by stoning for each sin, but God took away his sins and the two death sentences against him.

After Nathan left David, the baby boy who had been born as a result of King David's sinful sexual affair with Bathsheba become very sick. David prayed for the baby and went into his house and stayed there. He lay on the ground, refusing to eat with his family. On the seventh day, the baby died. (Reference; II Samuel 12:15-18)

Soon after the boy's death, David expresses his broken heart's sorrow, and reveals God's love, mercy, grace, and faithfulness, in Psalms 51.

It begins with David crying out, "*Have mercy on me, O God,*

CHAPTER 8 - REPENTANCE - GOD'S FIRST R-GATE OF SALVATION

according to your unfailing love; according to your great compassion, blot out my transgressions. Wash away all my iniquity and cleanse me from my sin. For I know my transgressions, and my sin is always before me. Against you, you only, have I sinned and done what is evil in your sight; so, you are right in your verdict and justified when you judge." (Reference Psalms 51:1-4).

David felt deep regret, guilt, sorrow, and grief for committing adultery with Uriah's wife and orchestrating Uriah's murder. He was burdened with torment for his transgressions, iniquity, and sin. He pleaded with God, *"Cleanse me with hyssop, and I will be clean; wash me, and I will be whiter than snow. Let me hear joy and gladness; let the bones you have crushed rejoice. Hide your face from my sins and blot out all my iniquity."* (Reference Psalms 51:7-9).

David expressed these descriptions to show the seriousness of sin and the great lengths that God goes through in separating, purging, and cleansing us from all our sins, if our confession is sincere and from the heart.

David wanted his joy back. He wanted his relationship with Jesus and Father God back the way it was prior to committing the sins of adultery and murder. When he said, *"Wash me, and I will be whiter than snow,"* David's request came from his heart. He was asking God for His mercy. This is the only appropriate request a confessing sinner can make to ask God to forgive him and mean it from the heart.

Once King David repented, he asked God; *"Create in me a clean heart, O God. Renew a loyal spirit within me. Do not banish me from your presence, and don't take your Holy Spirit from me. Restore to me the joy of your salvation, and make me willing to obey you.*

Then I will teach your ways to rebels, and they will return to you. Forgive me for shedding blood, O God who saves; then I will joyfully sing of your forgiveness. Unseal my lips, O Lord, that my mouth may praise you." (Psalms 51:10-15).

David was sincere, and he promised God he would use his experience to bring others to the knowledge of God's love, mercy, and salvation. It was God's grace that brought David a renewed motivation to sing with his tongue about God's forgiveness. David's desire to be forgiven, his desire for peace, and his desire for the message of hope that he could communicate to others is an example we must follow. We need to compare our confession of sin to David's.

Today, many of us come to God, professing our belief in Jesus. We spend three or four-minutes asking God to forgive us for our entire lifetime of rebellious sin, iniquity, and transgressions we've committed against him. But we don't make any promises or vows to God like King David did.

Instead, we immediately begin asking for stuffs; money, a job, a home, food, a good husband or wife. We need to ask ourselves; "does my confession of sin simulate the pain, regret, guilt, and suffering David displayed? Do I feel convicted to serve the Lord Jesus and Father God in doing kingdom work and telling others of God's, love, mercy, and forgiveness?"

If we don't feel painful regret and remorse for our transgressions against God, then we're not sincerely confessing from our heart. We're under the conviction of wanting something from God.

When David repented, he made a commitment to die to his sinful nature in exchange for a newly created and clean heart from God. David was sincere in confessing his sins and promised to serve God by telling others of God. God did what David asked Him to do! And David kept his vows and promises to God.

If we are going to follow Jesus, we must lay down our old sinful lifestyle of pleasing the flesh and the vanity of this world. We must die to it and live for God's plan of salvation. If we don't, God will not forgive us of our sins.

"Do not love the world or the things in the world. If anyone loves the world, the love of the Father is not in him. For all that is in the world; the lust of the flesh, the lust of the eyes, and the pride of life is not of the

CHAPTER 8 - REPENTANCE - GOD'S FIRST R-GATE OF SALVATION

Father but is of the world. And the world is passing away, and the lust of it; but he who does the will of God abides forever." (I John 2:15-17)

King David said to God, *"You do not delight in sacrifice, or I would bring it; you do not take pleasure in burnt offerings. My sacrifices, O God, is a broken spirit; a broken and contrite heart you, God, will not despise."* (Psalms 51:16-17)

David told us the truth; Father God does not desire or take delight in or find pleasure in burnt sacrificed animals. God finds pleasure and delight in you and me becoming a restored person, reconciled to Him.

A contrite heart is a heart that feels regret and expresses pain, sorrow, and guilt for sins and iniquities committed against God. David knew what pleased God. It was a person who comes to God with a contrite and broken heart. David's desire to be forgiven, his desire for peace, and his desire for the message of hope that he could communicate to others is an example that we must follow.

The completion of repentance is when we willfully surrender our old lifestyle of sin, our goals of pleasing ourselves, and accept Jesus as our Savior and Master of our life. We cannot please God and the desires of our flesh at the same time.

"Those who live according to the flesh have their minds set on what the flesh desires; but those who live in accordance with the Spirit have their minds set on what the Spirit desires. The mind governed by the flesh is death, but the mind governed by the Spirit is life and peace. The mind governed by the flesh is hostile to God; it does not submit to God's law, nor can it do so. Those who are in the realm of the flesh cannot please God." (Romans 8:5-8)

The greatest promise God gives us, is the assurance that when we repent from our sins, He is faithful to forgive us all our sins and removes all our sins away from us, as far as the East is from the West.

Once sin is removed, God gives us His Holy Spirit to reside in us, giving us peace and joy, and declares to us that we are His righteous and holy Children.

Many of us are wondering why our life is like a spiritual roller-coaster ride with all the problems we have with finances, jobs, health, children, and our recurring doubts of whether God even hears our prayers. We even wonder at times if we're saved. Our checkpoint is the Cross at Calvary, daily.

If you do not repent and ask for forgiveness for your sin daily, and **if you have not forgiven all who sinned against you**, that may explain your spiritual roller-coaster ride in your relationship with God.

God will not forgive your sins unless you forgive others who have sinned against you. You see, salvation is a daily task, not an once-in-a-lifetime event. Repentance isn't just about wiping your slate clean. It's about finding renewed purpose and receiving a refreshing from Father God.

"Now repent of your sins and turn to God, so that your sins may be wiped away. Then times of refreshment will come from the presence of the Lord, and He will again send you Jesus, your' appointed Messiah." (Acts 3:19-20)

God loves you just as much as He loved King David. But you must humble yourself, turn from your wicked ways, and have an attitude of repentance from your heart, like King David did. God is calling for you to repent. He created you and loves you dearly.

However, in the spiritual realm, you are Children of the Wicked One, separated from and enemies of God.

The only way God can take His rightful position in your life is; *"If you declare with your mouth, "Jesus is Lord," and believe in your heart that God raised him from the dead, you will be saved. For it is with your heart that you believe and are justified, and it is with your mouth that you profess your faith and are saved."*

"For everyone who calls on the name of the Lord will be saved." (Romans 10:9-10, and 13)

CHAPTER 8 - REPENTANCE - GOD'S FIRST R-GATE OF SALVATION

You may be wondering "**Why do I need to confess my sins with my mouth out loud**? Why can't I just think it?" "God knows everything including the motives of our heart." **So why do I need to say it out load**?

You are correct, God knows everything about you, including the intentions of your heart. However, Satan and his evil forces do not know your heart's intentions, and he cannot read your mind. Satan needs to hear you say, "I want Jesus as Master and Lord of my life."

Since the downfall of Adam and Eve in the Garden of Eden, every human baby born from the seed of a man is spiritually born as **a son or daughter of the Wicked One**, the **Devil**. Every human being is born bound to Satan's legally binding spiritual contact over us. Satan truly is our spiritual father.

God has no authority to operate in your life **until you give Him permission to do so**.

You see, God really did give the authority and dominion over planet Earth, to Adam. And when Adam sinned, Adam gave away that authority and dominion to Satan who became our spiritual father.

All human beings, born on earth from the seed of man, are children of the Wicked One. Born as sons and daughters of Satan.

Even though God created us, He has no authority to come into our life unless we ask God to do so.

The only way this spiritually binding contract of Satan's head-ship over you can be broken, is by you believing in Jesus, the Son of God. You must declare through your mouths, out loud into the atmosphere that Jesus is your Lord and Savior.

When you confess your sins with your mouth and mean it from your heart, you are asking the Father to forgive you, and set you free from Satan and his evil forces. It's your confessing and asking that gives God the permission to take His rightful place as your Spiritual Father.

Now Satan recognizes you are a child of God, and he knows he has no authority to breathe on you, or touch you, or come near you, unless God, the Father allows it or unless you speak with your mouth and say

CHAPTER 8 - REPENTANCE - GOD'S FIRST R-GATE OF SALVATION

something that opens a door in the spiritual realm, allowing Satan and his evil forces permission to operate in or around you.

When you confess your sins, Satan realizes you have fired him and he no longer is your spiritual father. You now belong to Father God and are citizens of His kingdom of Heaven.

Satan just heard you – confess your sins to God and Satan heard you ask God to forgive you.

Satan heard you – ask God to forgive you and wash you in the blood of Jesus Christ.

Satan heard you – ask God to become a child of God and fill you with His Holy Spirit.

You just fired Satan. He no longer is your spiritual father.

Satan heard you vow to live the rest of your life becoming a disciple for Christ Jesus and doing the will of God.

Satan is not happy. He knows you now have been born again with God's Holy Spirit, "the Spirit of Truth," is now in you. Satan knows he lost an evil soul to God's goodness. He's extremely angry because:

Satan no longer has any legal, moral, or spiritual authority to be near you.

When Satan heard you ask God for His Holy Spirit to live in you and have His way in your life, you were immediately born-again with God's Holy Spirit in you.

You are now a Child of God and Satan cannot touch you without God's permission.

On the Cross at Calvary is where Jesus exchanged His life for your lives. He sacrificed His freedom and life, so you could choose to be free and become born again through God's Holy Spirit.

Two thousand years ago, Jesus asked these two important questions: *"What good is it for a man to gain the whole world, yet forfeit his soul?*

Or what can a man give in exchange for his soul?" (Reference Mark 8:36-37)

Because Jesus died on Calvary's Cross for our sins, we are able to choose to believe, accept, and obey, the plan of salvation God has provided for us. The cost for our salvation is; we must be willing to die to ourselves and exchange our life here on earth, for a loving obedient relationship with God through Jesus.

Would You Like to Start Life all over again?

God is willing and ready to forgive you, but you must declare with your mouth out loud, and mean it from your heart that you desire to have God become your spiritual Father, instead of Satan.

If you want Jesus to save you from hell, and set you free from Satan and all his addictions, he has you bound to— pray this prayer out loud and mean if from your heart.

"Heavenly Father, I believe that Jesus is the Son of God and I want Jesus to become my Savior. I believe Jesus died on the Cross at Calvary to save me, and I believe that your Holy Spirit raised Jesus from death, back to life, and that Jesus is alive today in heaven, sitting on your throne.

From the bottom of my heart, I am sorry for living my life in sin. I confess all the sins that I remember, and those sins I cannot remember. I ask you to please forgive me. I want to become a new person. Father, wash me and cleanse me in the blood of Jesus, yours son. I love you Jesus, thank you for saving my soul. I love you Father God, thank you for making me whole.

The proof of repentance is change

We cannot remain the same person once we exchange our life. The Bible says, *"Don't you realize that your body is the temple of the Holy Spirit who lives in you and was given to you by God? You do not belong to yourself, for God bought you with a high price. So, you must honor God*

CHAPTER 8 - REPENTANCE - GOD'S FIRST R-GATE OF SALVATION

with your body." (I Corinthians 6:19-20)

Our body becomes a temple of the Holy Spirit, whom we receive from God. Therefore, we must honor God with our bodies. Apostle Paul told us, *"I have been crucified with Christ and I no longer live, but Christ lives in me. The life I live in the body, I live by faith in the Son of God, who loved me and gave himself for me."* (Galatians 2:20)

Jesus became flesh, just like you and me. It was his pure, holy, righteous blood that provided a way and a right for you and me to be set free from Satan's controlling head-ship and become children of God. Only the blood of Jesus can redeem you. The choice is yours!

The price of your soul is Jesus' blood that He shed on the Cross at Calvary, for the reconciliation of your soul.

"So, what makes us think we can escape if we ignore this great salvation that was first announced by the Lord Jesus himself and then delivered to us by those who heard him speak?" (Hebrews 2:3)

CHAPTER 9

Reconciliation

God's Second R-Gate of Salvation

Reconciliation is the Second "R-Gate" in God's plan of salvation. It occurs **the moment we sincerely repent**. The blood of our Lord Jesus Christ shed on the Cross at Calvary has made possible reconciliation for all human beings.

Reconciliation involves a change in the relationship between God and man. It signals a change from living a hostile life toward God, separated from God, and being an enemy of God to a relationship of peace, fellowship, and becoming a Child of God.

When Adam and Eve disobeyed God's command and ate the forbidden fruit from the Tree of Knowledge of Good and Evil, the human race became separated from God and enemies of God. At that time, no provision or right existed for Adam and Eve to repent of their sin.

No ransom had been established for human's sin that would allow

God to forgive human's sin. There was no advocacy in heaven that could testify on behalf of the human race and justify God's desire to reconcile the human race back to Him. This is why Jesus stepped out of eternity and came to Earth to be born a divine human being, without a rebellious sinful nature in Him.

He came to provide all peoples of all nations a way and the right to become Children of God by believing in Him. Salvation can be found only in the name of Jesus Christ of Nazareth, *"for there is no other name under heaven given among men by which we must be saved."* (Acts 4:12)

"For God in all His fullness was pleased to live in Christ, and through him God reconciled everything to Himself. He made peace with everything in Heaven and on earth by means of Christ's blood on the cross." (Colossians 1:19-22)

A good way to understand how God reconciles you and me to Him is to look at what Jesus did on the Cross at Calvary as our mediator, interceding between God the Father and the human race. There is a scripture in Proverbs 17:12 that says, *"Better to meet a bear robbed of her cubs than a fool in his folly."*

Imagine, for a moment, being in a beautiful forest on a warm, sunny late-spring day, stream fishing for trout and salmon. You hear splashing in the water and look downstream to see two small lovely cub bears playing in the stream less than fifty feet from you.

Suddenly you come alive with fear as you remember the advice that an old woodsman taught you about surviving bear encounters in the woods of Maine. He said "if you encounter bear cubs in the woods, stop, don't move, and slowly look around for momma bear. Be very careful that you have not interceded between a momma bear and her cubs. Because if you do, there's fixing to be a meeting, and you're going to be on the receiving end of the meeting. And that meeting will be downright ferocious.

This is what happened to Satan at Calvary. It would have been better

CHAPTER 9 - RECONCILIATION GOD'S SECOND R-GATE OF SALVATION

for Satan to have met a mother bear robbed of her cubs, than to have met Jesus at Calvary. God the Father sent Jesus to intercede and reconcile His cubs back to Him.

Intercession and mediation require a meeting where delegation and authority are discussed between the differing parties. These meetings can become violent at times.

On Calvary's Cross, Jesus conducted two different intercessory meetings:

The first intercessory meeting Jesus had was with Satan, and it was a dis-uniting meeting.

It was a violent and ugly meeting because Satan had come between Father God and His children. Satan should never have done that because, after 4000 years of pent-up fury, Jesus interceded on our behalf in the meeting of all meetings. Satan's worst nightmare came true at Calvary as the spiritual battle between Good and Evil meet head on.

Evil spilled over into the physical realm. The sky grew dark, the earth shook, rocks split into pieces, the graves were opened, and many bodies of the saints who had died were raised out of the grave.

When God's Holy Spirit raised Jesus from death, back to life, *"They left the cemetery after Jesus' resurrection, went into the holy city of Jerusalem, and appeared too many people."* (Matthew 27:53)

All this happened as;
- Love met hate,
- Goodness met evil,
- Light met darkness,
- Truth met lies,
- Righteousness met sin.

It was at this dis-uniting meeting at Calvary, when Jesus interceded between Satan and humanity and destroyed Satan's strongholds, principalities, powers and head-ship over mankind and took the keys of death and the grave away from Satan.

The second intercessory meeting Jesus conducted at Calvary was a uniting meeting. It took place as Jesus was nailed to the cross and then lifted up and hung in the air between the sinful human race and Father God.

As he hung on the cross, Jesus mediated a peace treaty between humanity and God the Father. God's plan of salvation provided all peoples of all nations a way and the right to become reconciled to Him as His children. *"Yet to all who did receive him, to those who believed in His name, He gave the right to become children of God; children born not of natural descent, nor of human decision or a husband's will, but born of God."* (John 1:12-13)

It was about three o'clock in the afternoon when, *"Jesus cried out* It was about three o'clock in the afternoon when, *"Jesus cried out with a loud voice, in Aramaic saying, "Eli, Eli, lama sabachthani?" that is, "My God, My God, why have You forsaken Me?"* (Matthew 27:46)

On the Cross, Jesus took our place, becoming our scapegoat by volunteering to take our death sentence for sin. He suffered all of God's wrath against sin. He endured all the sinful bondage that Satan had you and me bound and shackled in. All sicknesses, diseases, illnesses, addictions, and sinful bondage that Satan has us chained and bound to, all of it was heaped onto Jesus as He hung on the Cross at Calvary.

It was extremely difficult for Jesus to have His Father, God, turn awayfrom and abandon Him when all the past, present, and future sins of all humanity were heaped on Him as He hung on the Cross.

This uniting meeting Jesus had, on our behalf, was good and pleasant for you and me, but it cost Jesus much pain, suffering, and a bloody physical death.

Jesus put into effect a Peace Treaty between God and the human race, on the Cross of Calvary while we were still sinners as, "*Mercy and truth have met together; Righteousness and peace have kissed.*" (Psalms 85:10)

Humanity's Peace Treaty with God is the **New Blood Covenant**, and it's for all mankind.

Only God could have planned such an event and have it turn out perfect. I find it ironic that the Serpent Satan, who accomplished his greatest victory in the Garden of Eden from a tree, the Tree of Knowledge of Good and Evil, also suffered his greatest defeat from a tree, the Cross of Calvary. That's where Jesus sacrificed His life for you and me.

You may be asking yourself what makes Jesus' bloody death on the Cross at Calvary so special. Billions of people over the years have been killed or died in one way or another, so why is Jesus crucifixion so special? That's true, but that's not where Jesus' story ends. Because three

CHAPTER 9 - RECONCILIATION GOD'S SECOND R-GATE OF SALVATION

days later, He arose from the grave of death to live again.

When God's Holy Spirit raised Jesus back to life from the dead, Jesus defeated death and the grave because He never died again. He ascended into heaven, to sit with Father God on His throne. Jesus promised us, *"To the one who is victorious, I will give the right to sit with me on my throne, just as I was victorious and sat down with my Father on his throne."* (Revelations 3:21)

Christians cannot know the victory of the resurrection without experiencing our own crucifixion on the cross with Jesus. This is why Apostle Paul told us, *"I have been crucified with Christ and I no longer live, but Christ lives in me. The life I now live in the body, I live by faith in the Son of God, who loved me and gave himself for me."* (Galatians 2:20)

The key to our salvation is the **Cross at Calvary**. We must check ourselves daily to see if any sin is in us. If we wish to follow Jesus and be His disciple, we must deny ourselves, set aside our selfish interests, and take up His cross daily, expressing a willingness to endure hardships, suffering, and perhaps even dying because of our faith in Jesus.

Disciple John wrote these words to us: *"But whoever keeps His* word, truly the love of God is perfected in him. By this we know that we are in Him. He who says he abides in Him ought himself also to walk just as He walked." (I John 2:5-6)

If we believe in Jesus, we are instructed to obey His teachings. And when we obey His teachings, the love of God is perfected in us. God's love empowers us to live and walk as Jesus walked. During Jesus' ministry, He told his disciples; *"Whoever wants to be my disciple must deny themselves and take up their cross and follow me. For whoever wants to save their life will lose it, but whoever loses their life for me will find it."* (Matthew 16:24-25)

God deals with sin in two ways:

1. The wicked, those who do not believe in Jesus as the Son of God and Savior of the world, receive God's condemnation.
2. The righteous, those who believe in Jesus and obey His teachings, receive God's undeserved mercy.

We become united with Jesus in our spiritual death to sin at the cross of Calvary. We cannot be reconciled to Father God with sin in us. God is holy, and sin cannot coexist with God's holiness.

This is why Paul says, *"Those who belong to Christ Jesus have crucified the flesh with its passions and desires."* (Galatians 5:24).

The removal of our sins is not a process. It is done immediately. The Bible says, *"He has removed our sins as far from us as the east is from the west. The Lord is like a Father to his children, tender and compassionate to those who fear Him. For He knows how weak we are; He remembers we are only dust." "Therefore, if anyone is in Christ, he is a new creation; old things have passed away; behold, all things have become new."* (Psalms 103:12-14 and II Corinthians 5:17)

We must die a spiritual death to sin, while we are alive on Earth. Sin will never enter the kingdom of God.

Salvation is a lifelong journey, in which we come to the cross daily and check ourselves for sin and to repent. Just as Jesus' crucifixion marks the death of our old, sinful nature, Apostle Paul assures us; *"Now if we died with Christ, we believe that we will also live with him. For we know that since Christ was raised from the dead, he cannot die again; death no longer has mastery over him."* (Romans 6:8-9)

"And, if the Spirit of Him who raised Jesus from the dead is living in you, He who raised Christ from the dead will also give life to your mortal bodies because of His Spirit who lives in you." (Romans 8:11)

When we die to our old sinful life and live for Christ while we are still alive on Earth, this is our first death. So, when a believer of Christ Jesus breathes their last breath and dies physically, this is our second death. And, immediately our soul is with Jesus in Paradise.

How can I be sure God has forgiven me for my sins?

God's forgiveness of our sins is based exactly what the Holy Bible says:

1. Ask God for forgiveness.

The Bible says, *"If you confess with your mouth the Lord Jesus and believe in your heart that God has raised Him from the dead, you will be* saved. *"For "whoever calls on the name of the* LORD *shall be saved."* (Romans 10:9 and 13)

2. Love God with all your heart, all your soul, and all your mind.

We must sincerely love God more than our parents, our wife, and even more than our children. One day a Pharisee asked Jesus, ***"Teacher, which is the great commandment in the law?"*** *Jesus said to him, "You shall love the* LORD *your God with all your heart, with all your soul, and with all your mind. This is the first and great commandment. And the second is like it: 'You shall love your neighbor as yourself.' On these two commandments hang all the Law and the Prophets."* (Matthew 22:36-40).

3. Love others as much as you love yourself.

"So now I am giving you a new commandment. *"Love each other." Just as I have loved you, you should love each other. Your love for one another will prove to the world that you are my disciples."* (John 13:34-35)

"You have heard that it was said, 'You shall love your neighbor and hate your enemy. But I say to you, love your enemies, bless those who curse you, do good to those who hate you, and pray for those who spitefully use you and persecute you, that you may be sons of your Father in Heaven; for He makes His sun rise on the evil and on the good, and sends rain on the just and on the unjust." (Matthew 5:43-45)

4. Forgiving others completely.

Jesus told us: *"For if you forgive other people when they sin against you, your heavenly Father will also forgive you. But if you do not forgive others their sins, your Father will not forgive your sins."* (Matthew 6:14-15)

Jesus set the highest standard possible for forgiving others as He hung dying on the Cross at Calvary, when he said, ***"Father, forgive them, for they do not know what they are doing."*** (Luke 23:34)

Stephen, the First Christian murdered because of teaching the

"Gospel Message of Jesus," to a crowd in Jerusalem, was dragged out of the City and stoned to death. As they stoned him, Stephen prayed; *"Lord Jesus, receive my spirit." He fell to his knees, shouting, "Lord, don't charge them with this sin!" And with that, he died.* (Acts 7:59-60)

To emphasize how important God's command for us to forgive others is, Jesus told this story. The kingdom of heaven is like a king who wanted to settle accounts with his servants. As he began the settlement, a man who owed him 10000 talents was brought to him. Since he was not able to pay, the master ordered that he and his wife and his children and all that he had be sold to repay the debt. The servant fell on his knees before him. *"Be patient with me,"* he begged, *'and I will pay back everything.'* The servant's master took pity on him, cancelled the debt, and let him go. (Reference; Matthew 18:24-27)

Two thousand years ago, the value of one talent was about 6000 days' wages. 10,000 talents equaled 60 million days' wages. Jesus was making it very clear that it is **impossible** for a farmer, a merchant, or any person **to repay 164,000 years of debt wages – during their lifetime on earth**.

Jesus continued telling the story, saying, when that servant who had been forgiven went out, he found one of his fellow servants who owed him a hundred denarii. He grabbed him and began to choke him. *"Pay back what you owe me!"* he demanded. His fellow servant fell to his knees and begged him, *"Be patient with me, and I will pay you back.*" But he refused. Instead, he went off and had the man thrown into prison until he could pay the debt. (Reference Matthew 18:28-30)

At that time, a denarii's value was a day's wage. 100 denarii was a debt that could be repaid in a reasonable time frame. When the other servants saw what had happened, they were greatly distressed, they went away, and told their master everything that had happened. The master called the servant in. *"You wicked servant,"* he said. *"I cancelled all that debt of yours because you begged me to. Shouldn't you have had mercy on your fellow servant just as I had on you?"* In anger, his master turned him over to the jailers to be tortured, until he should pay back all he owed. (Reference; Matthew 18:30-34)

At the end of this story, Jesus tells us, "*This is how my heavenly Father will treat each of you unless you forgive your brother or sister from your heart.*" (Matthew 18:35)

Because Jesus shed His holy, righteous, pure blood, for humanity, you are able to exchange your addictions, habits, and bondage as sons and daughters of the Devil, to becoming a child of God and citizens of the kingdom of Heaven, destined to live with Jesus in wondrous peace, joy, and harmony for all eternity.

Or you can reject Jesus and continue to remain sons and daughters of the Devil, destined to spend eternity with Satan and his demons in the Lake of Fire, prepared for the Devil by Almighty God. Hell is a home of continuous pain, agony, endless torment, and there is no second chance or means of escaping, it's your destination **for all of eternity**.

If you make the commitment to accept Jesus Christ as your Savior, at that instant, God's attitude toward you changes from – that of an enemy – to that of a son or daughter. This is the beginning of your wonderful new relationship with God, made possible **through the blood of the Lord Jesus Christ.**

CHAPTER 10

Redemption

God's Third R-Gate of Salvation

Repentance was the First "R-Gate" we entered.

Reconciliation was the Second "R-Gate".

Redemption is God's Third "R-Gate" in His perfect plan of Salvation for us. Redemption is the fruit of what a redeemer does.

The picturesque story of redemption began in Egypt. After four hundred and thirty years of being enslaved in harsh bondage by Egypt, God birthed a new beginning for the descendants of Abraham, Isaac, and Jacob, in Exodus Chapter 12.

The theme of Passover is redemption, when God redeemed his people from slavery in Egypt. We miss the full implications if we don't understand the ancient meaning of the word, **redeemed**.

When the Children of Israel were delivered from Egypt, they wondered for forty years in the wilderness. When God allowed Joshua to lead them into the "Promised Land," they began practicing the Law God gave to Moses.

In **the Law of Moses**, God made provisions for a Hebrew family member called a kinsman, to redeem a family member, or entire family, who had become enslaved to another Hebrew. But only a closely related Hebrew male, who was willing to become the family redeemer could qualify as a kinsman to buy back the freedom of his relatives.

Once the family kinsman paid the ransom price in full to redeem his relative, "the relative who was redeemed was specifically bound to his redeemer. Bound not as a slave, but as one who owed his life to the redeemer. As an example, Boaz acted as kinsman redeemer to Ruth, and she became his wife (Ruth 4:9-10).

God was using this image of redeemer, when He told Moses to say to His people, *"I am the LORD, and I will bring you out from under the burdens of the Egyptians, and I will deliver you from their bondage. I will also redeem you with an outstretched arm and with great judgments. Then I will take you for My people, and I will be your God." (Exodus 6:6-7)*

The first Passover took place in Egypt at twilight, on the fourteenth day of the first month of the Hebrew year, that is when God instructed the entire community of Israel to slaughter the lamb at twilight. " (Exodus 12: 6).

God told Moses, *"Then they are to take some of the blood and put it on the sides and tops of the doorframes of the houses where they eat the lambs."*

That same night they are to eat the meat roasted over the fire, along with bitter herbs, and bread made without yeast. Do not eat the meat raw or boiled in water, but roast it over a fire—with the head, legs and internal organs.

*Do not leave any of it till morning; if some is left till morning, you must burn it. This is how you are to eat it: with your cloak tucked into your belt, your sandals on your feet and your staff in your hand. Eat it in haste; it is **the LORD's Passover**.* (Exodus 12:7-11)

*"On that same night, I will pass through Egypt and strike down every firstborn of both people and animals, and I will bring judgment on all the gods of Egypt. I am the LORD. The blood will be a sign for you on the houses where you are, and **when I see the blood, I will pass over you**. No destructive plague will touch you when I strike Egypt."* (Exodus 12:12-13)

And that is exactly what happened on the first Passover. "At midnight the LORD struck down all the firstborn in Egypt, from the firstborn of Pharaoh, who sat on the throne, to the firstborn of the prisoner, who was in the dungeon, and the firstborn of all the livestock as well. Pharaoh and all his officials and all the Egyptians got up during the night, and there was loud wailing in Egypt, for there was not a house without someone dead.

During the night, Pharaoh summoned Moses and Aaron and said, *"Up! Leave my people, you and the Israelites! Go, worship the LORD as you have requested. Take your flocks and herds as you have said and go. And also bless me."* (Exodus 12: 29-32).

God told Moses to tell the Children of Israel, *"This is a day you are to commemorate; for the generations to come you shall celebrate it as a festival to the LORD; a lasting ordinance."* For seven days you are to eat bread made without yeast. ***On the first day remove the yeast from your houses***, for whoever eats anything with yeast in it from the first day through the seventh must be cut off from Israel.

On the first day hold a sacred assembly, and ***another one on the seventh day***. Do no work at all on these days, except to prepare food for everyone to eat; that is all you may do. (Exodus 12:14,-16)

"Celebrate the Festival of Unleavened Bread, because it was on this very day that I brought your divisions out of Egypt. Celebrate this day as a lasting ordinance for the generations to come."

"In the first month you are to eat bread made without yeast, from the **evening of the fourteenth day until the evening of the twenty-first day.**" *For seven days no yeast is to be found in your houses*. And anyone, whether foreigner or native-born, who eats anything with yeast in it must be cut off from the community of Israel. (Exodus 12: 17-18,)

God instructed Moses to tell the Children of Israel. The **14th day** of Nissan (Aviv) is the Lord's Passover. The redemption of the first born of all of the Israelites that obeyed God's instructions occurred on **Passover Day,** which is a **one** day (one meal) Festival unto the Lord, for when God saw the Blood of the Passover Lamb smeared on the door post and frames of their homes — He passed over the home, sparing the death of the first born male children and animals, in that home.

Then, on the evening of **the 15th**, the very next day following Passover, the **Festival of Unleavened Bread** began in the evening (at twilight).

I am making this point to clarify that the **Passover festival,** and the **Festival of Unleavened Bread** are **two Festivals that merge together over eight (8) consecutive days**.

During Moses time and for hundreds of years after, the Passover was celebrated and followed immediately by the festival of Unleavened Bread.

However, by the time Jesus began His ministry, the Passover was referred to, in the Gospel Books, as "**Preparation Day**." "

"**The Passover**" and "**Preparation Day**," are one in the same. The name change is associated for preparing the homes of the Israelites to be totally free of all yeast, because of God's instruction, **no yeast shall be found in your homes for seven (7) days.**

Before Jesus came from eternity to Earth to shed His blood and die for us at Calvary, God required the Children of Israel to use animals as sacrifice for their sins. The criteria for selecting an animal to be used as a sacrifice to God were:

- The animal had to be the first animal born from the mother's womb.
- The animal had to be a one-year old male.
- The animal had to be perfect without any blemishes or deformities.
- The animal had to be selected from the person's own flock.
- The head of the family would bring the selected sacrifice to the altar in the tabernacle, (and later the Temple), and present it to the priest.
- The priest would place his hand on the head of the animal, which symbolized the transferring of sins from the family to the animal. The priest would then place the animal on the altar and sacrifice it by slitting his throat with a sharp knife, allowing the blood to flow down over the altar.
- The head of the family and his family had to have an attitude of repentance and worship in their hearts toward God. If they did God forgave their sins. God required this type of sacrifice as the redemption price to forgive their sins.

After the death of Aaron's two sons, who died after they entered the LORD's presence and burned the wrong kind of fire before Him, the LORD said to Moses, *"Warn your brother, Aaron, not to enter the Most Holy Place behind the inner curtain whenever he chooses; if he does, he will die. For the Ark's cover, the place of atonement, is there, and I Myself am present in the cloud above the atonement's cover."*

This is when God established, once a year, on the tenth day of the seventh month, the most solemn and important holy day of the Jewish calendar to take place, **the Day of Atonement.** On this day, the High Priest of Israel was to sacrifice a bull as a sin offering to purify himself and his family, making them right with God. After sacrificing the bull, he dipped his finger in the bull's blood and sprinkled it on the east side of the atonement cover. He sprinkled blood seven times with his finger in front of the atonement cover. (Leviticus Chapter 16)

The High Priest would then depart from the Holy Place and take two goats, which were chosen by casting sacred lots. He presented them at the door of the tabernacle for the corporate sins of and for the nation of Israel.

One of the goats, called **"The Lord's Goat,"** was offered as a blood sacrifice. The blood of the slain goat was taken into the Holy of Holies. Behind the sacred veil, the goat's blood was sprinkled over on the mercy-seat lid of the Ark of the Covenant and in front of it, just as with the bull's blood.

After the blood sacrifice was presented to Father God, the High Priest confessed the sins of the Israelites to God. If the High Priest followed God's instructions, he would not die and would be able to leave the Holy Place alive.

Once outside the Holy Place, the High Priest would go and lay his hands on the head of the second goat, called **"The Scapegoat."** This symbolized that all of the sins and guilt of the Children of Israel were placed on the head of the scapegoat, which was then led out into the wilderness and released, never to be seen again.

CHAPTER 10 - REDEMPTION GOD'S THIRD R-GATE OF SALVATION

This scapegoat represented the sins of the nation of Israel being taken away. Once a year, on the Day of Atonement, the sin of the nation was thus "atoned for" by the two goats, "**The Lord's Goat**" and "**The Scapegoat**." (Reference; Leviticus 16:10-22)

However, animal sacrifices were required over and over again during the year because people were continuously sinning. But because the blood of animals and birds are of a lower nature than human blood, the sacrifice of animals and birds was a remedy only in the Law of Moses. The blood of animals offered no real redemption, it only covered the sins the Children of Israel had already committed.

Animal sacrifices appeased Father God, but He could still see they were sin-stained, and because sin and the sinful nature was not removed from their body, God's Holy Spirit could not dwell in the bodies of the Children of Israel.

The only way for His Spirit to dwell in humans, like He did with Adam and Eve in the Garden of Eden prior to their sin, is for sin to be removed from us. And God's plan for sin to be removed from humanity required a ransom to be paid that would appease the Father's wrath against sin, **once and for all**.

This ransom price to remove the sinful nature within human beings was a far greater sacrifice than any perfect animal or any sinful human could ever pay. God required a Family Redeemer, who could pay the redemptive death penalty price in full, allowing Father God to forgive and remove sin from our human body. We needed a perfect human sacrifice who could justify and advocate for us, before God.

God required a first-born male human-being redeemer who was holy, righteous, and pure, without any sin and defects whatsoever, to volunteer to accept the death sentence and die one time as a human scapegoat sacrifice to God for the sins of the entire human race. This is why John the Baptist announced, **"Behold the Lamb of God, which taketh away the sin of the world."**

Redemption means the buying back from captivity by paying a ransom. Two thousand years ago, one way to buy back a slave was to offer an equivalent or superior slave in exchange.

And that's the way Father God chose to buy us back, by offering Jesus, his Only Begotten Son, in exchange for you and me. *"But when the set time had fully come, God sent His Son, born of a woman, born under the law, to redeem those under the law, that we might receive adoption to son-ship."* (Galatians 4:4-5)

What Adam and Eve lost in the Garden of Eden; no human being born from the seed of man could restore. That's why Jesus stepped forward and became our family redeemer.

Peter tells us, *"For you know that God paid a ransom to save you from the empty life you inherited from your ancestors. And it was not paid with mere gold or silver, which lose their value. It was the precious blood of Christ, the sinless, spotless Lamb of God. God chose him as your ransom long before the world began, but now in these last days he has been revealed for your sake."* (I Peter 1:18-20)

The Law of Moses could not do this. Jesus did not come to abolish the Law or the Prophets but to fulfil them. He redeemed us and provided a way and the right for each human being to choose to be born again of the Father's Holy Spirit and become a Child of God.

Probably on a Thursday evening approaching twilight, on the 14th day of Nissan (Aviv) of the Jewish calendar, about 1500 years after the first Passover Day, when Jesus celebrated the Passover meal with His disciples in Jerusalem.

He took some unleavened bread, gave thanks, broke it, and gave it to his disciples, saying, *"This is my body given for you; do this in remembrance of me."* In the same way, after the supper, he took his cup, saying, *"This cup is the new covenant in my blood, which is poured out for you."* (Luke 22: 19-20)

After the supper, late that Thursday's night, Jesus was arrested and taken away like a lamb being prepared for sacrificial slaughter.

The most brutal soldiers on Earth beat His head, face, and body, with their fist and wooden staffs until blood flowed from His swollen head and face down over His body.

They stripped him and whipped him with a whip that had sharp pieces of metal tips in the ends of the leather tines. It was specifically designed to tear the flesh from his back, to weaken him and make more blood flow.

Jesus' blood was splattered each time the tips from the whip ripped into the flesh on his back and sides. Blood poured from the wounds on his head, face, shoulders, and back, down over his body and onto the ground in the city of Jerusalem.

More blood flowed from His head, down onto the purple robe, and onto the ground. The beatings lasted all through the Thursday night and into the early morning hours of Thursday. Then they sent Jesus to Pilate.

Imagination for a moment, Jesus standing before Pilate as He is rejected by his own people. Jesus may have thought back to the cheering that the people of Jerusalem had heaped on him as He entered their city a few days earlier.

They had spread their cloaks on the road, cut palm branches from the trees, and laid them on the road for the colt carrying Jesus to walk on. The crowd hailed him like a king as He entered Jerusalem.

They had spread their cloaks on the road, cut palm branches from the trees, and laid them on the road for the colt carrying Jesus to walk on. The crowd hailed him like a king as He entered Jerusalem.

The whole city of Jerusalem was stirred as people asked, *"Who is this?"* The crowds answered, "This is Jesus, the prophet from Nazareth in Galilee, the one with mighty miracles.

Now, just a few days later, as Jesus stood before Pilate, He heard the crowd yelling, *"Away with Him, Away with Him! Crucify Him!" "His Blood is on us and our children."*

On the first Passover Day, Pharaoh finally honored the command God had given to him through Moses to, *"Let my people go,"* by allowing Moses to lead the Exodus of the Children of Israel up out of their bondage of slavery in Egypt, to a journey toward freedom.

Nearly 1500 years later, on this Passover Day, they led Jesus, *"The Lamb of God,"* outside the city walls of Jerusalem to a hill named Calvary.

CHAPTER 10 - REDEMPTION GOD'S THIRD R-GATE OF SALVATION

They nailed both of His hands and feet to a wooden cross. The little blood He had left in His body dripprf from the Cross onto the ground, outside the city of Jerusalem. All the horrific sin, sickness, diseases, addictions, and sins that Satan had put on the entire human race were heaped on Him.

As the last bit of His lifeblood flowed from His body, Father God's will, the new Blood Covenant, was put into effect that very day. Jesus' blood paid in full the ransom price for God's four thousand years of fury and wrath against sin. The prophetic picture was made complete as God's command to Satan was, "Let My People Go."

On Calvary's Cross, Jesus redeemed you and me from the spiritually binding contract of enslavement that bound us to Satan. He paid the price in full for each and every one of us.

Jesus fulfilled both types of the goats sacrificed in the Old Testament. Jesus was led out of Jerusalem like the scapegoat, carrying the sinful burdens of the entire human race. He was our scapegoat, who volunteered to take our death sentence for sin and be punished for the wrongdoings for all mankind. He was nailed to the Cross as the Lord's Goat, shedding His blood as a one-time atonement for all of humanity's sins, so that we may exercise our right to become adopted into the Family of God as His Children.

Only Jesus' blood can wash away our sins, cleanse us, and make us spotless in the Father's sight. Paul tells us, *"Praise be to the God and Father of our Lord Jesus Christ, Who has blessed us in the heavenly realms with every spiritual blessing in Christ. For He chose us in Him before the creation of the world to be holy and blameless in His sight. In love, He predestined us for adoption to son-ship through Jesus Christ, in accordance with His pleasure and will, to the praise of His glorious grace, which He has freely given us in the one He loves. In him we have redemption through his blood, the forgiveness of sins, in accordance with the riches of God's grace."* (Ephesians 1:3-7)

It is my prayer and hope that God's Holy Spirit reveals to all of us God's love that allowed Jesus to die for us so we could become adopted as His children.

Today I hear people ask, *"Did Jesus really need to shed His blood and die at Calvary, for us?* It seems so barbaric! *Why didn't God simply forgive us?"*

To better understand what Jesus' death actually did for us, let's imagine we're in a courtroom scene in which we are on trial for our sins against God the Father.

Our sins and sinful nature are capital crimes, and according to divine law, the minimum sentence for our crimes is the death penalty. In our sinful state, we were judged and found guilty and have been sentenced to death by God Himself! God's meaning of death is: we are enemies and separated from Him. Our spiritual father is the Wicked One, Satan. But God loved us so much that He sent Jesus to become the family redeemer for the human race; to take our death sentence and die in our place on the cross at Calvary, so that God the Father could forgive all of humanity's sins.

Jesus did this to please His Father. He came from eternity to Earth, to teach us how to do the Father's will. Once Jesus finished His work, he

CHAPTER 10 - REDEMPTION GOD'S THIRD R-GATE OF SALVATION

accepted our sentence of death, shedding his blood until he died for our sins.

Jesus took our punishment of death and offered us His Father's righteousness. God the Father poured out His judgment and unleashed His wrath on Jesus, sparing me and you that awful fate. Jesus was separated from His Father on the cross at Calvary!

God did all of this for you and me! He did it so we could choose to repent of our sins, confess with our mouth that Jesus is our Lord and Savior, and believe in our heart that the Father's Holy Spirit raised Jesus from the dead. If you believe this, then you are saved. This is the true Gospel of Jesus Christ and the kingdom of Heaven.

Jesus' blood made peace between the Father and humanity's sins. It is Jesus' blood that God the Father used to remove all our sins and wash our garments clean, making them white as snow. Then God sees us with no sin. We are righteous and pure in His eyes.

This is why in Heaven, they sing a new song: "*You are worthy to take the scroll and to open its seals, because you were slain, and with your blood you purchased men for God from every tribe and language and people and nation."* (Revelations 5:9)

Jesus is offering all of you a choice: by faith, you may exchange all your sins, iniquities, and your death penalty for a righteous and loving relationship with God the Father and spend eternity with Him and Father God. *"Salvation is found in no one else, for there is no other name under Heaven given to mankind by which you must be saved."* (Acts 4:12)

This is the Good News.

It is available for all peoples of all nations. If you do not accept Jesus as the Father's Peace Treaty, then your sinful nature is still at war with Father God, and you are an enemy of God, destined to spend eternity in the Lake of Fire with the Devil.

You can come to the Father only through Jesus. He told us, *"I am the way and the truth and the life. No one comes to the Father except through me. If you really know me, you will know my Father as well."*

"Believe me when I say that I am in the Father and the Father is in me; or at least believe on the evidence of the works themselves." (John 14:6-7, and 11).

Are you ready to enter through the Narrow Gate?

CHAPTER 11

Rebirth

God's Fourth R-Gate of Salvation

Jesus said, "*I tell you the truth, no one can see the kingdom of God unless he is born again*" "*No one can enter the kingdom of God unless he is born of water and the Spirit. Flesh gives birth to flesh, but the Spirit gives birth to spirit.*" (John 3:3 and 5-6)

Rebirth is when God the Father makes us complete and whole, like we were prior to sin in the Garden of Eden. Our rebirth" is a spiritual, holy, and heavenly new birth, which results in our being made alive spiritually in Christ Jesus. It happens when we repent. The Bible says, *"Repent, and let every one of you be baptized in the name of Jesus Christ for the remission of sins; and you shall receive the gift of the Holy Spirit.* (Acts 2:38)

Immediately, the redeeming blood of Jesus cleanses us from our sins, and we are born again with a new spiritual birth, from God. His **Holy Spirit comes into our body and dwells is us**.

When we are born again, our relationship with God changes. God sees us differently. We no longer are separated from and enemies of God. Apostle Paul tells us, *"The mystery that has been kept hidden for ages and generations, but is now disclosed to the Lord's people. To them God has chosen to make known among the Gentiles the glorious riches of this mystery, which is Christ in you, the hope of glory.* (Colossians 1:26-27)

"He redeemed us, in order that the blessing given to Abraham might come to the Gentiles through Christ Jesus, so that by faith we might receive the promise of the Spirit." (Galatians 3:14)

"So, you are no longer a slave, but God's child; and since you are His child, God has made you also an heir." (Galatians, 4:7)

"Because you are His sons, God sent the Spirit of His Son into our hearts, the Spirit who calls out, "Abba Father." (Galatians 4:6)

We are witnesses of these things, and so is the Holy Spirit, whom God has given to those who obey Him." (Acts 5:32)

God's Holy Spirit dwelled in the bodies of Adam and Eve in the Garden of Eden, until they rebelled and defied God's instructions regarding the forbidden fruit. When they disobeyed God, He removed His Spirit from their human bodies.

Several hundred years later, God chose a nation's small group of people, the Children of Israel, to be His Children and He would be their God. He did so to teach them His ways so they could become His Priest for the other nations of the Earth to learn about the only Most High God.

God provided Moses and His Children a place where they could come to give thanks, praise, celebration, sacrifice, and to worship Him. The first dwelling place was the tabernacle, which travelled around with Moses. This is where Moses would meet God in the Holy Place, at the "Mercy Seat" of the "Ark of the Covenant." After meeting with God, Moses' face glowed and this caused the people to be afraid of him.

Years later, King Solomon built the Temple as a permanent place in Jerusalem for the people to come and give thanksgiving, praise, celebrate, worship, and bring their animal sacrifice to the Priest.

CHAPTER 11 - REBIRTH GOD'S FOURTH R-GATE OF SALVATION

Two thousand years ago, Jesus stepped off His Father's throne and left all His glory to come from eternity to Earth. He was born in a barn and laid in an animals' feeding troth with a bed of straw and hay as His mattress. Mary wrapped baby Jesus in hand-me-down rags to keep Him warm.

Jesus came to Earth to teach, demonstrate, and speak His Father's Will to the entire human race. Then He offered Himself up as a one-time atonement, a perfect human sacrifice, for you and me. He took our death sentence and died in our place, on the cross.

Three days and **three nights** after His death, Jesus arose out of death's tomb, alive. That very evening, Jesus visited His disciples for the first time since He'd been killed by crucifixion. When He saw them, ***He "breathed on them*** and said, "*Receive the Holy Spirit.*" (Reference; John 20:22)

Today, God's Spirit still requires a special holy place set apart where He can meet with His Children and where we can meet and commune with Him to give Him thanksgiving, praise, and to worship Him. But that special place is not a church, or Temple, or Mosque, or any physical building. This special holy place is our body, being submitted to God in a spiritual state of worship.

Apostle Paul told us, "*Therefore, I urge you, brothers, in view of God's mercy, to offer your bodies as living sacrifices, holy and pleasing to God, this is your spiritual act of worship. Do not conform any longer to the pattern of this world, but be transformed by the renewing of your mind. Then you will be able to test and approve what my Father's will is His good, pleasing and perfect will.*" (Romans 12:1-2)

Have you ever wondered why God wants us as a living sacrifice?

In Psalms Chapter fifty-one, King David, after repenting for his sins against God and Israel adultery with Bathsheba and the pre-meditated murder of her husband, Uriah, David did not ask God for anything. Instead, he made a pledge to God, saying, *"Restore to me the joy of Your salvation, and uphold me by Your generous Spirit. Then I will teach transgressors Your ways, and sinners shall be converted to You. Deliver me from the guilt of bloodshed, O God, The God of my salvation, and my tongue shall sing aloud of Your righteousness. O Lord, open my lips, and my mouth shall show forth Your praise."* (Psalms 51:12-15)

David was a wealthy king, but God didn't want David's wealth. God expected and wanted the very best sacrifice David could possibly give Him; a broken humble soul. David told God, *"You do not delight in sacrifice, or I would bring it; you do not take pleasure in burnt offerings. The sacrifices of God are a broken spirit; a broken and contrite heart."* David gave God the very best sacrifice he could give; He gave himself to God.

David's revelation and understanding of pleasing God is an amazing example that we must follow. David knew exactly what God wanted and desired from him. A contrite, broken heart that feels regret, expresses pain, sorrow, and guilt, for the sins and iniquities he'd committed against God. When David died to the sinful nature, God created a new and clean heart in him.

God wants us to die to our old self and live as citizens serving the kingdom of Heaven. Jesus gave His life for us. God requests and expects the same from me and you. This is why He told His disciples, *"Whoever wants to be my disciple must deny themselves and take up their cross daily and follow me. For whoever wants to save their life will lose it, but whoever loses their life for me will save it. What good is it for someone to gain the whole world, and yet lose or forfeit their very self*?" (Luke 9:23-24)

God will only accept our very best sacrifice. The two hours of time on Sunday, the one hour at weekly prayer meeting, the few seconds we spend in prayer, blessing our food daily, and our tithes and financial love gifts that we give to God; all of this is nice. But that's not our best. God wants our life totally committed to Him. **This is God's expectation!**

One day during His ministry, "Jesus sat down near the collection box in the Temple and watched as the crowds dropped in their money. Many rich people put in large amounts. Then a poor widow came and dropped in two small coins. Jesus called his disciples to him and said, '*I tell you the truth, this poor widow has given more than all the others who are making contributions. For they gave a tiny part of their surplus, but she, as poor as she is, has given everything she had to live on*.'" (Mark 12:41-44)

We must commit our life to God, to **serve** and **live for His divine purpose**. Any other sacrifice we give God, apart from all of our heart, is unacceptable.

Today, many of us repent to God, tell Him we're sorry, and make a promise to reform, but we really don't mean it in our hearts. We want to keep living the same sinful lifestyle of sin and have God's blessings and goodness also. However, God's Holy Spirit cannot come and dwell in our body while we are committed to living a sinful lifestyle of rebelling against God.

Please understand: **God's Holy Spirit cannot coexist with sin**. We cannot knowingly continue to sin and serve God at the same time. Sin must be removed from us before God's Holy Spirit can have His way in our lives.

Jesus told us, "*No one can serve two masters; for either he will hate the one and love the other, or he will be devoted to the one and despise the other. You cannot serve God and mammon* [money, possessions, fame, status, or whatever is valued more than the Lord]." (Matthew 6:24 AMP Bible)

Apostle Paul tells us, "*Don't you realize that those who do wrong will not inherit the Kingdom of God? Don't fool yourselves. Those who indulge in sexual sin, or who worship idols, or commit adultery, or are male prostitutes, or practice homosexuality, or are thieves, or greedy people, or drunkards, or are abusive, or cheat people, none of these will inherit the Kingdom of God.*

Run from sexual sin! No other sin affects the body as this one does.

For sexual immorality is a sin against your own body. (I Corinthians 6:9-11)

"Don't you realize that your body is the temple of the Holy Spirit, who lives in you and was given to you by God? You do not belong to yourself, for God bought you with a high price. So, you must honor God with your body." (I Corinthians 6:18-20)

The time has come to ask yourself: Have I crawled up on the Cross with Jesus, and crucified myself with Christ, nailing my sins to the Cross and surrendered my whole life to God?

"When you came to Christ, you were circumcised, but not by a physical procedure. Christ performed a spiritual circumcision; the cutting away of your sinful nature. For you were buried with Christ when you were baptized. And with him, you were raised to new life because you trusted the mighty power of God, who raised Christ from the dead.

You were dead because of your sins and sinful nature was not yet cut away. Then God made you alive with Christ, for He forgave all our sins. He cancelled the record of the charges against us and took it away by nailing it to the cross. In this way, He disarmed the spiritual rulers and authorities. He shamed them publicly by His victory over them on the cross." (Colossians 2:11-15)

CHAPTER 11 - REBIRTH GOD'S FOURTH R-GATE OF SALVATION

Each day, the Cross at Calvary is our checkpoint. Have we come to the Cross and asked God for forgiveness of our sins daily?

Satan has seduced many of us into believing we can live our Christian life while knowingly committing a few small sins. Satan plants thoughts in our minds that persuade us that a little bit of sin is not so bad, and besides, removing sin from us is a process. It takes time. **This is a lie from hell**. God removes our sin instantly and gives us His Holy Spirit, which empowers us to say no to sin.

Paul said, *"I have been crucified with Christ; it is no longer I who live, but Christ lives in me; and the life which I now live in the flesh I live by faith in the Son of God, who loved me and gave Himself for me."* (Galatians 2:20).

We have been "born again." We are born of God's Holy Spirit, indwelling in us. God's Holy Spirit's personality is very sensitive to our human will. He will never force us to do anything. He won't argue or debate with us. We must learn to live and to submit, and willingly allow the Holy Spirit to have control of our life.

Many Christians don't know how to act or treat God's Holy Spirit. Spiritually, we live life doing what we want to do, instead of surrendering and allowing the Father's Holy Spirit to lead us. We cannot treat the Holy Spirit this way. When we do this, the Holy Spirit has no choice but to back off and allow us to take back the control of our life. It's the way God created and structured us, with **our own free will to choose**.

God's will and desire for us is to seek Him and establish a sincere loving relationship with Him. But we must learn **to allow** his Holy Spirit to guide and lead us through our Christian journey. However, **this cannot be done with sin in us**. It can be done only by repenting and then being obedient like Joshua, David, Peter, and Paul were.

The Bible says, *"But whoever keeps His word, truly the love of God is perfected in him. By this we know that we are in Him."* (I John 2:5)

"Now hope does not disappoint, because the love of God has been poured out in our hearts by the Holy Spirit who was given to us." (Romans 5:5)

When we obey God's word, it's like God's Holy Spirit is pouring gasoline on our heart's fire, and we are consumed by a loving desire to please Him in all we do.

We must love God with all our heart. We must read, study, and obey His instructions, so God's Holy Spirit can teach us all things, remind us, guide us in all our ways, comfort us in all persecutions, and lead us where God sends us.

We must be accessible to Him for the purpose of harvesting souls for the kingdom of Heaven.

God's Holy Spirit is proof that He lives in us and is our guarantee that God will give us the inheritance He promised us. Apostle Paul told us, *"And now you Gentiles have also heard the truth, the Good News that God saves you. And when you believed in Christ, He identified you as His own by giving you the Holy Spirit, whom He promised long ago. The Holy Spirit is God's guarantee that He will give us the inheritance He promised and that He has purchased us to be His own people. He did this so we would praise and glorify Him."* (Ephesians 1:13-14)

But we cannot keep pushing God's Holy Spirit away from guiding us spiritually and physically in our relationship with God. We must obey Jesus teachings. He told us, *"Remain in me, and I will remain in you. For a branch cannot produce fruit if it is severed from the vine, and you cannot be fruitful unless you remain in me. Yes, I am the vine; you are the branches. Those who remain in me, and I in them, will produce much fruit. For apart from me you can do nothing.*

"Anyone who does not remain in me is thrown away like a useless branch and withers. Such branches are gathered into a pile to be burned.

But if you remain in me and my words remain in you, you may ask for anything you want, and it will be granted! When you produce much fruit, you are my true disciples. This brings great glory to my Father. (John 15:4-8)

All Christians should strive not to sin. But we are going to sin. <u>And when we do sin</u>, we should remember what Disciple John said: *"I write this to you so that you will not sin. But if anybody does sin, we have an advocate with the Father; Jesus Christ, the Righteous One. He is the atoning sacrifice for our sins, and not only for ours but also for the sins of the whole world. We know that we have come to know him if we keep his commands.*

*Whoever says, 'I know him,' but does not do what he commands is a liar, and the truth is not in that person. But if anyone obeys his word, the love for God is truly made complete in them. This is how we know we are in Him: Whoever claims to live in Him **must live as Jesus did**."* (I John 2:1-6)

All Christians, should come to the cross daily to confess our sins and seek God's forgiveness. Some of us have areas of vulnerability in our lives, where temptation is strong and habits are hard to conquer. These weaknesses may give the Devil a foothold if we are not diligent in our obeying God's Word.

This is why Disciple John cautions and warns Christians who are struggling with a sin, and where victory over sin is not complete yet. **Do not make sin a practice, and do not look for ways to justify our sin.** Because we have been born again with God's Holy Spirit, **God's seed is in us,** we have the strength to say "no" to sin and defeat it in our lives.

John tells us, *"The one who does what is sinful is of the devil, because the devil has been sinning from the beginning. The reason the Son of God appeared was to destroy the devil's work. No one who is born of God will continue to sin, because God's seed remains in them; they cannot go on sinning, because they have been born of God."* (I John 3:8-9)

It's our sin that pushes the Holy Spirit away from us. As a Child of God, when we knowingly choose to sin and choose to live in sin, and not turn away from sin, **we break our agreement with God's Holy Spirit**.

When we do this, we open up spiritual doors for Satan's forces to enter into.

Holiness is attained when we believe in Jesus and obey the Father's will that Jesus taught and demonstrated on Earth.

If we don't do our part, how can the Holy Spirit remind us of all things?

How can He teach us if we're not reading the Word?

How can He remind us to pray against spiritual and physical attack?

The Cross at Calvary is the key, it's our daily checkpoint. **Did we repent from our heart?**

Have we forgiven others who sinned against us?

Did we surrender, submit, and commit our life to God?

Am I walking in obedience to Jesus' teachings?

Today, Jesus is knocking at your heart's door. If you unlock your heart to Him, He will come in and establish a closer relationship with you.

In Hebrews the Bible gives us this advice, *"We must pay the most careful attention, therefore, to what we have heard, so that we do not drift away. For since the message spoken through angels was binding, and every violation and disobedience received its just punishment,*

Then, the author of Hebrews poses a serious question to you. He asks, *"How shall we escape if we ignore so great a salvation? This salvation, which was first announced by the Lord, was confirmed to us by those who heard him.*

God also testified to it by signs, wonders and various miracles, and by gifts of the Holy Spirit distributed according to his will. (Hebrews 2:1-4)

It's time to "Enter through the Narrow Gate.

CHAPTER 12

Regeneration

God's Fifth R-Gate of Salvation

Since the death of Jesus disciples and apostles of the First-Century Church, Satan has been extremely successful in keeping millions of Christians blinded to the mission Jesus gave us**,** "go and make disciples of all peoples and all nations." And the authority Jesus gave us to complete this mission. **We are saved to save others**!

Today's Church, is at a critical intersection because many Christians don't know the Father's Will, regarding their true mission as Christians. Today's Church is not producing Disciples of Christ, like the First-Century Church did. The truth is making Disciples is not a priority of most Christian churches today. It's not even in their mission statement!

God expects His Children to develop a relationship with Him and to cultivate their knowledge and understanding of His Will, so that they can please Him and flourish from small Children into becoming mature disciples. To accomplish this, we must spend time with

God's Holy Spirit while reading and studying the bible, praying, and allowing God's Holy Spirit to teach us.

Today, Christians don't expect the Holy Spirit to display the same powerful signs, wonders, and miracles, as He did with the First-Century Church. **What Happened?**

We need to revisit the teachings, the miraculous signs and wonders, and the expectations, that Jesus taught His disciples — and compare them — to the watered-down teachings and expectations being fed to us today by most Christian Church's and false Teachers and Prophets. Do you see signs wonders and miracles in your Church today? **Why not?**

Marian Webster's Dictionary defines regeneration as: ***an act or process of regenerating: the state of being regenerated***.

For example; Genesis Chapter's one and two tell us, **Regeneration** was created and established by God for all living vegetation, trees, birds, fish, sea creatures, animals that crawl and walk on the ground, and for human beings. When God created them He spoke the seed of regeneration into everything containing life. Everything is created to regenerate after their own kind—with Good Seed. It's a concept and structure of God's Creation and it was ALL GOOD! **God is a God of Good Seeds.** God is incapable of creating EVIL.

The Bible teaches us prior to the fall of the Adam, God created the angels as spiritual beings, holy, righteous, intelligent, having diverse spiritual shapes and sizes, with names and responsibilities. They lived with God in the heights of heaven performing worship and being around God and all His Glory.

Lucifer was one of the angels created by God as the model of perfection, perfect in all his ways, full of wisdom, and beautiful.

God ordained and anointed him as the mighty angelic guardian. Lucifer had access to God's Holy Mountain, and he walked among the stones of fire. God created Lucifer holy, righteous, and good.

The Bible says, "You were blameless in all you did from the day

CHAPTER 12 - REGENERATION GOD'S FIFTH R-GATE OF SALVATION

you were created ***until the day evil was found in you***." "Your heart was filled with pride because of all your beauty. Your wisdom was corrupted by your love of splendor. So I threw you to the ground and exposed you to the curious gaze of kings." (Ezekiel 28:15 and 17)

Evil was found in the heart of Lucifer. **Pride** overcame Lucifer. Prophet Isaiah tells us, *"How you have fallen from heaven, morning star, son of the dawn!*
You have been cast down to the earth, you who once laid low the nations! You said in your heart,
"I will ascend to the heavens;
I will raise my throne above the stars of God;
I will sit enthroned on the mount of assembly, on the utmost heights of Mount Zaphon.
I will ascend above the tops of the clouds;
I will make myself like the Most High." (Isaiah 14:12-14)

In all of God's creation—Evil was birthed—in the heart of Lucifer when he devised a plan of leading one-third of heavens angelic beings, who sided with him, in an all-out assault on the throne of God his creator, and rule everything by **forcibly taking control of God's Throne**.

It is **vitally important** for you to know and understand—that **God is Holy**. And, It is impossible for **evil** (Lucifer and his evil angelic forces) **to coexist** at the same time and or in the same place **with GOD!**

There was no room for Lucifer and his host of angelic forces in heaven any longer. W**ar broke out in heaven**. Archangel Michael and his angels went to battle against Evil Lucifer, also known as the Red Dragon, and his evil host of angels. Satan and his evil forces were literally ejected from God's throne with all the quickness and power of lightning—down to earth. Jesus referred to this when he said, "*I saw Satan fall like lightning from Heaven*. (Luke 10:18)

As a result of his atrocious sin against God, Lucifer and his evil host of angels were cast to Planet Earth. Banished from living in the highest heavens, which belong to God. He became corrupt, and his name changed from Lucifer (morning star) to **Satan** (adversary). His power became completely perverted

So, **Iniquity** [Evil, Sin, and Pride] **was birthed** in the heart of Satan before — Adam and Eve's Sin and fall from God's grace in the Garden of Eden.

When Eve sinned, she believed the words spoken by Satan through the Serpent – instead — of obeying the Words of God. And, Adam sinned by listening to his help-mate Eve — instead of listening and obeying God's Words. This is when a evil rebellious nature against God was birthed in the hearts of humanity. Satan's nature entered into the hearts of Adam and Eve –and there was no plan in effect for human beings to be reconciled back to God.

God's Holy Spirit could not co-exist – with the sinful rebellious nature of man, whom He had created. So, when Adam and Eve chose to believe Satan's Word and ate the forbidden fruit – That God had commanded them not to eat. God removed His Holy Spirit from dwelling in the bodies of mankind.

Then, God quickly banished them from the Garden of Eden, so they could not eat from the **Tree of Life.**

The second definition for Regeneration in the Webster's dictionary is: ***Spiritual renewal or revival.***

Much like the physical seeds regenerate by being planted and rooted into good ground; **Spiritual seeds** planted in belief and faith will also take root and grow producing Good Fruit or Bad (Evil) Fruit. **God is a God of Good Seeds. Satan is a prince of Evil - Bad seeds.**

Jesus, the Minister of reconciliation, was sent by God the Father with authority to do the Father's will here on Earth. Jesus told us, *"For I have come down from Heaven not to do my own will, but the will of Him who sent me.* (John 6:38)

CHAPTER 12 - REGENERATION GOD'S FIFTH R-GATE OF SALVATION

During His ministry Jesus taught His disciples and dedicated followers about the kingdom of heaven, and he also demonstration the authority His Father God, had given Him. Everywhere Jesus went sign wonders and miracles followed His teachings. For example, Jesus walked on water, He rebuked the wind and the raging waves of water by telling them to be *"quiet and still."* One day, after teaching a large multitude of people for 3 days in the countryside—He fed 5000 hungry men, (not counting the women and children with them)—with 5 loaves of bread and 2 small fish. When they had finished eating they had 12 baskets of food left over. He drove demons out of human beings, and one day when a funeral possession was passing by him carrying the dead body of a widow's only son Jesus raised the dead son back to life.

The Bible tells us, *"Jesus did many other things as well. If every one of them were written down, I suppose that even the whole world would not have room for the books that would be written."* (John 21:25)

Jesus disciples and dedicated followers believed Jesus was truly the Messiah, they learned fast and also performed signs wonders and miracles—before Jesus was crucified.

What authority did Jesus give to his disciples?

Soon after Jesus started his ministry on earth, he called his twelve disciples to him and gave them authority to drive out impure spirits and to heal every disease and sickness. He gave the twelve disciples these instructions: *"Do not go into the way of the Gentiles, and do not enter a city of the Samaritans. But go rather to the lost sheep of the house of Israel. And as you go, preach, saying, "The kingdom of Heaven is at hand." Heal the sick, cleanse the lepers, raise the dead, and cast out demons. Freely you have received, freely give."* (Matthew 10: 5-8)

Jesus gave the authority Father God gave him – to his disciples and they performed the Father's will.

A short time after this, Jesus appointed seventy-two others and sent them two by two ahead of him to every town and place where He was about to go. He told them, *"The harvest is plentiful, but the workers are few. Ask the Lord of the harvest, therefore, to send out workers into His harvest field. Go! I am sending you out like lambs among wolves."*

"Whoever listens to you listens to me; whoever rejects you rejects me; but whoever rejects me rejects Him who sent me." (Luke 10:1-3 and 16).

Jesus <u>gave them the authority</u> **before** He <u>was crucified on the Cross.</u>

The Bible says, "The seventy-two returned with joy and said, *"Lord, even the demons submit to us in your name."* He replied, *"**I saw Satan fall like lightning from Heaven**. I have given you authority to trample on snakes and scorpions and to overcome all the power of the enemy; nothing will harm you. However, do not rejoice that the spirits submit to you, **but rejoice that your names are written in Heaven**."* (Luke 10:17-

On another occasion, during his ministry, Jesus was teaching His disciples one day and asked them, *"**Who do you say I am**?* Simon Peter answered, '*You are the Messiah, the Son of the living God.'* Jesus replied, *"Blessed are you, Simon son of Jonah, for this was not revealed to you by flesh and blood, but by my Father in Heaven.*

*And I tell you that you are Peter, and on this rock, I **will build** my church, and the gates of Hades will not overcome it. **I will give you** the keys of the kingdom of Heaven; whatever you bind on earth **will be bound in Heaven**, and whatever you loose on earth **will be loosed in Heaven**."* (Matthew 16:15-19). (Notice Jesus speaks this in the **future** tense.)

Shortly after this, Jesus once again reinforced the authority that His disciples **will have**. He told them a second time, *"Truly I tell you, whatever you bind on earth **will be** bound in Heaven, and whatever you loose on earth **will be** loosed in Heaven.* (Matthew 18:18).

Jesus used the future tense of **"will be"** in the two scriptures above because His mission was not completed yet. (Jesus had not yet been

CHAPTER 12 - REGENERATION GOD'S FIFTH R-GATE OF SALVATION

crucified for the forgiveness of humanity's sins when he said this).

When Jesus finished teaching, demonstrating, and speaking the Father's will here on Earth, He was crucified on the Cross, taking the sinful death sentence for every human being. He became a one-time, perfect atoning sacrifice for us, which appeased God's wrath against all human sins.

The <u>evening before Jesus was crucified</u>, He **explained some of the expectations that God the Father has for each one of us** who believe in Jesus and have become born-again Children of God. Jesus told His disciples, "*I tell you the truth, anyone who believes in me **will do** the <u>same works I have done</u>, and even greater works, because **I am going** to be with the Father. You can ask for anything in my name, and **I will do it**, so that the Son can bring glory to the Father. Yes, ask me for anything in my name, and **I will do it**!* (John 14:12-14).

Did the Authority Jesus gave to His Disciples have an expiration date?

Nowhere in the Bible does Jesus tell us that there is an expiration date for the authority or the mission—he spoken into his disciples and followers 2000 years ago.

If there was an expiration date – would our Salvation also expired? How? Why? Would a person believe suck a foolish teaching?

Is the Authority Jesus gave to His Disciples 2000 years ago---for Today's Disciples?

The evening before Jesus was arrested to be crucified, He revealed the value that exists **in his name** and all that Father God has invested in him when he gave us the unqualified **use of His name**. He told his disciples, "*At that time you won't need to ask me for anything. I tell you the truth, you will ask the Father directly, and He will grant your request because you use my name. You haven't done this before. Ask, using my name, and you will receive, and you will have abundant joy.*" (John

16:23-24)

"In that day, you will ask in my name. I am not saying that I will ask the Father on your behalf. No, the Father Himself loves you because you have loved me and have believed that I came from God. I came from the Father and entered the world; now I am leaving the world and going back to the Father." (John 16:26-28).

In these verses, Jesus put His name and prayer on <u>a spiritual legal basis</u> and **gave legally gave us the spiritual right and authority to use His Name.** Once again, Jesus is teaching them in the **future** tense.

Today, our courts of law use the phrase **"Power of Attorney."** And that is exactly what Jesus did for me and you two thousand years ago! He gave all of His believers "The "Power of Attorney" **to use His Name**.

Many Christians believe the authority Jesus gave His disciples to use His name to accomplish miracles, signs, and wonders, <u>expired like a quart of milk does</u>, with the death of Jesus' original disciples and the First-Century saints.

Is this true? Was the authority only for the twelve disciples, the eyewitnesses, and the apostles of Jesus' time? Or is it for you and me today?

After Jesus gave His disciples the legal authority to use His name, that same evening, just before He was arrested, He went into the Garden of Gethsemane in Jerusalem and prayed to Father God, saying, *"My prayer is not for them alone.* ***I pray also for those who will believe in me through their message****, that all of them may be one, Father, just as You are in me and I am in You. May they also be in Us **so that the world may believe that You have sent me. I have given them the glory that You gave me, that they may be one as We are One; I in them and You in me, so that they may be brought to complete unity***.

Then the world will know that You sent me and have loved them even as You have loved me." (John 17:20-23)

Jesus is praying this portion of his prayer in the **future** tense, for **future believers**. When Jesus prayed this prayer to His Father, He gave

CHAPTER 12 - REGENERATION GOD'S FIFTH R-GATE OF SALVATION

the authority **for all who would believe in Him to use His name**. Jesus' prayer covered the believers of the First-Century Church and Christian believers today.

If the value, power, and authority, in Jesus' name had expired and died with the disciples and apostles of the first century**, there would be no salvation for you and me**. This why Jesus prayed, "*I pray also for those who will believe in me through their message, that all of them may be one, Father, just as You are in me and I am in You. May they also be in Us so that the world may believe that You have sent Me*."

If we were in a court of law, a competent attorney would use the words Jesus spoke in John Chapter 16 and Jesus' prayer to His Father, God, in John Chapter 17, as clear, unequivocal evidence that Jesus gave all who love and obey His teachings "the power of attorney," meaning, we have the authority to use His Name.

In the legal and business world, a person who has received "the power of attorney" to represent another person has the same legal rights and privileges as the person who gave them the authority. It's as if the person who originally gave it is right there speaking and doing the work himself.

Today, if you gave me Power of Attorney over your bank accounts to address your personal will and affairs, the bank would honor the authority you gave me and allow me to perform any and all transactions, because I now represent you. You authorized it. My power is not the issue. Your supreme power to authorize me, to use your name, is the ultimate authority that the bank recognizes.

If you have one million dollars in your account, and I write a check from your account for nine hundred thousand dollars, the bank will honor the check I wrote from your account because I have your authority to do so. You gave me the "Power of Attorney."

Jesus did not only gave us the authority to use His name, He also declared that prayer in His name will receive His special attention. Whatever we ask of the Father in Jesus' name, He will endorse it, and the Father will give it to you. Nothing has changed since Jesus prayed, except us and our beliefs. The Bible says, "*Jesus Christ is the same yesterday and today and forever.*" (Hebrews 13:8).

We know that the Father always hears Jesus, and when we pray in Jesus' name, it is as though Jesus Himself was doing the praying. When we pray, we take Jesus' place here to carry out the Father's will on earth, and Jesus takes our place, before the Father.

Prayer for a disciple of Jesus is like a rifle, to a soldier in the army. Jesus' name will not only cover us in our prayer life, we will also be able to use it in our combat against the unseen forces that surround us.

As Disciples of Christ today, what is our Mission?

Imagine for a moment how Jesus felt after spending three days and nights in the heart of the earth and then stepping out of death's tomb and standing before Heaven, Earth, and Hell, as the undisputed victor over man's ancient destroyer, Satan and sin.

He was alive and full of joy, because He had provided the way and the right for peoples of all nations to believe in Him, as their redeeming Savior, so they could become Children of the only true God, by choosing to believe in him they would be born again of God's Spirit.

Jesus had destroyed the legal spiritual binding contract of Satan's head-ship over the human race for all who believe in Him.

God's Holy Spirit had been absent from dwelling in mankind since the Garden of Eden for more than four thousand years. So the same evening Jesus arose from the dead, He went to visit His disciples to show them he had defeated death and the grave, and to confirm what He had taught them. *"That Sunday evening the disciples were meeting behind locked doors because they were afraid of the Jewish leaders. Suddenly, Jesus was standing there among them! "Peace be with you," he said. As he spoke, he showed them the wounds in his hands and his side. They were filled with joy when they saw the Lord. Again, he said, "Peace be with you. As the*

Father has sent me, so I am sending you." Then **he breathed on them** and said, *"Receive the Holy Spirit."* (John 20:19-22)

Jesus expects you and me to become sent ones. We are saved to lead others to the Cross at Calvary to meet Jesus face to face. You're asking yourself, *"Is he talking to me?"* **Yes, I am talking to you**.

Paul asks you and me, *"But, how can they call on him to save them unless they believe in him? And how can they believe in him if they have never heard about him? And how can they hear about him unless someone tells them? And how will anyone go and tell them without being sent? That is why the Scriptures say, 'How beautiful are the feet of messengers who bring good news!'"* (Romans 10:14-15).

Jesus was a sent One, sent by the God the Father! *"We are therefore* **Christ's ambassadors,** *as though God were making His appeal through us. We implore you on Christ's behalf: Be reconciled to God. God made him who had no sin to be sin for us, so that in him we might become the righteousness of God."* (II Corinthians 5:19-21)

An ambassador is someone who is sent with the authority to represent and speak on behalf of <u>the one who sent him</u>. An ambassador needs to believe, trust, love, and obey the person who is sending them.

An ambassador is not a producer; he doesn't produce anything. An ambassador <u>is a distributor</u>; he is sent by the sender to distribute the message of the sender, or to perform the deed that the sender sent him to do.

For example: the leader of your country has chosen you as an ambassador and sends you to a foreign country with authority to represent the leader and speak on his behalf. When you arrive at the country you were sent to, it is your responsibility to speak the message your leader instructed you to speak or to perform the deeds he sent you to do. It's as if the one who sent you is there, speaking through you.

The power, ability, and conditions to carry out, produce, or enforce the message that you speak, on his behalf, is not your responsibility. It is the responsibility of the one who sent you.

Do We Have the Same Authority the disciples had in the First Century Church?

It is extremely important for us to understand to whom Jesus gave the authority (Power of Attorney) to accomplish His mission of reconciliation.

To answer this question, let's read what Jesus said to His disciples after God's Holy Spirit resurrected him from death to life.

A few days before Jesus ascended into Heaven, he met with his disciples on a mountain in Galilee and told them, "*All authority (all power of absolute rule) in Heaven and on Earth has been given to Me. Go therefore and make disciples of all the nations [help the people to learn of Me, believe in Me, and obey My words], baptizing them in the name of the Father and of the Son and of the Holy Spirit, teaching them to observe everything that I have commanded you; and lo, I am with you always [remaining with you perpetually, regardless of circumstance, and on every occasion], even to the end of the age.*" (Matthew 28:18-20 AMP Bible).

The mission Jesus spoke to His disciples in the scripture above is; **present** tense, *go "I am with you"* ... And, **future** tense "*even unto the end of the age.*"

In the book of Mark, the same **present** tense is used when Jesus gives his disciples these directions, "*Go into all the world and preach the Good News to everyone.*" (Mark 16:15)

But, then Jesus speaks in the future tense. "*Anyone who believes and is baptized will be saved. But anyone who refuses to believe will be condemned. These miraculous signs will accompany those who believe: They will cast out demons in my name, and they will speak in new languages. They **will** be able to handle snakes with safety, and if they drink anything poisonous, it won't hurt them. They will be able to place their hands on the sick, and they will be healed.*"

CHAPTER 12 - REGENERATION GOD'S FIFTH R-GATE OF SALVATION

When the Lord Jesus had finished talking with them, he was taken up into heaven and sat down in the place of honor at God's right hand. (Mark 16:16-19)

Jesus is clearly speaking to His disciples who **would believe, this includes you and me**.

When Jesus had completed His Father's majestic plan of salvation for humanity, He sent His disciples with all authority in Heaven and on Earth to represent him here on earth, to speak in his place, and to use his name.

Before we go any further, we must understand the definition and difference of authority and power.

The definition of **authority** is "having the power to command or act."

While the definition of **power** is "having the authority to act with strength, energy, and ability."

The only one with the authority to give power to command or act is God the Father.

Jesus came to earth as a sacrificial lamb, but the truth is **he was a Lion**. He destroyed Satan's strongholds, his powers and principalities in dark places, and took back the authority that Satan held over the human race. Jesus provided the right for every human being to come through him as "the way", to be born again by God's Spirit and become Children of God.

To those who believe in Jesus and obey His teachings, He has given the authority to use the power that exists in His name, to represent the kingdom of heaven and tell others about the Good News of Jesus.

If Jesus destroyed the devil's strongholds, why does He need me to do His work of reconciliation for Him?

The answer to this question lies in our understanding of what Jesus actually accomplished when He defeated Satan's powers, principalities, and strongholds.

Contrary to what many Christians believe, Jesus did not remove any of Satan's power. Satan still has all his power, cunningness, lies, and threats. What Jesus took from Satan was the keys of **death**, and **hades**, and his authority to use his power <u>on those of us</u> who **believe, love**, and **obey**, Jesus' teachings and make Jesus **the Lord of our lives**.

Satan is capable of doing **only evil**. He is a liar, who takes the truth and twists it so that it's distorted and then uses it masterfully in accusing you. He is a thief, a lawbreaker, and a murderer, who masquerades as an angel of light. This is why Jesus told us, *"He was a murderer from the beginning. He has always hated the truth, because there is no truth in him. When he lies, it is consistent with his character; for he is a liar and the father of lies."* (John 8:44).

<u>Satan is not a lion</u>; the Bible says he goes around **like** a roaring lion, **but Satan is no lion**.

Today, <u>Jesus is in Heaven, sitting on his Father's throne</u>. Jesus is sending you and me to represent Him and the kingdom of Heaven in our victory at Calvary.

Reason with me for a moment: when we drive a vehicle on our highways, there are speed limits that we are required by law to obey. Signs are posted periodically informing us of the maximum speed we are not to exceed. However, the signs don't stop people from speeding and breaking the law. In fact, many of us disregard the speed-limit signs and travel at a faster speed than the law permits. In doing so, we are breaking the law by speeding. But nothing happens to the lawbreakers because no one is there to enforce the law.

So to enforce the laws, the states and municipalities have trained, equipped, and sent state police, city police, and county sheriffs, with governmental authority and power to enforce the laws.

Just as the government has sent police, Jesus is sending you and me to enforce the Victory and Peace Treaty that His blood put into effect at Calvary. God has trained, equipped, and sent us with all the spiritual gifts we need to enforce our victory.

In the book of Joshua, Chapters 9 and 10, Joshua led the Army of Israel in battle and defeated five different kings and kingdoms all at once.

After the victory, what Joshua did and said to his army was a prophetic picture of what Jesus is doing for us today.

During the battle, the five kings escaped and hid in a cave. The Israelites covered the opening of the cave with large rocks and placed guards at the entrance to keep them inside while the army continued the slaughter of the Amorites. Once the destruction of the Amorites was complete, Joshua ordered the five kings to be brought out of the cave, to him. When they brought them out, he made the kings lie on their backs on the ground. Joshua was about to perform a very familiar custom, which was to place his foot on the necks or heads of his captives to display their triumphant victory.

In the history of war, it was common for defeated captives to be marched before the conquering king or general as he displayed his successful victory over them. This is what Apostle Paul was referring to when he wrote, *"And having disarmed the powers and authorities, made a public spectacle of them, triumphing over them by the cross."* (Colossians 2:15)

But after Joshua's victory, Joshua did something very different and extremely prophetic. Joshua celebrated the fulfillment of Israel's conquest over the five kings and their armies, but rather than placing his foot on the necks of these kings, "he beckoned some of his soldiers to come forward and put their feet on the kings' necks."

After the battle, Joshua told his army commanders, *"Come here and put your feet on the necks of these kings."* So, they came forward and placed their feet on their necks. *"Don't ever be afraid or discouraged. Be strong and courageous, for the Lord is going to do this to all of your enemies."* (Joshua 10:24-25)

What Joshua did is a powerful prophetic picture of what took place at Calvary, when Jesus defeated Satan and his principalities of darkness with which Satan held humanity captive in sin. Calvary is not His victory alone, it is our victory also.

Today, Jesus is calling me and you; his army of believers, to come out and celebrate the Victory. Jesus is telling us to put our feet on our enemies and enforce the "Victory of Calvary" by believing in and using the authority He gave us in His name, "the Name of Jesus." This is why Paul told us, *"The God of peace will soon crush Satan under your feet."* (Romans 16:20)

Jesus has put the enemy under our feet legally, but we must believe in and exercise the authority that Jesus has given us to use his name in individual situations to impose the literal execution of the Father's will on Earth.

Jesus is telling you and me, "***All authority** in Heaven and **on earth** has been given to me.* (Matthew 28:18)

Jesus is telling you, *"Go into all the world and preach the gospel to all creation.* (Mark 16:15)

"Whoever believes and is baptized will be saved, but whoever does not believe will be condemned." (Mark 16:16)

Jesus is telling you, *"And these signs will accompany those who believe: **In my name** they will drive out demons; they will speak in new tongues;* (Mark 16:17)

"They will pick up snakes with their hands; and when they drink deadly poison, it will not hurt them at all;" (Mark 16:18)

"They will place their hands on sick people, and they will get well." (Mark 16:18)

Jesus is telling you, *"And surely, I am with you always, to the very end of the age."* (Matthew 28:20)

Perhaps now we can better understand how Jesus operates on Earth through us. Jesus has given us the **authority** to bind (forbid) and to loosen (permit) when dealing with the agents and gates of Hell.

Don't be intimidated or fearful by the size of the cancer, the demon, or the life-threatening sicknesses. All we have to do is represent Jesus and do what He instructed us to do. Don't be afraid of past failures. Demons must be cast out. Cancers must be prayed over and destroyed. Death sentences that have been passed out by doctors must be bound and rebuked. People must be told about God's love for them. We are Christ's ambassadors, armed with the Gospel message about Jesus and the spiritual gifts that God's Holy Spirit has given us. We are sent with the authority of the Kingdom of Heaven to represent Jesus, the King of Kings, and Lord of Lords.

God the Father was in His Son Christ Jesus, reconciling the world to Himself. And he gave us this wonderful message of reconciliation. So, *we are Christ's ambassadors*; God is making his appeal through us. God has given us this task of reconciling people to Him. We speak for Christ when we plead, "*Come back to God*!" (Reference; II Corinthians 5:18-20).

We are saved to save others. You are **a Soldier in the Army of God** and you need to put on **all the armo**r of God so that you may stand against your enemy; Satan, and his evil forces.

Our mission is to tell others the Gospel Message of Jesus' salvation. And when we do, God's Holy Spirit will liberate prisoners of war that Satan has bound, by breaking every chain and setting them free. "*Those whom the Son sets free, are free indeed.*" (John 8:36). You and I don't need to do anything except speak the true Good News that Jesus saves!

The reason why the First-Century Church came together was the **name of Jesus**. They came together to worship, pray, and teach in the **name of Jesus**. Jesus' name was the center around which everything evolved.

Salvation is in the name of Jesus. When sinners cry out from their heart "the name of Jesus," it catches the Father's attention. The name of Jesus is the only name that a sinner can use to approach Father God. Jesus said, "*I am the way and the truth and the life. No one comes to the Father except through me.*" (John 14:6)

Peter told us, *"Salvation is found in no one else, for there is no other name under Heaven given to mankind by which we must be saved."* (Acts 4:12)

–Jesus Words Did Not Expire -- Jesus did not change

Jesus Christ is the same yesterday and today and forever. (Hebrews 13:8)

Prayer is done in the Name of Jesus. We pray to God the Father "in Jesus' Name."

Prayer, from a soldier in the kingdom's army, is like firing a heat-seeking missile. Jesus' name does not only covers us in our prayer life, we are also to use it in our combat against the unseen forces that surround us. When we pray, we need to expect explosions to take place.

In the Name of Jesus, I pray that Christians know **the value** of the **authority** and **power** that exist in the **Name of Jesus**. I pray that we are enlightened with the understanding and spirit of John the Baptist, Peter, and Paul, so that we may be revived and on fire as the Saints of the First-Century Church were.

Unveil our minds and hearts, Father, that we may realize the **value that is in the Name of Jesus**. For everything you have done, are doing, and will do for us and through us, is done in Jesus' name. We are truly your ambassadors for the kingdom of Heaven. In Jesus' name I pray, Amen.

CHAPTER 13

DON YOUR ARMOR

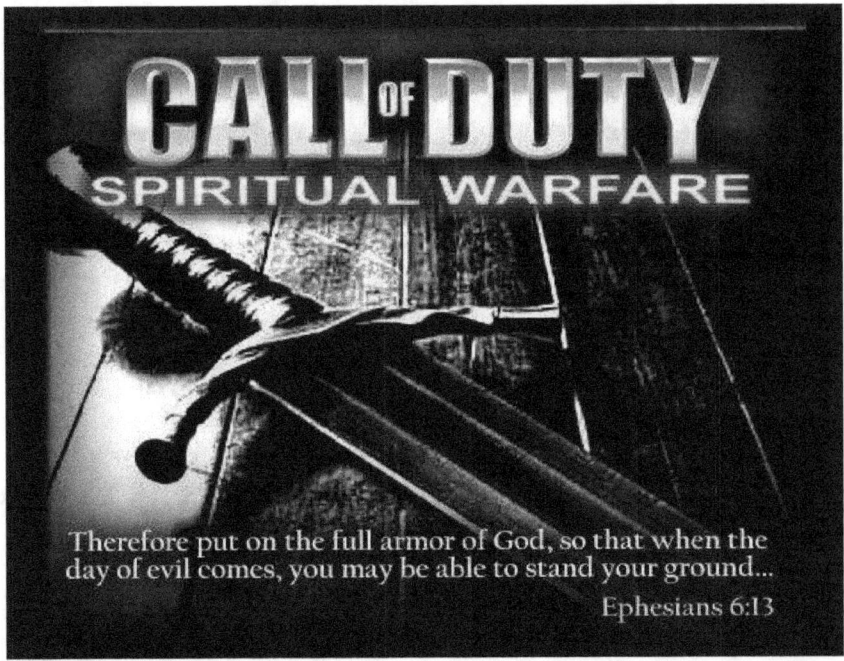

Near the end of Apostle Paul's life two thousand years ago, he was in Rome at his residence under house arrest, guarded by Roman soldiers in full battle dress, as he waited for his trial before Caesar. It was at this time that God's Holy Spirit inspired Paul to use the Roman soldier's battle armor to contrast with the spiritual armor believers in Jesus should be clothed in, so we can stand and fight against the Devil and his evil forces.

Paul may not have physically looked the part of a mighty warrior, but he was. Paul understood that spiritual warfare resulted and manifested itself in the physical realm. So, when he battled for the city of Ephesus, he did it spiritually, knowing it was not a physical battle that required a military army to win the fight.

Paul knew he needed to pray and declare God's will to be done in

Ephesus, so that the spiritual victory he declared by faith would manifest into the physical realm. This is why Paul told us, *"For though we live in the world, we do not wage war as the world does. The weapons we fight with are not the weapons of the world. On the contrary, they have divine power to demolish strongholds. We demolish arguments and every pretension that sets itself up against the knowledge of God, and we take captive every thought to make it obedient to Christ. And we will be ready to punish every act of disobedience, once your obedience is complete."* (II Corinthians 10:3-6)

Paul was strategic in his warfare because he understood his battle was against spiritual powers and that what was happening physically was a result of the ongoing spiritual warfare. So, when Paul preached the Good News about Jesus and the kingdom of heaven, souls were saved, people changed, miracles took place, and lives were affected, as the Gospel spread through the city of Ephesus.

Paul knew he had the authority to use the **name of Jesus**. He knew the value and power that existed in the **name of Jesus**, and he knew how to use it.

Paul may have looked weak, but he was a mighty spiritual warrior in God's army. He fought for the city of Ephesus, which was not just any ordinary city. Ephesus was the Roman capital city of Asia, a giant cultural city of trade and influence. This is where Paul established his strategic base of operations for teaching the Good News Gospel about Jesus. He was behind enemy lines, occupying enemy territory, and engaged in spiritual warfare for the city of Ephesus. He battled the demonic realms which controlled the city of Ephesus by using the *authority* and *power* in the **name of Jesus** to pull down Satan's spiritual strongholds.

As a result of Paul's spiritual declarations, prayer, and faith, a major victory was won. The people in the city of Ephesus stopped buying idols, and *"many of those who had practiced magic brought their books together and burned them in the sight of all. And they counted up the value of them, and it totaled fifty thousand pieces of silver. So, the word of the Lord grew mightily and prevailed."* (Reference Acts 19:19-20)

Another major spiritual battle was won about 3100 years ago, when God used a young teenage shepherd boy named David to bring down the mighty Philistine warrior Goliath, who was a giant of a man at 9 feet 9 inches tall. That battle was a spiritual battle that manifested itself into a physical victory.

Goliath's appearance overwhelmed Israel. He wore a bronze helmet on his head and a bronze coat of armor weighing 125 pounds. His shins were covered with bronze armor, and a shield bearer carried his shied. No one in the whole army of Israel, including King Saul, who was a head taller than any of the others, had the courage to fight such an awesome specimen of humanity.

David was a teenage boy shepherding his father sheep, when he went to visit his three brothers who were enlisted in Israel's Army. David was too young to be in the Army of Israel because you had to be twenty years old to join. So, when David visited his brothers, the Israeli Army was under siege by the powerful Philistine army, led by champion Goliath.

For 40 days, Goliath taunted the Army of Israel, shouting, *"Why are you all coming out to fight?"* he called. *"I am the Philistine champion, but you are only the servants of Saul. Choose one man to come down here and fight me! If he kills me, then we will be your slaves. But if I kill him, you will be our slaves! I defy the armies of Israel today! Send me a man who will fight me!"* (I Samuel 17:8-11)

When Saul and the Israelites heard this, they were terrified and deeply shaken. Goliath's appearance and words had defeated the minds and hearts of Israel's Army, because they looked on his outward appearance and listened to and believed his words.

But when David saw and heard Goliath, he knew it had nothing to do with the giant's appearance and vicious words. David knew **this battle was the Lord's battle.** So, he looked to God to deliver this giant into his hands.

David had faith in God. He could not understand why the Israelite Army allowed this huge man to taunt and challenge the people of God and why no one had the courage to stand and fight this pagan giant. God heard the astonishment in David's voice as he asked the army soldiers, *"Who is this uncircumcised Philistine, that he should defy the armies of the living God?"* (I Samuel 17:26)

Some of the army soldiers overheard David's comments and his other questions, so they reported it to King Saul, and Saul sent for him. David met with King Saul and told him that the armies of Israel had nothing to fear. *"Let no one lose heart on account of this Philistine; your servant will go and fight him."*

Saul replied, *"You are not able to go out against this Philistine and fight him; you are only a young man, and he has been a warrior from his youth."*

But David responded, *"Your servant has been keeping his father's sheep. When a lion or a bear came and carried off a sheep from the flock, I went after it, struck it, and rescued the sheep from its mouth. When it turned on me, I seized it by its hair, struck it, and killed it.*

Your servant has killed both the lion and the bear; this uncircumcised Philistine will be like one of them, because he has defied the armies of the living God. The Lord who rescued me from the paw of the lion and the paw of the bear will rescue me from the hand of this Philistine." Saul told David, *"Go, and the Lord be with you."* (I Samuel 17:32-37)

David saw **Israel as the Lord's army**, and he saw himself as a **soldier in the Lord's army**. David trusted in the Lord's ability to deliver the Philistine giant into his hand.

King Saul tried to fit his own armor on David, but after trying it on, David rejected it. He didn't need it, because he was wearing the **armor of God** and relying on God's ability.

David collected five stones from the river. Then, armed with his shepherd's staff, five stones, and his sling, he started across the valley to fight the Philistine. David brought stones and a sling to a sward fight

Goliath walked out toward David with his shield bearer ahead of him, sneering in contempt at this ruddy-faced boy, saying, *"Am I a dog that you come at me with a stick?"* And he cursed David by the names of his gods. *"Come over here, and I'll give your flesh to the birds and wild animals!"* Goliath yelled. **Goliath also understood the spiritual battle**. That's why he cursed David by the names of his gods and declared, *"I'll give your flesh to the birds and wild animals!"*

David replied to the Philistine, *"You come to me with sword, spear, and javelin, but I come to you* **in the name of the LORD** *of Heaven's Armies —* **the God** *of the armies of Israel, whom you have defied.*

Today the LORD will conquer you, and I will kill you and cut off your head. And then I will give the dead bodies of your men to the birds and wild animals, and the whole world will know that there is a God in Israel! And everyone assembled here will know that the LORD rescues his people, but not with sword and spear. This is the LORD's battle, and he will give you to us!"

As Goliath moved closer to attack, David quickly ran out to meet

him. Reaching into his shepherd's bag and taking out a stone, he hurled it with his sling and hit the Philistine in the forehead. *The stone sank in, and Goliath stumbled and fell face down on the ground.*

Then, David ran over and pulled Goliath's sword from its sheath. David used it to kill him and cut off his head. When the Philistines saw that their champion was dead, they turned and ran. (I Samuel 17:41-49, and 51)

David trusted in the Lord's power and strength. He understood the battle was not his, but the Lord's. David was a faithful warrior. David's motive for doing what he did was not to please and bring glory to himself, but to bring glory to the God of Israel.

David's outward appearance was that of a young teenage shepherd boy, without armor.

Paul's outward appearance made him look, to others, like a weak man.

But, both of them saw themselves as warriors, fighting giants. They fully trusted God for their victory and knew God would come through. **Why?**

Because they did it for God's Will and purpose. They had **no hidden motive of their own for doing God's work**. God has always used people the world may perceive as weak to do extraordinary things.

For example:

Abram, an old childless man who became Abraham, the forefather of nations.

Gideon, a farm boy, defeated the armies of Midian (Judges 8:4).

Sampson, blind, weak, chained, object of ridicule, destroyed thousands his last day alive.

Joseph, the Egyptian slave, became head over all Egypt.

Daniel the Babylonian hostage became a ruler in Babylon and Persia.

Peter, a fisherman, became a leader in Christ's Church.

Paul, a murderer, an enemy of God, became the apostle to the Gentiles and author of one-half of the Holy Bible's New Testament.

They all experienced different troubles, circumstances, and situations in their lives. But one thing they all had in common was that they <u>all learned through their weaknesses to obey and trust in God's might</u> and not in the wisdom and power of themselves or other men.

Obeying and trusting in God is putting on the armor of God, and they all learned to **put on** God's armor. And, when they did, God operated through them to accomplish **His will** here on Earth.

Two thousand years ago, Paul used the Roman Soldier's battle armor to contrast the spiritual armor that Christians need to put on order to do God's Will.

The training and discipline the Roman legions employed 2000 years ago, was extremely demanding physically and mentally. It took a new Roman soldier six months of conditioning by running, jumping, and swimming with packs twice as heavy as those used in real service and wooden swords double the weight of the common ones, before they could become part of the Roman army.

When they became a part of the Imperial Roman Legion Army, the training was just as severe. They trained from early morning until midnight by running, chopping down trees, and maneuvering through obstacle courses. And, three times each month, a legionary had to march an 18-mile route carrying 60 pounds of equipment, armor, and weapons. Along with fitness, the Roman soldiers were trained to use their weapons and armor in combat. During Paul's ministry, they were the most brutal and vicious soldiers on Earth.

A Roman soldier was an expert with his sword, but without his helmet, body armor, and shield, he was wide open and fully exposed and could be struck down at any time by a blow or an arrow from his enemies. In contrast, with the armor on, the soldier was able to stand firm and fight.

So, the Roman soldiers were always in full battle armor and trained proficiently in their ability to use their armor and weapons. No soldiers in the world could compare to them — they defeated all. They ruled the world.

Accordingly, Paul wrote a letter sharing his knowledge and tactics of spiritual warfare and described the armor of God that Christians must be clothed in at all times, so we can stand and fight against the Devil and his evil forces.

These are the warfare instructions Apostle Paul wrote: *"Be strong in the Lord and in his mighty power. Put on the full armor of God, so that you can take your stand against the devil's schemes. For our struggle is not against flesh and blood, but against the rulers, against the authorities, against the powers of this dark world and against the spiritual forces of evil in the heavenly realms.*

Therefore, put on the full armor of God, so that when the day of evil comes, you may be able to stand your ground, and after you have done everything, to stand.

Stand firm then, with the belt of truth buckled around your waist, with the breastplate of righteousness in place, and with your feet fitted with the readiness that comes from the gospel of peace.

In addition to all this, take up the shield of faith, with which you can extinguish all the flaming arrows of the evil one. And you will need the helmet of salvation and the sword of the Spirit — which is the Word of God." (Ephesians 6:10-17)

Paul's instructions are especially true for the Army that God is raising up today. If we do not put on our Godly armor daily, we could suffer wounds and bruises as a result of spiritual warfare conducted by Satan and his forces of evil, to exposed areas that God's armor would have protected us.

Our Spiritual Armor consists of:

A. The **Helmet** of **Salvation** and **the Sword of the Spirit.** *Put on salvation as your helmet, and take the sword of the Spirit, which is the word of God.* (Ephesians 6:17)

These two pieces of our armor are critical to our becoming Children of God. When we repent from our heart and exchange our old lifestyle of rebellious sin for our gift of salvation and make Jesus Lord of our life, that's when we put on the **helmet of salvation**.

The sword of the Spirit, the Word of God, is the power of our salvation.

If we reject Jesus and His teachings we have no helmet of

salvation. We are separated from God; we are enemies of God, and we remain sons and daughters of the wicked one, the Devil.

The Gospel Message of Jesus is the source of power that brings salvation from God to everyone who believes. Jesus is in every piece of the armor that we put on.

In Paul's day, the design of the Roman helmet protected the soldier's head, temple, and neck. The helmet also made him look taller and more intimidating. With the helmet on, if a soldier received a strike to the head from a sword, flaming arrow, spear, ax, or hammer, the head was protected. The soldier might be stunned, but he could still stand his ground and fight.

But without a helmet, the head was unprotected and an open, inviting target. Any strike to the head from any weapon would knock the soldier off his feet, causing a serious wound, disabling or killing the soldier.

B. The **Belt** of **Truth:** *"Stand firm then, with the belt of truth buckled around your waist."*

The belt a Roman soldier of the first century wore was not a simple leather strap, such as we wear today. It was a thick, heavy, leather and metal band, with a protective piece that was buckled tightly around the waist. Hanging down from the belt were hard strips of leather that protected the lower abdomen, groin, and the upper legs and thighs of the soldier. Attached firmly to the belt was a sheath that protected and carried the soldier's sword. Other weapons could also be attached to the belt.

Truth, in the life of a Christian, is of the greatest importance. When a person puts on Jesus, the belt of truth will prepare and protect us for the battles that are part of our everyday Christian life. Jesus said, *"I am the way and the truth and the life. No one comes to the Father except through me.* (John 14:6)

I can do all this through him who gives me strength. (Philippians 4:13)

No weapon forged against you will prevail, and you will refute every tongue that accuses you. This is the heritage of the servants of the LORD, and this is their vindication from me," declares the LORD. (Isaiah 54:17)

We must actively put truth on and use it. The belt of truth is a crucial piece of defensive armor guarding our innermost being in the battle against the lies and deceptions of the enemy. Without an understanding of truth, we are left vulnerable to being "carried about by every wind of doctrine, by the trickery of men, and by craftiness in deceitful scheming." The schemes of the devil, who is the father of lies, will surely overpower us.

C. The **Breastplate** of **Righteousness**: Apostle Paul instructed us to, *"Stand therefore, having girded your waist with truth, having put on the breastplate of righteousness,"* (Ephesians 6:14)

"But let us who are of the day be sober, putting on the breastplate of faith and love, and as a helmet the hope of salvation." (Thessalonians 5:8)

In Roman times, the breastplate was made of hard leather or metal that was overlapped. It had a section that covered the front of the body from the top of the shoulders to the waist, and a second piece that covered the back of the body, from the top of the shoulders to the waist.

These two pieces were attached securely at the top of each shoulder, affording protection to all the vital organs of the upper body, protecting both the front and the back.

God's Righteousness comes to us when we turn away from our sinful rebellious life, face God, repent of our sins, and ask Jesus to come into our heart and be Lord of our life. The moment we repent, Father God cleanses us from all our sins and exchanges our sin for his righteousness. Paul tells us, *"For I am not ashamed of the gospel, because it is the power of God that brings salvation to everyone who believes: first to the Jew, then to the Gentile. For in the gospel the righteousness of God is revealed — a righteousness that is by faith from first to last, just as it is written: 'The righteous will live by faith.'"* (Romans 1:16-17)

As we wear God's breastplate of righteousness, it circumcises and purifies our heart, causing us to conform and take on the character of God's righteousness. It's God's righteousness that allows us to make godly choices that protect us from the evil attacks of Satan and his forces.

However, when we misuse our armor or wear it incorrectly, it will malfunction. For example: When we knowingly tolerate sin in our lives,

we are abusing God's grace. When we refuse to forgive others, or when we disobey the teachings of Jesus Christ and do not repent and turn away from these sins, then, we, in effect, take off the breastplate of righteousness and allow our heart to be exposed to our enemy, Satan.

D. **Shoes** of **Peace**. For shoes, *put on the peace that comes from the Good News so that you will be fully prepared.* (Ephesians 6:15)

Our shoes of Peace come from the Good News message about Jesus and the Father's Kingdom of heaven.

In Paul's day, the covering for the feet of a Roman soldier was critical. If a soldier slipped or stumbled and sprained, cut, bruised, or broke his foot, or if he was bitten by a scorpion or a poisonous snake, he would be maimed and slowed down. His limp would expose him to the enemy, and he would fall behind the rest of the army and be an easy prey.

So, the protection covering and providing grip for a Roman soldier's feet was of great importance. This is why they were covered with hard-studded footwear that not only protected their feet from sharp objects that may cut or bruise their feet but also allowed the Roman soldiers to stand firmly without slipping, so he could fight the enemy. The Romans soldier's feet were well supported and protected.

Today, you and I must cover our feet with the Good News Blood

Covenant of Jesus so we can stand against the ploys of Satan. We need to be able to run forward and attack, like David, because we have God's Holy Spirit in us, the Spirit of Truth. Paul told us, *"How beautiful are the feet of them that preach the gospel of peace;"* "The *God of peace will soon crush Satan under your feet."* (Romans 10:15 and 16:20)

E. **The Shield of Faith:**

"In addition to all this, take up the shield of faith, with which you can extinguish all the flaming arrows of the evil one." (Ephesians 6:16)

A typical Roman shield 2000 years ago was used against all weapons. Flaming arrows could not penetrate the fireproof hard leather or metal shield that the Roman soldiers used.

The First-Century Christian's faith in God was amazing, as they literally trusted Jesus for their lives. Thousands of First-Century Christians were persecuted and killed because they believed and declared Jesus as their Lord and Savior. **Yet,** the Good News Gospel of Jesus spread throughout the known world, and, about 300 years after Jesus was raised from the dead, the Roman government declared Christianity as the world's Religion. Saints of the First-Century Church **trusted** God for their food, shelter, clothing, healing, and for everything and anything. **They were hot and on fire for Jesus!**

The majority of us Christians today are not using our shield of faith. We are using the shield of our own understanding. Our breastplate of armor is of our own righteousness, **not God's.** As a Church Body, our faith lacks a great deal compared to the faith the believers of the First-Century Church displayed daily.

Today, Christ's Church is lukewarm at best. Many people who say they believe in Jesus believe only in their mind — **not their heart**. And, our understanding and faith in God's Holy Spirit lacks a great deal. We say we believe in Jesus and God's Holy Spirit, but our fruit does not match what we claim. **Where is the Power of God's Holy Spirit in us?**

A few minutes before Jesus was taken up into heaven, He told His disciples, *"But you will receive power when the Holy Spirit comes on you; and you will be my witnesses in Jerusalem, and in all Judea and Samaria, and to the ends of the earth."* (Acts 1:8 NIV) **Before they would be able to evangelize the world, they must receive the power of the Holy Spirit**.

In describing the power of the Holy Spirit, the word translated as "power" in the English Bible is the Greek word DYNAMIS, from which we get the word DYNAMITE.

God wants to sanctify us. The Holy Spirit possesses a dynamite bomb-like power that works within a believer to blast out anything that is not righteous and God like. The Holy Spirit's power does not exalt one person above others. The Holy Spirit does not manipulate or control others. Instead, the Holy Spirit's power **breaks us**, so God can remake and remold us. The more self we allow the Holy Spirit to blow away, the more we will yield to the Father's will being done in our lives.

It's like gasoline being poured onto a fire and an explosion happens. Immediately after the explosion, we are on fire for God. The bible says, *"And hope does not put us to shame, because God's love has been poured out into our hearts through the Holy Spirit, who has been given to us."* (Romans 5:5)

God wants to purify us of our selfish, rebellious, sinful nature of pleasing ourselves, and our fleshy human desires, and remove them from us, so He can pour Himself into us and use us to reach others. God wants to use us as a conduit or a channel through which He is able to pour Himself out through us to others.

The Holy Spirit empowers us to live in a way that pleases God. He enables us to meet fully the demands and pressures of life, and to resist temptation. The power of the Holy Spirit is the only power that is sufficient to win spiritual battles against our own selfish desires and the wiles of Satan.

The Holy Spirit empowers us to be witnesses of God's love. This is why Apostle Paul said, *"My message and my preaching were not with wise and persuasive words, but with **a demonstration of the Spirit's power,** so that your faith might not rest on human wisdom, but on **God's power**."* (I Corinthians 2:4-5)

"Because our gospel came to you not simply with words but also with power, with the Holy Spirit and deep conviction." (I Thessalonians 1:5)

Imagine with me for just a moment that we are traveling together, we run into Apostle Paul, he asks us if we have received the Holy Spirit, and we answer honestly, **no**. We are confused and don't really know what God's Holy Spirit is. Paul might ask us, "Then what baptism did you experience?" We probably would say **the baptism by water**.

This actually happened in the Bible as Paul traveled from Corinth, Greece, through the interior regions until he reached Ephesus, which is in modern-day Turkey. There he found several believers. Paul asked them, *"Did you receive the Holy Spirit when you believed?"*

"No," they replied, *"we haven't even heard that there is a Holy Spirit."* *"Then what baptism did you experience?"* he asked. And they replied, *"The baptism of John."* Paul said, *"John's baptism*

called for repentance from sin. But John himself told the people to believe in the one who would come later, meaning Jesus." As soon as they heard this, they were baptized in the name of the Lord Jesus. Then when Paul laid his hands on them, the Holy Spirit came on them, and they spoke in other tongues and prophesied. There were about twelve men in all. (Acts 19:2-7)

In order for Christians to know the victory of the resurrection and power of God's Holy Spirit, we must experience our crucifixion with Jesus, on the cross. Apostle Paul told us, *"I have been crucified with Christ and I no longer live, but Christ lives in me. The life I now live in the body,* **I live by faith in the Son of God***, who loved me and gave himself for me."* (Galatians 2:20)

God loves you and me as much as He loved Apostle Paul and King David. *"For God so loved the world that He gave His only begotten Son, that whoever believes in Him should not perish but have everlasting life."* (John 3:16)

The only way God can take His rightful position as our heavenly Father **is sin must be removed** from us; we must humble ourselves, turn from our wicked ways, have an attitude of repentance in our heart, and confess with our mouth our sins and declare that Jesus is our Lord.

If we believe in our heart that God the Father raised Jesus from the dead, **then,** *we will be saved. "For it is with your heart that you believe and are justified, and it is with your mouth that you profess your faith and are saved. For, everyone who calls on my name, of the Lord Jesus, will be saved.* (Romans 10:10 and 13)

If you're ready to *Enter Through the Narrow Gate* and accept Jesus as your Savior, take a few minutes and speak to Jesus right now. He is knocking on your heart's door, asking to come in. Get your hand off the doorknob, unlock your heart's door, and invite Jesus in for supper.

At the very moment we choose to believe in Jesus and obey his teachings, we become **a soldier in God's Army**. Soldiers need to be in great spiritual condition; we must be well trained in righteousness and equipped with spiritual gifts to be used as weapons against our enemy, Satan.

"Because of Christ and our faith in him, we can now come boldly and confidently into God's presence." (Ephesians 3:12)

"Without faith*, it is impossible to please God, because anyone who comes to him must believe that he exists and that he rewards those who earnestly seek him."* (Hebrews 11:6)

Paul encourages us to fight the good fight of faith. To take hold and embrace tightly to the eternal life to which God has called us to. The measurement of our faith is ***hope***.

Let us never forget what Jesus did to the Devil, who trusted in his own armor. The Bible says, *"When a strong man, fully armed, guards his own house, his possessions are safe. But when someone stronger attacks and overpowers him, he takes away the armor in which the man trusted and divides up his plunder."* (Luke 11:21-22)

Jesus is in every piece of the armor that we put on.

Prayer is the last thing Apostle Paul mentions regarding our armor. He said, *"**Pray** in the Spirit at all times and on every occasion. Stay alert and be persistent in your prayers for all believers everywhere."* (Ephesians 6:18)

CHAPTER 14

Why Pray?

Do My Prayers Really Matter?

Many Christians wonder, "Do my prayers really matter?"

Other Christians ask, "If I don't pray, will that hinder God from accomplishing His will here on Earth?

When it comes to prayer, most Christians believe God's going to do what He wants to do, when He wants to do it, whether we pray or not. If this is true, then He doesn't need us to waste our time praying, does He?

Christians need to know if our prayers really do make a difference. We need to know if God really needs us to pray, or does He just want us to pray because He said so?

God's answer to why our prayer is necessary lies in His original plan of creation. The scriptures clearly indicate that we are God's representatives here on earth. We really are in charge. What we, as Children of God, speak with our mouth carries authority in the spirit realm, here on Earth. The Bible says, *"The highest Heavens belong to the LORD, but the earth He has given to man."* (Psalms 115:16)

Jesus' teaching on prayer is the key to answering our questions. Jesus taught his disciples, *"This then, is how you should pray 'Our Father in Heaven, hallowed be Your name, Your kingdom come, Your will be done on earth as it is in Heaven. Give us today our daily bread."* (Mathew 6:9–11)

Although God is sovereign, all knowing, omnipotent, and all-powerful, scripture tells us that concerning human affairs, God limited His Will being done on Earth to working through human beings.

Our prayers must be in line with God's Will. Jesus taught us, *"If you remain in me and my words remain in you, ask whatever you wish, and it will be done for you. This is to my Father's glory, that you bear much fruit, showing yourselves to be my disciples."* (John 14:7-8)

"Very truly I tell you, whoever believes in me will do the works I have been doing, and they will do even greater things than these, because I am going to the Father. And I will do whatever you ask in my name, so that the Father may be glorified in the Son. You may ask me for anything in my name, and I will do it." (John 14:12-14)

"Truly I tell you, if you have faith and do not doubt, not only can you do what was done to the fig tree, but also you can say to this mountain, 'Go, throw yourself into the sea,' and it will be done. If you believe, you will receive whatever you ask for in prayer." (Matthew 21:21-22)

One Day Jesus was teaching his disciples on prayer. He told them to, **"Ask the Lord of the harvest, therefore to send out workers into His harvest field."** (Matthew 9:38)

Aren't these things God's will?

Wasn't God already planning to do what they asked?

Why then, did Jesus teach us to ask God the Father for something He already wants to do?

Is it, by us asking God, it somehow allows God to do it?

Has God limited Himself to operating on Earth through human beings? If this is true, is God depending on us to ask for His kingdom to come?

I firmly believe scriptures teach us that the answer is, **"Yes!"** In First Kings 18:1, the Bible says, *"After a long time, in the third year, the word of the LORD came to Elijah: 'Go and present yourself to Ahab, and I will send rain on the land.' So, Elijah went to present himself to Ahab."*

Whose will or idea was it to cause rain? The answer is not Elijah's, but God's will.

Why did it take a human's prayer to stop the rain?

And why did it take a human's prayer to bring the rain?

Did Elijah's prayers really produce the rain, or was it simply coincidental that he happened to be praying when God sent the rain?

The answer to this question is found in the book of James. *"Elijah was a man just like us. Elijah was a human being, even as we are. He prayed earnestly that it would not rain, and it did not rain on the land for three and a half years. Again, he prayed, and the Heavens gave rain, and the Earth produced its crops."* (James 5:17-18).

The only logical answer to the necessity of Elijah's prayer is that **God needs to work with and through human beings to accomplish His will on Earth.**

Throughout scripture, whenever God wanted something done, He used a human to speak His will. Whenever a human spoke what God instructed them to say, it always came forth, in God's time.

God revealed to Ezekiel some shocking information. He told him, *"Your priests have violated My instructions and defiled My holy things. They make no distinction between what is holy and what is not. And they do not teach My people the difference between what is ceremonially clean and unclean. They disregard My Sabbath days so that I am dishonored among them. Your leaders are like wolves who tear apart their victims. They actually destroy people's lives for money! And your prophets cover up for them by announcing false visions and making lying predictions. They say, 'My message is from the Sovereign LORD,' when the LORD hasn't spoken a single word to them. Even common people oppress the poor, rob the needy, and deprive foreigners of justice.*

*"I looked for someone who might rebuild the wall of righteousness that guards the land. I searched for someone to stand in the gap in the wall so I wouldn't have to destroy the land, **but I found no one.** So now I will pour out my fury on them, consuming them with the fire of My anger. I will heap on their heads the full penalty for all their sins. I, the Sovereign LORD, have spoken!"* (Ezekiel 22:26-31)

The implications of this portion of scripture are shocking. The passage clearly says that, while God's justice demanded judgment, His love wanted forgiveness. Had He been able to find a human to ask Him to spare these people, He could have. It would have allowed Him to show mercy, but because He found no one, He had to destroy them.

God's holiness, integrity, and uncompromising truth prevent Him from simply excusing sin, it must be judged. On the other hand, God is also love. And His love always desires to redeem, restore, and show mercy.

I don't like to consider that God has limited Himself to operating on Earth through human beings. But in light of hundreds of passages, the condition of the Earth, and the evil in people, the only logical conclusion to why we should pray is, <u>God needs us to pray so He can accomplish His will here on Earth</u>.

He is waiting on us to ask Him for His will to be done on Earth, as it is in Heaven. Not praying may result in lost souls for the Kingdom. Not praying may hinder God from accomplishing His will for someone. Not praying may result in someone suffering instead of God being able to heal them.

God's giving is directly connected to our asking. God needs us to pray, and we need to know how to pray. Knowing why we need to pray can be a great motivating force for us to pray. And not knowing why may cause us not to pray.

Why did Jesus teach His disciples to pray? He taught them to pray because He passed the ministry of reconciliation on to us. We are an extension of Jesus' ministry of reconciliation, and it is our responsibility and duty to pray to God the Father in Jesus' name. We are to ask for reconciliation in the lives of our family, friends, neighbors, and enemies.

Our prayers of intercession are an extension of the intercessory work that Jesus did while He was on Earth. Apostle Paul told us, *"For God was in Christ, reconciling the world to Himself, no longer counting people's sins against them. And He gave us this wonderful message of reconciliation. So, we are Christ's ambassadors; God is making His appeal through us. We speak for Christ when we plead 'Come back to*

God!'" (II Corinthians 5:19-20)

We don't have to produce anything. It's already been produced by Jesus. Our function is not to replace God but <u>to release Him</u>. We are here to distribute the provisions of God's new will, the Gospel of Jesus. Jesus is in Heaven interceding on our behalf, presenting us to the Father as righteous and one of His own.

We're Jesus' Awesome-mites on Earth, representing Jesus' awesomeness. We don't deliver anyone. We don't defeat the enemy. We don't reconcile anyone to God. But we must ask for the release and application of all these things from God the Father **in the Name of Jesus**. And when we do this, we are enforcing the victory of Calvary.

There are no magic words or special phrases that God requires when we pray. God listens to our heart. All we need to do is pray from our heart **in the Name of Jesus**.

We need to cry out to Father God when our brothers and sisters need help. Our prayers make the difference between life and death and between Heaven and hell for some people.

When someone asks you to pray for them, you must pray for them. The reason is two-fold.

1. First, those asking for someone else to pray for them may not have confidence in their own prayers for themselves and for others. In fact, they may not pray at all.

2. The second reason is because God asks us to, and He needs us to pray.

When we ask God to do something, He will do it. And when He does, something supernatural (a miracle) will happen. All we have to do is ask God and wait for His promise.

Prayer is the key that unlocks faith in our lives.

Effective prayer needs both the attitude of **complete dependence on God** and the **action of asking God**.

Prayer demonstrates our reliance on God as we humbly invite him to fill us with faith and power. There is no substitute for prayer especially in circumstances that seem impossible.

CHAPTER 15

How to Pray

Learning how to pray can be awkward and intimidating for many believers, especially new Christians. Some of us may be fearful and confused about how to talk to God in prayer. Many of us feel it's the kind of activity that is best left to pastors and church leaders. However, scripture teaches us that prayer is an everyday activity for everyday people.

Prayer, **in the name of Jesus,** brings us close to God and deepens our relationship with God the Father, through Jesus. In Chapter Eleven of this book, we learned about the value that is in the name of Jesus and how to use His name. Jesus not only gave us the use of His name, he also told us the only way to approach our Heavenly Father is in **His name**.

In other words, we know that the Father always hears Jesus, and when we pray in Jesus' name, it is as though Jesus Himself is doing the praying. So when we pray, we take Jesus' place here on Earth, to carry out the Father's will, while Jesus takes our place before the Father in Heaven.

One day, Jesus was praying, and when he finished, one of his disciples said to him, "Lord, teach us to pray, just as John taught his disciples." He told them, *"When you pray, say: "Father, hallowed be Your name, Your kingdom come. Give us each day our daily bread. Forgive us our sins, for we also forgive everyone who sins against us. And lead us not into temptation*." (Luke 11:1-4) This teaching was several months before Jesus was crucified on the cross.

We should prepare to enter into prayer with thanksgiving and praise in our hearts. Sometimes I sing a song to prepare my heart. The Bible says, *"Enter His gates with a song of thanksgiving and His courts with praise. Be thankful to Him, bless and praise His name."* (Psalms 100:4 AMP).

When we say, "Father, in the name of Jesus I come to you," the name of Jesus opens Heaven's gate to us and welcomes us to approach Father God.

When we pray, we should elevate God for Who He is. Jesus said, ***"When you pray, say: "Father, hallowed be your name."*** We should tell God how much we love and adore Him for all He has done for us. We should thank Him for all His accomplishments, which allow us to be redeemed and be in His Presence.

We may thank God for the birds in the sky; for the water we drink; the air we breathe; the food we have to eat; the parents we have; the country we live in; and on and on we go, giving God thanks. We may spend 10 or 20 minutes just giving thanks to God and telling Him how awesome He is.

We continue praising and elevating God to "The Lord of Lords" that He is. God is above all of our problems, above all our sicknesses, above all our jobs, and above all of our loved ones. When we praise His name, we need to remind ourselves that His name is holy; there is no one or anything like Him. His name is the name that is "above all names." Even when times are tough for us, we need to stand and give praise to God. Our salvation is in our praise of God. Our needs are fulfilled in our praise. Our deliverance is in our praise of God. Our healing is in our praise of God.

Jesus taught us to ask God for "***Your kingdom come.***" We are to call for the Kingdom of God to come into our homes, into our bodies, and say, "Lord, be the Lord of my life. Be the Lord of everything around me. I'm yours."

When we ask God for "***Your Kingdom come, your will be done on earth as it is in Heaven***," we bow down, we submit and surrender our life to Him, asking God for His will to be done in our lives, as it is in Heaven. When we do this, we no longer argue and debate with God. Instead, we desire to give Him things that we don't even have yet. Our relationship with Him is closer. Now God's presence is near us. God's presence is His Glory, and when God's Glory comes into a place, lives change. It is impossible to be in the presence of God and remain the same person. Our nature changes and we take on the characteristics of God. We lose our jealousy, lying, hatred, anger, and our selfishness, all is

CHAPTER 15 - HOW TO PRAY

removed in God's presence, because God's will is perfect and holy. It changes us, it's the only thing that can change us.

Sons and daughters of God's kingdom have the authority to ask the Father, in **Jesus' name**, for *His kingdom to come on Earth*. It is His desire that His will be done in our lives and in the lives of our loved ones, as it is in Heaven. Jesus told us, "*Therefore I tell you, whatever you ask for in prayer, believe that you have received it, and it will be yours.*" (Mark 11:24)

We need to ask God every day, "***Your kingdom come***; may your will be done in me." This is our daily task so that God's Will is being worked in our lives.

This is what walking in the Kingdom of Heaven is. As we speak and pray for God's will to be released, it's as if God is holding our hand as we walk on Earth. His holy, righteous, pure will is released in people's lives and in situations just as it is in Heaven. In fact, our words are the same as if Jesus were saying them, because He is. His Spirit lives in us. Apostle Paul told us, "*God has sent the Spirit of his Son into our hearts, prompting us to call out, 'Abba, Father.' Now you are no longer a slave but God's own child. And since you are His child, God has made you His heir.*" (Galatians 4:6-7)

As we talk to God in prayer and study God's word, the Holy Spirit reveals and teaches us the will of God and the expectations that God has for us. As we obey Jesus' teachings, our loving relationship with God deepens immensely as God's love is poured out into our heart by the Holy Spirit. However, "*If we say we know God but do not obey His commands, we are lying. The truth is not in us. But when we obey God's teaching, His love is truly working in us. This is how we know that we are living in Him.*" (I John 2:4-5)

"*And this hope will never disappoint us. We know this because God has poured out His love to fill our hearts through the Holy Spirit, He gave us.*" (Romans 5:5)

You see, it really is the will of the Father for us to walk and declare

His will *"to be done on earth, as it is in Heaven."* But in order for us to do this, we must obey what Jesus teaches. Jesus told us, *"Whoever has my commands and keeps them is the one who loves me. The one who loves me will be loved by my Father, and I too will love them and show myself to them."* (John 14:21)

Jesus ends his teaching on how to pray with a startling warning about forgiveness. He taught us to ask, *"Give us today our daily bread. And forgive us our debts, as we also have forgiven our debtors.*

*And lead us not into temptation, but deliver us from the evil one. For if you forgive other people when they sin against you, your Heavenly Father will also forgive you. But <u>if you do not forgive others their sins</u>, **your Father will not forgive your sins**."* (Matthew 6:11-15)

Our salvation is based on us knowing why and understanding what it means to forgive others. Apostle Paul told the Christians in Ephesus, *"Be kind and compassionate to one another, forgiving each other, just as in Christ God forgave you."* (Ephesians 4:32)

When we come to God in prayer, we need a sacrifice to give Him. As children of the Kingdom of Heaven, it's our daily duty to approach the Father and surrender our will by offering **ourselves as a living sacrifice to God**. Apostle Paul told us, *"Therefore, I urge you, brothers and sisters, in view of God's mercy, to offer your bodies as a living sacrifice, holy and pleasing to God; **this is your true and proper worship**."* (Romans 12:1)

"Do you not know that your body is the temple of the Holy Spirit who is in you, whom you have received from God? You are not your own;" *"You were bought at a price. Therefore honor God with your bodies."* (I Corinthians 6:19-20)

We need physical food to live, but more important is the spiritual nourishment that we need daily. When our spirit comes in contact and unites with God's Holy Spirit, we are in God's presence, and worship happens. Fellowship happens, and miracles, signs, and wonders happen.

CHAPTER 15 - HOW TO PRAY

When man's spirit and God's Holy Spirit unite, **true worship happens**. In true worship, God is present, and when God is present, anything can happen. God's Glory may come. However, God's presence and sin cannot coexist. Sin must be regretted, admitted, confessed, and removed in order for God's Holy Spirit to be present in us and with us.

Every day, we need to bring ourselves to God, **free of sin**. We are truly the only sacrifice that God wants and desires. But we must be free of sin. Then we can enter into His presence and ask what we want from Him. Anything may happen in God's presence.

There is a difference between thanking and praising God—versus worshipping God.

My Body and soul can praise God.

My body and soul can give thanks to God.

My Body and soul can dance, sing, yell, and submit to God.

But my body and soul cannot – Worship God.

Jesus told us, *"But the hour is coming, and now is, when the true worshipers will worship the Father in spirit and truth; for the Father is seeking such to worship Him. God is Spirit, and those who worship Him must worship in spirit and truth."* (John 4:23-24)

Worship is done with our spirit and the Holy Spirit. The Bible says, *"Oh, come, let us worship and bow down; let us kneel before the Lord our Maker for He is our God, and we are the people of His pasture, and the sheep of His hand."* (Psalms 95:6-7)

The Bible says, *"Do you not know that your bodies are members of Christ himself? Shall I then take the members of Christ and unite them with a prostitute? Never!*

Do you not know that he who unites himself with a prostitute is one with her in body? For it is said, 'The two will become one flesh.' ***But whoever is united with the Lord is one with him in spirit.****"* (I Corinthians 6:15-17)

In verse 16 above, the relationship with the prostitute is done with the body. In verse 17 above, when our spirit is united with God's Holy Spirit, we become one with Him in Spirit and worship happens.

In this state of worship, God touches us, our needs are met, and the requests we make for others are heard. He speaks to us, and we hear Him. We know what to ask for, and we know we shall receive it, because we believed when we asked, we were in His very presence.

Worshipping God is humanity's highest activity with God on Earth. Nothing we do on Earth exceeds our worshipping God. Human beings were created to worship God! Worship opens the door to a deep relationship with God. Worship is the way into the Holiness of God. In worship, our heart speaks to God. In worship, we hear God's voice.

Understanding **why you should pray,** will help you in your prayer life and walk with Jesus.

Not knowing why you should pray, may cause millions of people to remain enemies of God and separated from God, destined to spend all of eternity in hell.

You and I are here to distribute the provisions of Father God's will. All you have to do is ask God for His will to be done in you as it is in heaven. The bible says, *"Whatever you ask for in prayer, believe that you have received it, and it will be yours."* (Mark 11:24)

It's time to, "Enter through the Narrow Gate," and begin your Journey to discipleship.

CHAPTER 16

The Measurement of Faith Is Hope

When we were young children, many of us looked forward to Christmas morning, because we were filled with hope of receiving the gift we had asked for. The closer we got to Christmas morning, the more our expectation grew, so much so that we peeked in the closets, looked under beds, and in the attic or garage, expecting to get a glimpse of the gift we had asked our parents for. We had faith in our parents to do what they said they would do. We knew that if we were good and obeyed our parents, our hope of receiving the gifts we asked them for was very high.

Finally, early on Christmas morning, we got out of bed and ran to the Christmas tree and unwrapped the gifts we had waited so long to receive. *"Faith is the confidence that what we hope for will actually happen; it gives us assurance about things we cannot see"* (Hebrews 11:1)

The faith of a small child is powerful because it contains **hope**. As adult Christians, our faith must be like that of a young child who climbed high up in a tree and became fearful when they could not get down. But when the child looked down and saw the father with his arms open wide, saying, "*Jump, and I'll catch you,*" the fathers' words created faith in the young child. <u>Hope came alive</u> and overcame doubt and fear. Hope rekindled faith, as the child positioned their body to jump, expecting their father's arms to catch them.

Imagine how a father must feel when he yells to his child, "*Jump, and I'll save you.*" But the child's face shows fear. Their afraid and worried that the father will miss catching them when they jump, and they will fall to the ground and get hurt. The child lacks faith because the child's hope is dead.

How helpless God must feel when His own sons and daughters don't trust Him. Our relationship with God must be like that of a child who obeys his father and mother out of love and trust. When we hear the Gospel message of Jesus Christ, it feeds our heart faith. *"So then faith comes by hearing, and hearing by the word of God.* (Romans 10:17)

Most Christians today don't have a child's faith. We have adult faith. We say we believe in God, but we really don't. And the reason we don't believe is we have no hope, or we believe in our minds and not with our heart.

Today, most Christians act and behave like the non-believers in the world do. This is why Jesus told us that we must *have the faith of a child*, confident and full of hope that Jesus is who He said He is, and that He will do what He said He will do.

Jesus said, *"I tell you the truth, unless you turn from your sins and become like little children, you will never get into the Kingdom of Heaven."* (Matthew 18:3)

"Anyone who doesn't receive the Kingdom of God like a child will never enter it." (Mark 10:15).

The faith of a small child is powerful, because it contains **hope. Hope is the measurement of our faith**. When we hear the Gospel message about Jesus, it feeds our heart faith, and we come alive because, *"faith comes from hearing the message, and the message is heard through the word about Christ."* (Romans 10:17)

Faith was alive and demonstrated in the First-Century Church of Peter and Paul's time. They came together to praise and worship Jesus and God the Father, and if someone had a physical or spiritual need they prayed for them in the name of Jesus, and signs, wonders, and miracles were done because of their faith in God.

Today, there are very few churches where people are prayed for and healed. Many times, when we do see a believer praying for the physical and spiritual, the majority of people being prayed for <u>don't believe</u> in their heart <u>that God will heal them</u>. They say they believe, but they really don't.

There is something that professing Christians need to know and

CHAPTER 16 - THE MEASUREMENT OF FAITH IS HOPE

understand about faith, and that is *"faith by itself, if it is not accompanied by action, is dead." "As the body without the spirit is dead, so faith without deeds is dead."* (James 2:26)

Disciple James, the step-brother of Jesus, asked. *"What good is it, my brothers and sisters, if someone claims to have faith but has no deeds?* **Can such faith save them?**

James answers this question by telling us, *"Suppose a brother or a sister is without clothes and daily food. If one of you says to them, "Go in peace; keep warm and well fed," but does nothing about their physical needs, what good is it?*

*In the same way, faith by itself, if it is not accompanied by action, is dead." But someone will say, "You have faith; I have deeds." "Show me your faith without deeds, and I will show you my faith by my deeds. You believe that there is one God. Good! Even the demons believe that and shudde*r.

You foolish person, do you want evidence that **faith without deeds is useless?** *Was not our father Abraham considered righteous for what he did when he offered his son Isaac on the altar? You see that his faith and his actions were working together, and his faith was made complete by what he did. And the scripture was fulfilled that says, "Abraham believed God, and it was credited to him as righteousness," and he was called God's friend.*

You see that a person is considered righteous **by what they do** *and not by faith alone. In the same way, was not even Rahab the prostitute considered righteous for what she did when she gave lodging to the spies and sent them off in a different direction? As the body without the spirit is dead,* **<u>so faith without deeds is dead</u>**. (James 2:15-26)

Most professing Christians claim that they have faith in God, **but they don't**. Many Christians today make choices based on common sense, because they believe in what they see, feel, taste, smell, and hear, not based on their faith in God.

225

When Christians trust in their own or another human beings common sense, this leads them to doubt God, and eventually into darkness. The Bible says, *"Cursed are those who put their trust in mere humans, who rely on human strength and turn their hearts away from the LORD."* (Jeremiah 17:5)

We must understand that **our human mind is incapable of responding to or recognizing faith**. Our mind gathers information from the body's senses and from the knowledge, wisdom, memories, and imaginations of man's mind and then translates and transports the common senses' knowledge to the heart of man, which is our soul.

Only the soul of man is capable of recognizing faith. When I say, "the soul of man" or "the heart of man," I am referring to both the male and female genders that God created.

The soul responds to faith by believing and accepting Jesus Christ or by rejecting Jesus. God has given each person a measure of faith to believe in His Only Begotten Son, Jesus. If we accept and believe in Jesus, we do it by faith.

However, if we neglect to feed our soul the daily bread of God's Word, then our soul's only food source is the wisdom, knowledge, understanding, imagination, and memories **of our human mind**, and the emotions and senses of our body. Everyone who does not believe in Jesus has established their decision on faith of their human knowledge, reality, and reason of their mind.

In our everyday life, we buy items of value with currency. In America, the U. S. dollar is used for purchasing power. In Europe, they use the Euro; in some places in Africa, the shilling is used, in Pakistan the Rupee, and in Japan, the Yen is the currency used for purchasing things.

But, to receive something from our Heavenly Father, we need to be a citizen of the kingdom of Heaven, and we need the currency used in Heaven, which is faith in Jesus Christ. Our faith in Jesus is the only purchasing currency that God the Father recognizes, accepts, and

CHAPTER 16 - THE MEASUREMENT OF FAITH IS HOPE

responds to. Jesus said, "*I am the way, the truth, and the life. No one can come to the Father except through me.*" (John 14:6)

Faith is the currency Father God responds to. It's our faith in Jesus Christ that allows Father God to lift us up out of our physical, human realm of instincts and human senses, into the spiritual realm, where born-again Christians belong. Faith allows us to walk in step with the Spirit of God.

When we need something that is within the concepts and structure of God's Will for us, if we believe God will give it to us when we ask Him for it, and if we ask in Jesus' name, then He will give us what we asked for. We will receive it by faith from the spiritual realm, into the physical realm. But when we make our request to God, our faith must be like that of a child full of hope and expectation, believing that what we have asked Him for, He will provide to us, because He said he would.

2000 years ago, while Jesus was teaching a crowd, he asked them, "*When the Son of Man comes will he really find faith on the earth?*" (Luke 18:8)

What measurement or metric can we use to determine if we have enough faith to please God? Peter told us, "*Praise be to the God and Father of our Lord Jesus Christ! In His great mercy, He has given us new birth into a living hope through the resurrection of Jesus Christ from the dead*" (I Peter 1:3).

In this verse, Peter tied the measurement of faith to hope, a **living hope**. A living hope expects what we ask God for – will be fulfilled, even though we cannot see it. Apostle Paul tells us, "*For we were saved in this hope, but hope that is seen is not hope; for why does one still hope for what he sees? But if we hope for what we do not see, we eagerly wait for it with perseverance.*" (Romans 8:24-25)

We cannot hope for something that we already have. Hope believes and expects for something we do not have – to come to realization. Without **living hope**, we cannot have faith for things that haven't come to pass yet.

Because we are born blind spiritually, **living hope** can be experienced only by the Holy Spirit enlightening us and removing our spiritual blindness, so that the eyes of our heart will be opened and unveiled to see the hope of His calling. Apostle Paul told the Christians in Ephesus, "*I pray that the eyes of your heart may be enlightened in order that you may know the hope to which he has called you, the riches of his glorious inheritance in his holy people.*" (Ephesians 1:18)

This living hope that Apostles Paul and Peter are teaching us about is the **measurement of our faith.** If hope can be living and alive, hope can also be dying and dead. The condition of our hope determines the measurement of our faith. If our hope is alive, then our faith is strong.

Faith is like the battery in a cell phone. The cell phone needs a fully charged battery to make to allow it to call and text. If the battery is fully charged, the cell phone has life and functions well. But when the battery gets low and dies, the phone is dead. The phone still has a battery, but the battery is dead. It is impossible for the phone to function with a dead battery.

If you had a source of power you could plug into when the battery is dead – your phone will work. But without a power source — the phone is dead.

As Children of God, we operate similar to a cell phone. The phone battery is our faith, the battery is our hope and Jesus is our way to the Father. When the battery is dead it can only be charged up when it is plugged into a source of power. The source of power gives the battery power to operate and function.

When our hope gets weak and dies, it can only be brought to life when we are plugged into the word of God. Once we get plugged into the Word and get a little bit of Jesus in us, He ignites a spark of love, and our hope comes alive. **Once hope is alive**, it restores our faith. Without living hope there is no faith. "*And without faith it is impossible to please God, because anyone who comes to Him must believe that He exists and that He rewards those who earnestly seek Him.*" (Hebrews 11:6)

If our hope dies, then our faith is dead. Our human mind helps kill hope by calculating and reasoning within the limits of man's wisdom. **The human mind is incapable** of operating by faith.

Where does hope come from?

The love of God is what fuels our hope. Disciple John tells us, *"But whoever keeps His word, truly the love of God is perfected in him."* (I John 2:5)

Jesus told us, *"Love the Lord your God with all your heart and with all your soul and with all your mind." "This is the first and greatest commandment."* (Matthew 22:37-38)

"Anyone who loves me will obey my teaching. My Father will love them, and We will come to them and make Our home with them. Anyone who does not love me will not obey my teaching. These words you hear are not my own; they belong to the Father who sent me." (John 14:23-24)

To love God means totally surrendering ourselves to Him and obeying Jesus' teaching. It's our obedience to God that fuels the love of God in us. It's like gasoline being poured onto a fire. Its agape love, and the more we love God, the more attached to the Kingdom of God we become. Our relationship with God deepens, and we learn to lean on God for everything.

The hope and faith in most Christians today reminds me of stories I heard while serving as a U. S. Army Ranger in Vietnam. All of us soldiers had girlfriends or wives we left behind at home. They were faithfully waiting and hoping for us to return home from war. But after a few weeks went by and their boyfriends and husbands had not returned home, their hope began to fade, and doubt set in.

Doubt turned into fear and began to overshadow their hope, dimming it. A short time later, their hope flickered, and went out. The love they once had for their beloved husbands and boyfriends was dead. They gave up hope. No love remained in their hearts for their loved ones. Many of the wives and girlfriends had affairs with other men. And when they did, they wrote, "Dear John letters," saying goodbye. They found a new love.

Today, millions of us Christians who made a commitment to love, obey, and remain faithful to Jesus' and His teachings have allowed doubt and fear to enter our minds and hearts. We have endorsed the desire for wealth and routinely put the well-being of our family and loved ones ahead of God on our priority list. Our love and obedience to do the Father's will has died. We still speak and act in godly ways, but our faith and hope is in man's wisdom and the ways of man. When we approach God, we do it because we want something from Him.

There are a few Christians whose hope is still alive. We are waiting faithfully, expecting Jesus to return to us. We are the Disciples that God will use to advance His Kingdom in these last days. When we kneel down to pray, God pours spiritual "gasoline" on us. Our hope explodes with the love of Father God. When we enter His presence, anything can happen.

This is a mystery to the world. *"The mystery that has been kept hidden for ages and generations is now disclosed to the Lord's people. To them, God has chosen to make known among the Gentiles the glorious riches of this mystery, **which is Christ in you, the hope of glory**.* (Colossians 1:26-27

Without Jesus dwelling in us, **there is no hope.** Jesus is our love story that causes the Holy Spirit to pour out God's love into our hearts, creating a fire of desire in us to introduce Jesus to our relatives, friends, and people we meet.

The Key, to the Love of God being in us is <u>obeying Jesus' teachings</u>. When we do, God promises us hope will be poured out into our hearts. The Bible says, *"Now hope does not disappoint, because **the love of God has been poured out in our hearts by the Holy Spirit** who was given to us."* (Romans 5:5)

Maybe you have never ask Jesus to save you and meat it. Perhaps you were saved, and have turned your back on Jesus and fallen sin and fallen away from God.

No matter what you have done, God is ready and willing to forgive you of your sins—right now—right where you are.

Come back to Jesus, it's time for you to fall in love with Jesus and make Him your first love.

It's time for you to be obedient to the Father's will that Jesus taught you.

It's time for you to establish a loving and obedient relationship with God, right now! There is nothing on Earth as important as your relationship with God.

It's time to, "**Enter through the Narrow Gate**." Jesus said, "**I am the Gate**."

Jesus is telling those whose hope is alive, "*I am coming soon. Hold on to what you have, so that no one will take away your crown.*" (Revelation 3:11)

"*I am coming soon! Blessed are those who obey the words of prophecy written in this book.*" (Revelation 22:7)

"*I am coming soon, bringing my reward with me to repay all people according to their deeds.*" (Revelation 22:12)

"*Yes, I am coming soon!*" *Amen*! (Revelation 22:20).

CHAPTER 17

Can I Use Your Boat?

Today, many Christians have lost their desire to please God. Our flame has gone out. We are unable to discern whether we are walking with God and listening to His voice, or walking in the flesh and doing our own will pleasing ourselves. Something needs to happen to us. We need to be refined, to become mature children of God. We must be **refined by the Holy Spirit**, which is what happened to Peter and his fishing buddies during an overnight fishing trip on Lake Gennesaret.

In the Gospel of Luke chapter 5 verses 0ne to eleven, the author us about this fishing story, as Jesus is teaching a large crowd beside a lake. Luke says, "So it was, as the multitude pressed about Him to hear the word of God that He stood by the Lake of Gennesaret, and saw two boats standing by the lake; but the fishermen had gone from them and were washing their nets.

Then He got into one of the boats, which was Simon's, and asked him to put out a little from the land. And He sat down and taught the crowd from the boat. "When He had stopped speaking, He said to Simon, *'Launch out into the deep and let down your nets for a catch.'*

But Simon answered and said to Him, "*Master, we have toiled all night and caught nothing; nevertheless at your word I will let down the net.*"

And when they had done this, they caught a great number of fish, and their net was breaking. So they signaled to their partners in the other boat to come and help them. And they came and filled both the boats, so that they began to sink.

CHAPTER 17 - CAN I USE YOUR BOAT?

When Simon Peter saw it, he fell down at Jesus' knees, saying, *"Depart from me, for I am a sinful man, O Lord!" For he and all who were with him were astonished at the catch of fish which they had taken*; and so also were James and John, the sons of Zebedee, who were partners with Simon.

And Jesus said to Simon, "Do not be afraid. From now on you will catch men." *So, when they had brought their boats to land, they forsook all and followed Him.*" (Luke 5:1-11)

2000 years ago, fishing was a very hard job. They used large nets by throwing them into the water. As they drifted along, they hoped the nets trailing behind would capture several fish. Or if they spotted a school of fish swimming fast, with fins sticking above the surface making a boiling-like effect on the surface on the water, they would throw the nets out in hopes of catching a large quantity.

After working all day or night, the fish needed to be cleaned and prepared. The nets needed to be washed and mended and then folded away, ready for the next trip. It was very a labor intensive hard work that produced a low wage.

Peter had fished all night long and caught nothing. They were cleaning the nets when Jesus came by the shore. A large crowd had followed as they listened to Him. So Jesus got into Peter's boat, sat down, and asked him to push him out a little way from shore, so He could speak to the crowd.

Just imagine what might have been going through Peter's mind when Jesus requested to use his boat. He had been fishing all night long; perhaps his back was aching, and he was tired and hungry. Most likely he just wanted to go home. Even though he was tired, Peter was sensitive and obedient to Jesus' request. He made himself available by doing what Jesus asked. He pushed the boat out a way from the crowded shore, so Jesus could speak to the crowd.

When Jesus finished speaking to the crowd, He told Peter, "*Launch out into deeper water and let your net down*." Jesus may have wanted to bless Peter for being obedient and allowing Him to use his boat. Peter was reluctant and perhaps frustrated. He had fished all night long and caught nothing. And they had just cleaned, mended, and folded the nets for the next day's fishing. Peter knew it was a waste of time to lower the nets back into the water, but he was receptive to Jesus.

Even though he didn't believe they would catch any fish, he told Jesus, "*Master, we have toiled all night and caught nothing; nevertheless, at your word I will let down the net.*" Peter did not believe. He had no faith, not even a mustard-seed size of faith, that he was going to catch anything, but Peter told Jesus, "If you say so, I'll do it."

When Peter lowered their nets, *they caught such a large amount of fish that the nets began to break, so Peter signaled for his fishing partners in the other boat to come and help them. They came over and began filling their boats with fish.*

They kept selecting fish from the net and putting them in their boats until both boats began to sink. They had to stop because the boats could hold no more. "*When Simon Peter saw it, he fell down at Jesus' knees, saying, "depart from me, for I am a sinful man, O Lord!' For he and all who were with him were astonished at the catch of fish which they had taken; and so also were James and John, the sons of Zebedee, who were partners with Simon. And Jesus said to Simon,* '*Do not be afraid. From now on you will catch men.*' *So, when* they had brought their boats to land, they forsook all and followed Him." (Luke 5:8-11)

Right then and there, Jesus called Peter, James, and John to Discipleship. They parked their boats and all their fishing equipment on dry land and left to follow Jesus. Peter knew Jesus was the Lord. He didn't know all that was about to happen, but he knew Jesus was the Messiah.

Today, Jesus is asking me and you to allow Him to use our body for a boat. He wants to push us out of our comfort zone a little ways so He can speak through us. Will we hear His request and be receptive to it, like Peter?

All Christians are called by God to help accomplish one mission; the ministry of reconciling the world to Jesus. Are you willing to push out into the deeper water, away from the things of the flesh, and learn how to be receptive and obedient to His Word?

Some of us tell God we've tried it and haven't caught anything.

Others of us, tell God we will support and cheer others on from the shoreline. Many of us try to explain to God our tough situation and limitations, as if He doesn't know.

There are some disciples who are willing to push out a little way from shore, as long as their feet can still touch bottom, because we enjoy the comforts of our job, family, and friends, more than following the instructions of Jesus. We say we're scared of the deep water, but the truth is we enjoy the pleasures of this worldly life so much, that we are disobedient to God's calling. We want to keep one foot in the world and one foot in the boat.

We're not mature in Christ. Our desire is gone. We're willing to come to church and pray and listen to the Word once a week, but unwilling to go into deep water and allow Christ to use us.

There are a few Christians who are willing to go out into deeper water and sacrifice their body [boat] to tell others of the Good News of how Jesus freed us from addiction, lying, stealing, cheating, and healed all the pain caused by years of depression, recklessness, and acts of violence.

God wants us to become spiritually inclined to put on the life vest of righteousness and go out into deeper water. When we push our body (boat) out into deeper water, the water is over our head and our feet can no longer touch bottom so we can't control where we go. That's when we commit to loving God, being obedient, trusting, and depending on God's Holy Spirit to blow us where He wants us to go.

This is where we are being refined in Christ. We learn to lean on God to provide everything for our lives. We overcome our fears of this world. <u>The only fear we have is not pleasing God</u>. There are only a few disciples who are willing to put on the Holy Spirit's life vest and trust the wind to blow our body [boat] where God wants us to be.

Jesus told us, *"Enter through the narrow gate. For wide is the gate and broad is the road that leads to destruction, and many enter through it. But small is the gate and narrow the road that leads to life, and only a few find it."* (Matthew 7:13-14)

CHAPTER 17 - CAN I USE YOUR BOAT?

When we surrender our all to God, then it's all or nothing, and God can use us. His wind will blow us where He wants us. Peter told Jesus, *"Master, we have toiled all night and caught nothing; nevertheless, at your word I will let down the net."* When we say, **"nevertheless at your Word,"** we are being obedient. We must push ourselves into reading God's word, meditating, praying, and developing our relationship with Jesus and the Father. Then Jesus can use us to catch a lot of fish.

When we go **"all in,"** we become givers. Our entire life belongs to Christ. We may do it reluctantly at first, like Peter, but as we surrender and trust more and more on Jesus, our faithfulness will become noticeable to our Heavenly Father, and our relationship will become closer with Jesus. This is why Jesus said, *"If any of you wants to be my follower, you must give up your own way, take up your cross daily, and follow me. If you try to hang on to your life, you will lose it. But if you give up your life for my sake, you will save it."* (Luke 9:23-24)

As a Disciple of Christ Jesus, our life, our home, our finances, our food, our clothing, everything we have is for the Kingdom of Heaven.

Nothing on Earth; no husband, wife, child, or job, is as important as our relationship with Jesus.

God puts us through trials so we can learn to trust Him fully and develop a faithful relationship with Him. The Bible says, *"Consider it pure joy, my brothers and sisters, whenever you face trials of many kinds, because you know that the testing of your faith produces perseverance. Let perseverance finish its work so that you may be mature and be complete, not lacking anything.* (James 1:2-4)

When we trust God enough to get into the boat and push out into the deep water, God knows we have surrendered and allowed His will to be done in our lives. This is our time of refinement. His Holy Spirit is our life vest. No matter how rough the water gets, we are safe in Him, as long as that vest of righteous is in and around us.

I'm an example of a modern-day disobedient Child of God. It took me about 40 years until finally, at the age of 53, God broke me down enough to where I surrendered. I gave up and told God, "I love You; I will trust and obey You." I entered through the Narrow Gate, to me "it is all or nothing."

God refines every Christian. Every Child of God has a desert to cross, and that desert is where God refines us. We learn to lean on God for everything.

I have heard it would normally take about 20 to 30 days to walk across the desert in a straight path from Egypt to the Promised Land. But it took 40 years for the Children of Israel to become obedient to God and arrive at the Promised Land. God had to refine them.

Today, we are like the Children of Israel. Each one of us has a desert to cross. Crossing the desert is where we get rid of self and learn to lean on God. Crossing the desert is where refinement from flesh allows us to submit to God.

In Moses' day, the desert was an extremely dangerous place. There were bodies scattered all over the desert. We can still hear some of their voices saying, *"Oh, God wouldn't allow that to happen to me!"* In a way, they are correct. God doesn't just allow death to happen to us. It's our <u>sin</u>, our <u>disobedience</u>, our <u>lack of love</u>, and our <u>non-commitment to God</u> that causes our separation from God.

God needs to refine us. It's time to die to self, our own personal goals, and desires of this world, and become mature servants of our Savior, Jesus Christ. Apostle Paul tells us, *"I have been crucified with Christ; it is no longer I who live, but Christ lives in me; and the life which I now live in the flesh I live by faith in the Son of God, who loved me and gave Himself for me."* (Galatians 2:20)

It's time we come to Jesus like Peter did. And say, *"Nevertheless, at your word,"* and we push out into deep water, that's where the glory of God is. That's where miracles are. When God is in control of our body (boat), we become instruments of God, and we'll experience His Glory.

CHAPTER 17 - CAN I USE YOUR BOAT?

When God's glory begins to manifest in our life, we will be like Peter, James, and John, our body-boat will be overflowing, and we won't be able to put any more in our boat because we'll be so full. This may happen at any time when we're in God's glory.

As we get closer to God, He allows us to see ourselves as He sees us. We see the sin in our life and ask God to remove it, which allows us to get closer to Him. Our relationship deepens. That's what Peter did. He allowed God to be in full control of his life, and when he did, Jesus told Peter, "**Do not be afraid. From now on you will catch men**."

Jesus taught us this short parable: "The Kingdom of Heaven is like a fishing net that was thrown into the water and caught fish of every kind. When the net was full, they dragged it up onto the shore, sat down, and sorted the good fish into crates, but threw the bad ones away. *That is the way it will be at the end of the world. The angels will come and separate the wicked people from the righteous, throwing the wicked into the fiery furnace, where there will be weeping and gnashing of teeth.* "**Do you understand all these things**?" "*Yes,*" they said, "*we do.*" (Matthew 13:47-51)

Today, Jesus is asking you, "*Do you understand all these things*?" God expects us to be like Peter and say, "*Nevertheless, at your word,* I will obey you and do as you request."

2000 years ago, Peter and the others pulled their boats up on the shore, stowed away their equipment, and walked away, forsaking it all. They died to themselves, their old fishing habits, and their old way of life. It was "all or nothing," they went "all in," to follow Jesus and become fishers of men.

Jesus is asking you to leave your desires of pleasing the body behind and follow Him.

He is asking if He can use your body (boat) to speak to the people.

Jesus is asking if you'll launch out into deeper water and trust the Holy Spirit.

He is telling you, if we'll lower the nets into the deep water, He will overfill them. May your response be, *"**Nevertheless, at Your word, I will let down the net**."*

Every second that goes by 1.8 people die.

Every minute that passes 107 people die.

Every day 153, 425 people die and many of them are going to hell because they don't have a relationship with God the Father, through Jesus. They needed someone to tell them about Jesus one more time. There are people who will not go to Heaven unless you talk to them. It may be family, friends, co-workers, and others that Jesus will bring into our lives.

Are you willing to make a commitment and become a mature Christian fisherman of men by telling others about Jesus and His goodness and what he has done for you?

What is stopping you from doing the kingdom work God wants you to do?

Jesus is asking you, can I use your boat?

CHAPTER 17 - CAN I USE YOUR BOAT?

Father, in the name of Jesus, strengthen me as I turn my back on my old wicked ways of pleasing myself.

Today, I seek You and ask You to forgive my many sins, especially of neglecting You.

I ask You to give to me the strength and the gift to tell others about Jesus.

Heavenly Father, I surrender this day to You, submitting my will for Your will to be done in my life. Have Your way with me. Clean me, wash away my failures, and renew in me a clean heart that desires to love You more, to please You always, and to do Your will.

I ask for Your Holy Spirit to gift me to be a soul winner. Lord Jesus I pray Your Holy Spirit teach me to become a disciple for You. May I be obedient when You ask, **"Can I borrow your boat?"**

Father, make me a fisher of Men.

In the Name of Jesus, Amen!

Chapter 18

Rewards - Dead Or Alive?

Whenever I hear about rewards and recognition, I think of the World Olympic Games that are held every four years. I love listening to the Olympic theme song as the teams from each country march into the arena. I also enjoy watching the competition and the presentation of the gold, silver, and bronze medals to the winners at the awards ceremonies. This is a special moment in time when each competitor proudly stands alone on a pedestal to receive a reward for their accomplishments.

As I watch the competitors receiving their individual rewards, I imagine myself standing, bowing my head, and bending over slightly at the waist, while the medal is put around my neck. What a thrilling awesome ceremony it must be!

One day very soon, Jesus Christ will come on the clouds and gather together all of us who believed in Him.

*For the Son of Man will come in the glory of His Father with His angels, and then **He will reward each** according to his works.* (Matthew 16:27)

For we must all appear before the judgment seat of Christ, that each one may receive the things done in the body, according to what he has done, whether good or bad. (II Corinthians 5:10)

"For the Lord himself will come down from Heaven with a commanding shout, with the voice of the archangel, and with the trumpet call of God. First, the believers who have died will rise from their graves.

Then together with them, we who are still alive and remain on the Earth will be caught up in the clouds to meet the Lord in the air. Then we will be with the Lord forever. So encourage each other with these words." (I Thessalonians 4:16-18)

After we meet Jesus in the air, the believers that are caught up to meet Jesus, we will have our rewards' ceremony in heaven. It will take place right after Jesus comes for His Church, and only believers will attend this rewards ceremony.

Jesus first revealed his rewards for us, in His teaching known as "The Sermon on the Mount," when he said, *"Blessed are you when people insult you, persecute you and falsely say all kinds of evil against you because of me. Rejoice and be glad, because great is your reward in Heaven, for in the same way they persecuted the prophets who were before you."* (Matthew 5:11-12)

Can you imagine being glad and joyful because someone hates or insults you because of your belief in Jesus? I couldn't. I had read this scripture several times but didn't really understand what these verses meant.

There is another scripture where Jesus said, *"Blessed are you when men hate you, when they exclude you and insult you and reject your name as evil, because of the Son of Man. Rejoice in that day and leap for joy, because great is your reward in Heaven. For that is how their fathers treated the prophets"*. (Luke 6:22-23)

Once again, I could not imagine wanting to jump for joy or being joyful after someone excluded me or insulted me and called me evil, because of Jesus and my believing in Him.

Then, one day I was reading Luke Chapter 14 verses 1-14 and the Holy Spirit revealed to my heart about Jesus' rewards' program and what Jesus meant when he said, ***because great is your reward in Heaven***. I suddenly realized that there was a direct connection between **what I do for God** on Earth and **something great God will do for me in Heaven**.

Doctor Luke tells us, "One Sabbath, Jesus went to dinner with some distinguished guests at the home of a prominent Pharisee. Jesus watched the guests jockeying for the best seating positions for dinner, and then He offered some unsolicited advice to the Pharisee who was hosting the dinner, saying, *"When you give a luncheon or dinner, do not invite your friends, your brothers or relatives, or your rich neighbors; if you do, they may invite you back and so you will be repaid. But when you give a banquet, invite the poor, the crippled, the lame, and the blind.*" (Luke 14:12-13)

What Jesus said next brings us to the heart of the Bible's teaching on rewards: He said, "And, *you will be blessed. Although they cannot repay you, you will be repaid at the resurrection of the righteous.*" (Luke 14:14)

No one at the dinner table could have missed Jesus' astonishing revelation that God will repay us for our good work **after we are dead**.

This teaching contradicted what everyone in that room believed. At that time, the Jewish teaching was that God rewards only people on Earth for the good they do while alive on Earth.

But Jesus revealed just the opposite that you will be repaid at the "resurrection of the righteous" after you're dead and in Heaven.

Jesus words teach us that when you do a worthy deed for a person who cannot repay you:

1. You will be repaid
2. Your payment will come in eternity
3. When you receive your reward, you will be blessed

In this scripture, Jesus is teaching us that there is a direct connection between what we do for God on Earth and something great God will do for us in Heaven.

Jesus described it **as a reward for doing**, which makes it entirely different from the gift of salvation that we receive from believing. And the reward is personally ours if we behave in a particular way. However, the reward is not ours if we behave in a different way.

For example, let's imagine you're at work. Someone who knows you and has observed you comes to you, tells you they have cancer, and asks you questions about Jesus and for you to pray for them. The company policy at work forbids praying to Jesus and discussing about Jesus on company property because it may offend another person's belief. What would you do?

1 - Would you invite them to come to church and give them some scriptures to read?

2 - Or, would you take the time then or during lunch break to share about Jesus with them?

3 - Would u give them something to read?

4 – Invite them to Church?

God creates opportunities for us so that every believer on Earth, regardless of circumstance or ability, has an opportunity to please Him.

But if we do what God wants and has prepared for us to do, we will be rewarded. If we do not do what God wants and has prepared for us to do, we will not receive a reward.

The rewards Jesus has in store for us are not just a small charitable tip, or a "little something extra" like a company giving you a watch for 25-years of service. Jesus called it *"a reward"*, something you earn, resulting from something you do.

Every small deed done for the glory of God will be rewarded. No deed will be overlooked or unrewarded. For example: Private prayer is valuable to God. Jesus told us, *"But when you pray, go into your room, close the door and pray to your Father, who is unseen. Then your Father, who sees what is done in secret, will reward you."* (Matthew 6:6)

Giving; Jesus said, *"But when you give to the needy, do not let your left hand know what your right hand is doing, so that your giving may be in secret. Then your Father, who sees what is done in secret, will reward you."* (Matthew 6:3-4)

Fasting; Jesus taught us, *"But when you fast, put oil on your head and wash your face, so that it will not be obvious to men that you are fasting, but only to your Father, who is unseen; and your Father, who sees what is done in secret, will reward you."* (Matthew 6:17-18)

Receiving a Prophet, Jesus told us, *"Anyone who receives you receives me, and anyone who receives me receives the Father who sent me." If you receive a prophet as one who speaks for God, you will be* *given the same reward as a prophet. And if you receive righteous people because of their righteousness, you will be given a reward like theirs. And if you give even a cup of cold water to one of the least of my followers, you will surely be rewarded."* (Matthew 10:40-42)

There are two Bible verses that confirm Jesus' teaching of God's rewards program for His Children:

1. The first scripture is in Hebrews, and it reads, *"But without faith, it is impossible to please Him, for he who comes to God must believe that He is, and that He rewards those who diligently seek Him."* (Hebrews 11:6)

If you want to please God;

➢ Firstly, you must *believe that He is.*
➢ Secondly, you must believe "that *He rewards those who diligently seek Him.*

God's provision to save and His plan to reward is a display of His amazing grace and generous nature.

2. The second scripture that reveals Jesus' teachings of God's rewards for us, comes directly from the mouth of Jesus when He said, *"For the Son of Man is going to come in his Father's glory with his angels, and **then he will reward each person according to what he has done**."* (Matthew 16:27)

Jesus is clearly describing a series of events in every Christian's future that will alter our experience of eternity.

- ✓ Jesus will come again;
- ✓ He will bring rewards;
- ✓ Then the rewards will be given to each according to he has done.

Jesus is the only person to come from eternity to Earth, and then return to eternity. He knows the past, the present, and the future. He is the Alpha and Omega, no one else can teach us!

Webster's Standard Dictionary defines a reward as: "Compensation, as a commendable act, to recompense. Recompense is Compensation, as for services rendered; as for damages; to repay, as for damages."

It is our duty and privilege to serve God here on Earth. If Jesus thanks and rewards us, it is because He is gracious and generous, not because we deserve it. Jesus told us, *"So you also, when you have done everything you were told to do, should say, 'We are unworthy servants; we have only done our duty.'"* (Luke 17:10)

Jesus will be the judge at our Judgement and rewards ceremony. *"Moreover, the Father judges no one, but has entrusted all judgment to the Son."* (John 5:22)

Some Christians mistakenly believe they will be judged for sin in Heaven, or on Earth at the Great White Throne Judgment. But that is not true. Christians must die to sin – while we're alive on Earth. Sin will never enter God's Kingdom.

Apostle Paul confirmed this when he told the Christians at Corinth, *"For we must all appear before the judgment seat of Christ, that each one may receive what is due him for the things done while in the body, whether good or bad."* (II Corinthians 5:10)

When Paul says, *"that each one may receive,"* he is clearly indicating a reward or repayment. And when he says, *"things done in the body,"* Paul is telling us the rewards are for things we did while we were alive on Earth, in our body.

When Christians stand before Jesus to give an account of all our works and the deeds we performed as Christians, "whether good or bad," to enhance and advance God's Kingdom on planet Earth. *"So then, each of us will give an account of ourselves to God."* (Romans 14: 12)

Just imagine: your own judgment and rewards ceremony in eternity, for only Christians, and it comes hundreds of years before the final great Judgment Day. Jesus told us, *"Behold, I am coming soon! My reward is with me, and I will give to everyone according to what he has done."* (Revelations 22:12)

CHAPTER 17 - REWARDS - DEAD OR ALIVE?

What if today was your last day alive on Earth? Ready or not, in the blink of an eye, your life on Earth is over, and your soul is off into eternity to be with Jesus, in Heaven. Are you ready to stand before Jesus at your rewards' ceremony?

When we stand before Jesus, He will use three criteria's to judge and determine if the works and deeds we did while alive on Earth will endure His test.

The First Criterion for the test is our relationship with God.

Jesus defined eternal life as a relationship with God. He said, *"Now this is eternal life: that they know you, the only true God, and Jesus Christ, whom you have sent."* (John 17:3)

Our relationship with Jesus and Father God while we are alive on earth, will determine if our works will result in any reward in Heaven.

A relationship requires us to give our love, time, faithfulness, and our communication, to keep it alive and growing in all areas.

An affair is selfish and requires little to no love, no faithfulness, no self-sacrifice, and no heartfelt communication to maintain it, because it thrives only on "emotional gifts" and "emotional highs." An affair is temporary, only for certain times such as Sundays, while a relationship is all the time. An affair is secretive and is based on seduction, while a relationship is open and based on love.

It is my conviction that God wants and expects from us a loving obedient relationship, in which He is first in our lives. To be involved in a loving, faithful relationship with Father God, we must fall in love with Jesus. God will turn down all offers for an affair. He is not into having an affair with us.

Jesus told us, *"Those who accept my commandments and obey them are the ones who love me. And because they love me, my Father will love them. And I will love them and reveal Myself to each of them."* (John

14:21)

"All who love me will do what I say, my Father will love them, and we will come and make our home with each of them. Anyone who doesn't love me will not obey me. And remember, my words are not my own. What I am telling you is from the Father who sent me." (John 14:23-24)

It's time to ask yourself two important question.

3. Do I have a loving obedient relationship with God through Jesus?

4. Or, am I trying to have an affair with God?

The Second Criterion is our motive for doing our good deeds.

The **motive** we did the good deeds for others, will be used to judge and determine if our deeds will produce any rewards for us. What was the motive in our heart for doing the good deeds? Was it to benefit yourself and make you look good?

Apostle Paul told us, *"My conscience is clear, but that does not make me innocent. It is the Lord who judges me. Therefore judge nothing before the appointed time; wait until the Lord comes. He will bring to light what is hidden in darkness and will expose the motives of the heart. At that time, each will receive their praise from God."* (I Corinthians 4:4-5)

Disciple James, told us, *"When you ask, you do not receive because you ask with wrong motives, that you may spend what you get on your pleasures."* (James 4:3)

The Lord told Prophet Jeremiah, *"The human heart is the most deceitful of all things, and desperately wicked. Who really knows how bad it is? But I, the Lord, search all hearts and examine secret motives. I give all people their due rewards, according to what their actions deserve."* (Jeremiah 17:9-10)

CHAPTER 17 - REWARDS - DEAD OR ALIVE?

Our motive should be to serve God and bring Him glory. Even ordinary actions like eating and drinking can bring God glory. Yet, our most religious actions are worthless if our motive is to build up our own egos, pride, and reputations. Our motives must be to bring glory to God.

Jesus told us, *"Watch out! Don't do your good deeds publicly to be admired by others, for you will lose the reward from your Father in Heaven."* (Mathew 6:1)

Is God pleased with the attitude and motive you have in doing what you are doing?

The Third Criterion is our Love.

Unrestricted love that benefits others – will be used to determine if our good deeds will result in us receiving rewards in Heaven, at the rewards' ceremony. Disciple John told us, *"And this is love: that we walk in obedience to His commands. As you have heard from the beginning, His command is that you **walk in love**."* (II John verse 6)

Apostle Paul told us, *"If I gave everything I have to the poor and even sacrificed my body, I could boast about it; but if I didn't love others, **I would have gained nothing**."* (I Corinthians 13:3)

Good works that please God are always focused on sincerely trying to improve the well-being of another. Jesus told us, *"But love your enemies, do well to them, and lend to them without expecting to get anything back. Then your reward will be great, and you will be children of the Most-High, because He is kind to the ungrateful and wicked. Be merciful, just as your Father is merciful."* (Luke 6:35-36)

Did we perform our good works out of love? Without love, good deeds will not benefit us. So when we stand before Jesus at our judgment and rewards ceremony, we now know the criteria that Jesus will judge our good works and deeds by.

5. Our relationship with God
6. The motive in our heart for doing the deeds.

7. Our Love for others.

This is the criteria that Jesus will use to determine if our Good deeds and works as a Christian will endure **the Test** for us to receive rewards in Heaven.

You may be thinking, "Wait a minute! I thought the three criteria were the test."

No. Jesus will conduct **one test** on all our deeds and works. Our entire Christian life's works will be **tested by fire**.

Paul tells us, *"On the judgment day, fire will reveal what kind of work each builder has done. The fire will show if a person's work has any value. If the work survives, that builder will receive a reward. But if the work is burned up, the builder will suffer great loss. The builder will be saved, but like someone barely escaping through a wall of flames."* (I Corinthians 3:13-15)

Many believers do not believe or understand that some of us Christians may suffer the loss of our entire Christian career because we didn't have clean motives in our heart. But it's true. Apostle Paul told us if our works are burned up, we will suffer loss; we will be saved, but only as one escaping through the flames. Imagine leaving the rewards ceremony and escaping into Heaven with few or no rewards.

We may have done the good deeds to gain attention. Or we may have lacked and neglected God in our relationship with Him. Perhaps the motive for doing our good works and deeds was something other than love. Possibly we did it for the wrong motive. Perhaps this is why Disciple John warned us, *"Watch out that you do not lose what you have worked for, but that you may be rewarded fully."* (II John verse 8)

2000 years ago, Jesus taught His disciples "The Parable of the 10 Minas." This is a great motivating story for us to understand and apply to our lives today. It's from Luke 19:11-27.

In Jesus' time, a minas' value was equal to about three months' salary for the average worker. So 10 minas would be about two and one-half

CHAPTER 17 - REWARDS - DEAD OR ALIVE?

years' wages for the average worker.

The parable goes like this: There was a nobleman who was scheduled to travel to a far-off country, where he was to be made king and receive a kingdom. After he'd received it, he would return.

The nobleman called ten different servants to him, gave them each about two and one-half years' salary, and said to them, *"Put this money to work until I come back."*

And then he left and went to the far-off country, to his own people, but they didn't want him. They didn't receive him with favor. They hated him and formed a delegation and conspired against him. They said they didn't want this man to be their king. But the noble-man was made king and afterwards, returned home.

Upon his arrival, he sent for the ten servants he had given the two and one-half years' wages to in order to find out what they had gained with it.

The first servant said, *"Sir, your two and one-half years' wages has earned an additional two and one-half years' more money."* The Master replied, *"Well done, my good servant. Because you have been trustworthy in a very small matter, take charge of ten cities."*

The second servant said, *"Sir, your two and one-half years of wages has earned one-and-a-quarter-years more money.* The Master replied, *"Good work. Take charge of five cities."*

Then the third servant came and said, *"Sir, here is your two and one-half years wages you gave me; I have kept it laid away in a handkerchief.*

CHAPTER 17 - REWARDS - DEAD OR ALIVE?

I was afraid of you, because you are a hard man. You take out what you did not put in and reap what you did not sow."

This servant used the excuse of being afraid of the Master, but he wasn't really afraid of the Master. If he had been afraid, he would have put the money in the bank so it could have at least gained interest.

Instead, he completely ignored and failed to respond to the nobleman's command to *"Put the money to work until he came back."* He kept it laid away, hidden in a cloth.

The Master replied to the servant, *"I will judge you by your own words, you wicked servant! You knew, did you, that I am a hard man, taking out what I did not put in, and reaping what I did not sow?*

Why then didn't you put my money on deposit, so that when I came back, I could have collected it with interest?"

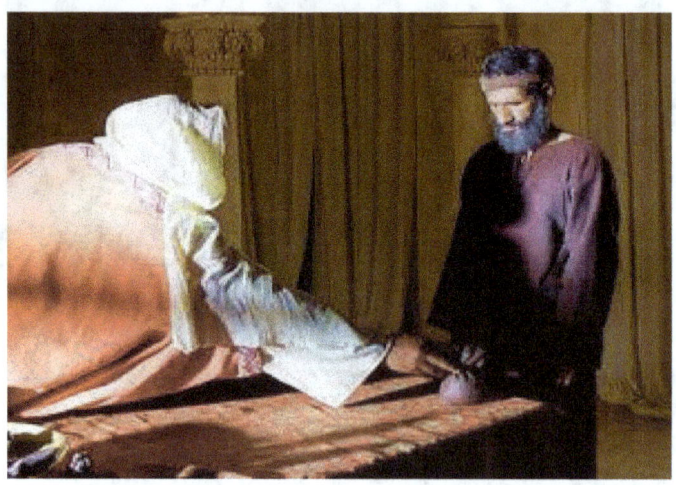

Then he said to those standing by, *"Take his minas away from him and give it to the one who has ten minas." "Sir,"* they said, *"he already has ten!" The Master replied, "I tell you that to everyone who has, more will be given, but as for the one who has nothing, even what he has will be taken away. "But those enemies of mine who did not want me to be king over them, bring them here and kill them in front of me."* (Luke 19:22-26)

This servant who buried and hid his money is a prophetic picture of many Christians today. We have hidden our talents and abilities that God gave us. Some of us have neglected God's calling, and failed to develop and utilized the spiritual gifts that God's Holy Spirit has given to us.

Instead of doing what Jesus told us, *"Put this to work until I come back"*, **we buried the gifts He gave us**.

If Jesus came and raptured the Church today, <u>some of us may be left behind</u>, while others would be in a state of shock because we would suddenly realize we are not prepared, **we're not ready to meet Jesus face to face**.

What are we going to say to Jesus when we stand before Him empty-handed with all our deeds and works laid bare before him? Then, all of a sudden, we will remember what Jesus told us: ***"Put this to work until I come back."***

Even though the consequences of missed opportunities and lost rewards will go with us into eternity, any regret, sorrow, or shame we might experience will not go into eternity with us. How can we be certain of this? Because God promises, *"He will wipe every tear from their eyes. There will be no more death or mourning or crying or pain, for the old order of things has passed away."* (Revelation 21:4)

The truth is, regardless of what happens at the ceremony, Jesus will not love us any less or any more than He loved us when He purchased our life with His own blood on the Cross of Calvary. No reward on Earth will compare to the pleasure of seeing joy on our Savior's face as He reviews the works we did as Christians and then leans forward to give us our rewards.

At that moment, we will completely see and understand:

- All that God has done **in us;**
- All that He has done **for us**;
- All he has done **through us;**

We will realize that, without Him, we could not have accomplished anything for Him. Our overwhelming response will be to cry out in thanks and praise to Him. Out of sheer joy and gratitude, we will want to fall at the feet of the Lord Jesus Christ in worship and give Him back everything He just has given to us.

It's time to ask ourselves, **"Am I ready to meet Jesus today?"**

"Salvation is found in no one else, for there is no other name under Heaven given to mankind by which we must be saved." (Acts 4:12)

All you need to do is ask Jesus to forgive you for all your sins and say, **"Jesus I want you to be my Savior."** The Bible tells us, *"If you declare with your mouth, 'Jesus is Lord,' and believe in your heart that God raised him from the dead, you will be saved.*

For it is with your heart that you believe and are justified, and it is with your mouth that you profess your faith and are saved." (Romans 10:9-11)

"Anyone who believes in him will never be put to shame" "For everyone who calls on the name of the Lord will be saved." (Romans 10: 13)

You can repent and believe that Jesus is – Who He says He is and spend eternity with Him in Heaven.

Or, you can reject Him and spend eternity in Hell with the Devil.

What is so great about all this is – you get to choose.

CHAPTER 19

The Condition of Today's Church

Two thousand years ago, Jesus asked his disciples, "***When the Son of Man comes will he find faith on the earth?***" (Luke 18:8)

What if Jesus left His Father's Throne in Heaven today, and came back to earth and heard the Good News Gospel Message of the kingdom of Heaven being preached and taught in Christian Churches all over the world. Would He find Faith?

What Would Jesus Say to Todays' Christian Church?

I truly believe Jesus would say, "I find the condition of today's Christian Church's lacking compared to the First century Churches of Peter, John, and Paul".

There are at least three keys areas that I believe Jesus would warn us to change immediately.

1. The Good News message about Jesus Christ and Salvation being preached and taught in today's Church is not the same message as what John, Paul, and Peter preached, to the First-Century Churches.

2. God is not pleased with the motives and attitudes of our heart. The problem God has with today's Church is not so much in what we are doing but in the motive and attitude we have in seeking Him. True repentance is missing.

3. The False Prosperity message that has manifested itself world-wide in today's Christian Churches is not part of the Good News Gospel Message, of the Kingdom of Heaven and salvation that Jesus ushered in and taught to His Disciples and the first Century Church over two thousand years ago.

Let's first look at how the Gospel Message of Jesus has changed over the past two thousand years. The key message of salvation for the saints of the first-century Church was **fear.**

- Fear of being separated from God and dead to Him.
- Fear of being an enemy of God
- Fear of spending eternity in hell.

To Christian believers two-thousand years ago, it was all about preparing for where they would spend eternity. You might be thinking, "Isn't hell eternal separation from God?" Yes, indeed it is, but we should fear separation from God now, today, not after we die.

When your mother gave birth to you, you were born as a son or daughter of the Wicked One, the Devil. If you were born Atheist, Baptist, Catholic, Muslim, Pentecostal, or no matter what religious belief, you were born into, you were born with a rebellious sinful nature separated from God and born as an enemy of God. (Reference Matthew 13:38-39)

You remain separated from God even when you mature. If you do not chosen to believe in Jesus, confessed your sins before Him, and ask him to be your Savior and Lord of your life, and you die a physical death, your soul will spend all of eternity with Satan in the Lake of Fire that God has prepared for him and his fallen angels.

Once you die, there is no second chance for amnesty in the spiritual realm. Our **belief** and **behavior,** while we're alive on earth, determine our destination for all of eternity. You not believing what the Holy Bible says doesn't change God's concept and structure of His creation and Plan of Salvation for you. **You not believing means you're lost**.

In fact, if we want to go to heaven but do not know and understand how our enemy status and our separation from God are affecting our life today, then we are embracing God's plan of salvation with no understanding of what we are being saved from. The Bible says, *"The fear of the Lord is to hate evil; Pride and arrogance and the evil way and the perverse mouth I hate."* (Proverbs 8:13)

Love for God and love for sin cannot coexist. When we harbor secret sins, we are tolerating evil within ourselves. We must make a clean break and turn away from evil and sin, putting it behind us by committing to God. We should fear being an enemy of and separated from God today while we are still alive on earth. We should fear spending eternity in hell.

The Bible says *"for all have sinned and fallen short of the glory of God."* (Romans 3:23)

And, *"the wages of sin is death, but the free gift of God is eternal life through Christ Jesus our Lord.* (Romans 6:23)

You see, God looks at us with love, while offering all human beings grace and mercy. Why? Because, if we're separated from God while we're alive walking around on planet earth, we are dead to Him. We should fear being dead to God now and we should also fear death itself because once we die, our life's destination for all of eternity is sealed. There is no second chance to change our minds.

God loves the human race so much that, *"He gave His one and only Son, so that everyone who believes in him will not perish but have eternal life. God sent His Son into the world not to judge the world, but to save the world through him,"* (John 3:16-17)

"And anyone who believes in God's Son has eternal life. Anyone who doesn't believe in the Only Begotten Son will never experience eternal life but remains under God's angry judgment." (John 3:36)

The eternal life Jesus is talking about is the Life that God breathed into Adam when he created Him. Adam and Eve lost their relationship, their eternal Life status, in the Garden of Eden when they rebelled against God's structure of Creation.

God told them, "***but you must not eat from the tree of the knowledge of good and evil, for when you eat from it you will certainly die***." (Genesis 2:17)

They died a spiritual death when they disobeyed God. So, there would be no misunderstanding of what Jesus meant by eternal life, He defined eternal life, for us, "*And this is eternal life, that they may know You, the only true God, and Jesus Christ whom You have sent."* (John 17:3)

2000 years ago, people were saved out in the streets. And then, once saved, they came out of the world, into the Church to fellowship, worship, pray, and grow from pilgrims into mature disciples.

The purpose and mission Jesus assigned to His Church was and still is, to make disciples of all peoples and nations. However, today, the majority of Christians have lost their faith and purpose.

Instead of teaching Christians to become Disciples of Christ Jesus and to walk as Jesus walked, most of today's Christian Churches have their eyes focused on making their Churches popular, rich, exciting, and entertaining. Their motive is to entice people to come be entertained and become members. They are trying to market God's plan of Salvation because more members, mean more money for the church's treasury.

In place of making disciples, today's Church has compromised God's plan of salvation to such an extent that the Gospel Message of Jesus is no longer offensive to the unbelievers of the world. They like the lukewarm entertaining plan of salvation. It makes them feel good.

Unbelievers are embracing today's Christian churches because:

- We stopped preaching against living a sinful lifestyle;
- We stopped preaching about being sons and daughters of the Wicked One;
- We stopped preaching about being enemies of God and our separation from God;
- We stopped preaching about fearing God, and His judgment and wrath against sin;
- We stopped preaching that we will spend eternity in Hell if we don't believe in Jesus,

Today's Church has replaced the old fashion first Century's Church message of Salvation, with a watered-down message of God's love and salvation, but without true fear and repentance. The results are millions

CHAPTER 19 - THE CONDITION OF TODAY'S CHURCH

of people, who claim to be Christians, don't know why they are saved, and what they are saved from!

Today, many of us come to the altar for salvation with no regret, no remorse, or sorrow in our heart, for the sinful lifestyle we have lived against God. Instead, we come to the altar with the motive to receive the Good Life plan of salvation that is being taught in many Christian churches today.

We didn't repent from our heart and turn away from our old sinful lifestyle. We didn't come to the altar of Christ Jesus and give Him our life to be saved from hell and living eternity in hell with our father the Devil.

The motive in coming to God and confessing is for us to receive something materialistic from God. So, we confess our sins for twenty to thirty seconds, and, as soon as we finish our confession, we begin asking God for the stuff we want. We even declare and claim things that don't belong to us. Things that if God allowed us to have, could harm or kill us.

In order for us to be born again of God's Holy Spirit, our sins must be separated and removed from us. God accomplished this by sending *"His Only Begotten Son"* to put into effect His perfect plan of salvation. Jesus became our scapegoat. It is the blood of Jesus that separates us from our sins and saves our soul from Satan and hell if we choose to believe in Him and repent.

In order for a true revival of God to happen today, there must be a call for repentance and revival to take place in church leaders and people professing to be Christians. We must repent and come back to our first love and build an intimate relationship with God the Father, through Jesus, the Messiah.

Nothing on earth is more important than our relationship with Father God! And, the only way to have a relationship with the Father is through Jesus His Only Begotten Son.

The true uncompromised Gospel message about Messiah Jesus

becoming our Lord and Savior by His death, His resurrection to life again, and His ascending into Heaven, was the key message of the First-Century Church.

The only message that will bring a true revival for today's Church is, *"Repent and be baptized, every one of you, in the name of Jesus Christ for the forgiveness of your sins. And you will receive the gift of the Holy Spirit. The promise is for you and your children and for all who are far off, for all whom the Lord our God will call."* (Acts 2:38-39)

"Salvation is found in no one else, for there is no other name under heaven given to mankind by which we must be saved." (Acts 4:12)

That was the message of the First-Century Church. Two thousand years ago, people were saved because:

- People feared being enemies of God.
- People feared being separated from God.
- People feared spending eternity in hell, with the Devil.

The First-Century Church's "Good News Message was that Messiah Jesus" had come and provided a way for all peoples of all nations to be saved from spending eternity in Hell.

What attitude and motive do we have when we come to God?

Today, millions of Christians come to God for salvation because they want something from God. This is happening because, in most Christian churches, the teachings and messages are fixed on divine providence in and about Christians having a prosperous earthly life.

I am not saying that some of their messages are not biblical, if and when spoken in context. However, just because someone is speaking from the Bible, that does not make the words they speak truthful and part of God's perfect plan of salvation.

Prosperity teachings are a sign that today's Church is living in fear.

CHAPTER 19 - THE CONDITION OF TODAY'S CHURCH

But it's not the same fear the First-Century Church had. Today's Church fears the same things the people of the world fear.

- Fear of the future;
- Fear of what might happen;
- Fear of losing what you have worked so hard to possess;
- Fear that you will not see your dreams and goals come true.

Many professing Christians are focused on finding their happiness from the wealth of this world. That's why many Churches have given up preaching about Jesus and <u>his coming kingdom as the ultimate hope</u>. Instead, many are preaching a hope that this declining world will get better. But that is not true. They have forgotten or don't believe the words our Savior, Jesus who spoke regarding God's wrath which is soon to come and will fall on this world.

Many Christians are trying to establish a relationship with God because they want God to do something for them.

- We come to God to fix our job problem.
- We come to God to fix our marriage issues.
- We come to God to fix our money problem.

But God sees our problems differently than we do. God envisions Sin as our problem. It's as if we are trying to have a flirtatious affair with God. But God is not interested in having an affair with us. He wants a committed, loving, and obedient relationship with us! And to do that, our rebellious, sinful, proud nature that is in our heart must be removed.

Jesus is the only way, he told us, *"I am the way, the truth, and the life. No one comes to the Father except through Me."* (John 14:6). We must repent from our heart, turn away from our evil sinful rebellious life-style, and believe in Jesus, making him Lord of our life.

The First-Century Church did not behave the way we do today. They were hot and on fire for Jesus. Their hope and expectations were alive. They waited, looked, and longed for Jesus' return.

The measurement of their faith was hope — hope that was alive! They were obedient to Jesus' teachings and because they obeyed, God's love was perfected in them. An explosion of love fueled the fire of the First-Century Church all because they obeyed and loved Jesus.

Disciple John told us, "Anyone *who says, 'I know Him' but does not obey His teaching is a liar. There is no truth in him. But whoever obeys His Word has **the love of God made perfect in him**. This is the way to know if you belong to Christ. The one who says he belongs to Christ should live the same kind of life Christ lived.*" (I John 2:4-6)

The Holy Spirit poured the love of the Father out into their hearts. It was like pouring gasoline onto an open fire. They were flames of fire. (Reference Romans 5:5)

Today's Christian Church is not on fire. We are lukewarm at best. There is imperfection in our knowledge and understanding of God's Plan of Salvation. We think we know and understand it, but we don't. We are not obedient to Jesus' teachings.

We are not seeking to please our Father God and do His will. Instead, we're asking God, for our will to be done. We are trying to accomplish our will by using God. We are trusting in ourselves, our money, our own wisdom, our own understanding, and the ways of this world. This not what Jesus taught his Disciples, and it is not what was done by the Disciples and Apostles of the First Century Church.

Disciple John told us, *"Do not love the world or the things in the world. If anyone loves the world, the love of the Father is not in him. For all that is in the world — the lust of the flesh, the lust of the eyes, and the pride of life — is not of the Father but is of the world. And the world is passing away, and the lust of it; but he who does the will of God abides forever."* (I John 2:15-17)

Because we desire to do our will and please ourselves, many Christians who think they are saved, are not! Jesus told us, *"Not everyone 'who says to Me, 'Lord, Lord,' shall enter the kingdom of heaven, but he who does the will of My Father in heaven. Many will say to Me in that day, 'Lord, Lord,*

CHAPTER 19 - THE CONDITION OF TODAY'S CHURCH

*have we not prophesied in Your name, cast out demons in Your name, and done many wonders in Your name?' And then I will declare to them, 'I never knew you; **depart from Me,** you who practice lawlessness!*" (Matthew 7:21-23)

Today, many Christians cannot understand why signs, wonders, and miracles are so rare in comparison to the miracles the First-Century Church routinely experienced.

One of the reasons is that many people don't believe that Jesus is the same today as He was 2000 years ago. They believe that signs, wonders, and miracles expired with the deaths of the Apostles. The only expiration date we need to be looking forward to and hoping for is Jesus' coming in the clouds, to rapture His Church.

The Bible teaches and promises that signs, wonders, and miracles were, are, and will be manifested, when the true Gospel message about Jesus Christ and the kingdom of heaven is preached and taught. "Jesus Christ is the same yesterday, today, and forever." (Hebrews 13:8)

Our Lord Jesus told us, "*Therefore, go and make disciples of all the nations, baptizing them in the name of the Father and the Son and the Holy Spirit. Teach these new disciples to obey all the commands I have given you. And be sure of this: I am with you always, even to the end of the age.*" (Matthew 28:19-20)

Signs, wonders, and miracles are not an option for Christ's Church today, they are a promise from God, just like they were in the First-Century Church.

If Jesus visited his Churches today, I believe He would be very upset. He might take a whip and tell us, "His house is a house of prayer." Jesus would tell us to repent from our heart, of these motives and attitudes. Jesus would tell us to remove the False Prosperity teaching of, "giving to receive."

"Quid Pro Quo," is a Latin term meaning; something is given or received for something else to be given or received.

Thousands of today's Christian churches are teaching this religious **"Quid Pro Quo," scheme**, promising that, because you give to God, God will give you something in return for your giving. So the attitude for giving is not what God spoke of in the Bible.

This teaching has infested many Christian churches, causing Christians to become deceived with a disease called "Worldly Possession Syndrome." The only known cure for this disease is a loving and obedient relationship with God the Father through Jesus Christ, with an attitude of worship.

"Giving to receive" is not a teaching of God. God asks and expects us to give. However, giving for the motive of receiving something is a sinful deed because our attitude and motive in our heart for giving is for us to receive something and not because we love God and want to please Him by being obedient. We might as well spend the money on ourselves.

God told Jeremiah to tell the Children of Israel, *"Take your burnt offerings and your other sacrifices and eat them yourselves! When I led your ancestors out of Egypt, it was not burnt offerings and sacrifices I wanted from them. This is what I told them: 'Obey me, and I will be your God, and you will be my people. Do everything as I say, and all will be well!'*

But my people would not listen to me. They kept doing whatever they wanted, following the stubborn desires of their evil hearts. They went backward instead of forward". (Jeremiah 7:21-24)

"Giving to God for the motive of receiving from Him is the same sinful attitude that the Children of Israel had in Jeremiah's time, when they gave their sacrifices without an attitude of worship. You might as well go ahead and spend the money sacrificed on yourselves.

God doesn't want our sinful sacrifice of money. Jerimiah is saying to us, if the motive in our heart for giving to God is, "giving to receive," then the attitude in our heart is "God owes us something." A sacrifice of, giving to receive, is worthless to God.

CHAPTER 19 - THE CONDITION OF TODAY'S CHURCH

Today's "Message of Prosperity" is causing millions of Christians to lose focus of their spiritual walk and relationship with God. It causes our eyes to fall back into the physical realm and pleasing ourselves with the treasures of this world, instead of pleasing God and doing His will.

Apostle Paul warned us about this, *"Do not be deceived: God cannot be mocked. A man reaps what he sows. The one who sows to please his sinful nature, from that nature will reap destruction; the one who sows to please the Spirit, from the Spirit will reap eternal life."* (Galatians 6:7-8)

Unless our love gift, tithe, or offering is accompanied by a sincere joyful obedience of giving from our heart, we are missing what God wants from us, a true attitude of worship. This is what the First-Century Church had. We should not be talked into giving. Give from and with a cheerful heart.

Apostle Paul told us, *"Remember this, a farmer who plants only a few seeds will get a small crop. But the one who plants generously will get a generous crop. You must each decide in your heart how much to give. And don't give reluctantly or in response to pressure. For God loves a person who gives cheerfully. And God will generously provide all you need. Then you will always have everything you need and plenty leftover to share with others."* (II Corinthians 9:6-8)

Our offerings, tithes, and love gifts are extremely important, but they are accepted by God only when given with **an attitude of love**, **obedience**, and **worship**. God looks at the attitude of our heart. We should never give to receive. Give because you love and worship God. And, because Jesus said, *"So you also, when you have done everything you were told to do, should say, we are unworthy servants; we have only done our duty."* (Luke 17:10)

The "Message of Prosperity" is not a new teaching. The Christians from the First-Century Church wanted money and worldly possessions, just like we do. But Paul told them, *"True godliness with contentment itself is great wealth. After all, we brought nothing with us when we came into the world, and we can't take anything with us when we leave it.*

So, if we have enough food and clothing, let us be content. People who long to be rich fall into temptation and are trapped by many foolish and harmful desires that plunge them into ruin and destruction. For the love of money is the root of all kinds of evil. And some people, craving money, have wandered from the true faith and pierced themselves with many sorrows.

"For the time will come when men will not put up with sound doctrine. Instead, to suit their own desires, they will gather around them a great number of teachers to say what their itching ears want to hear. They will turn their ears away from the truth and turn aside to myths." (I Timothy 6:6-10 NLT and II Timothy 4:3-4)

During Jesus' ministry on earth, He taught us His Father's will and demonstrated many signs, wonders, and miracles. He healed people from physical diseases, sicknesses, injuries, and death. On two different occasions, He fed a total of more than 9,000 men from 12 loaves of bread and a handful of fish, and had 19 full baskets of broken pieces of bread and fish left over.

Of all the miracles documented in the New Testament, there are none written where Jesus performed a miracle of making a poor person rich with earthly possessions, wealth, and the riches of this world.

Jesus did not come to earth to suffer a horrible death of crucifixion, be buried in a tomb for three days and three nights, then come back to life and ascend into heaven so we could have an abundant, rich life, enjoying the wealth of this sinful and fading world.

Jesus did all that he did so we could choose to believe in Him, and by believing in Jesus, we would be "born-again." **Born of God's Holy Spirit and enjoy an abundant life as Children of God**.

Born again, to live an abundant, **"Eternal Life**," enjoying the wealth of the Kingdom of Heaven. *"And this is eternal life, that they may know You, the only true God, and Jesus Christ whom You have sent."* (John 17:3)

CHAPTER 19 - THE CONDITION OF TODAY'S CHURCH

"Look, I am coming soon! Blessed are those who obey the words of prophecy written in this book." ... "Look, I am coming soon, bringing my reward with me to repay all people according to their deeds. I am the Alpha and the Omega, the First and the Last, the Beginning and the End." Blessed are those who wash their robes. They will be permitted to enter through the gates of the city and eat the fruit from the tree of life." (Revelations 22:7, 12-14)

God will provide all we need to perform our kingdom work on earth. Jesus told us, *"So don't worry about these things, saying, 'What will we eat? What will we drink? What will we wear? These things dominate the thoughts of unbelievers, but your heavenly Father already knows all your needs. Seek the Kingdom of God above all else, and live righteously, and he will give you everything you need."* (Matthew 6:31-33)

In addition to everything we need here on earth, Jesus also promised us that, when He returned, **"Great are your rewards in heaven."** In essence, Jesus is saying, "When you stand before me in heaven, I will pay you back in return for what you do for me and my Father here on earth." We are not citizens of this world. We are citizens and servants of the Kingdom of Heaven.

God is a generous and rewarding Father. *"But without faith, it is impossible to walk with God and please Him, for whoever comes near to God must necessarily believe that God exists and that He rewards those who earnestly and diligently seek Him."* (Hebrews 11:6 AMP Bible)

Today's eloquent false prophets of Prosperity, are wolves disguised as sheep. Their sleek questions are similar to those that Satan asked Eve in the Garden of Eden. **"Do you really believe God wants you to be poor?"** Before you can answer them, they answer the question by selecting Bible verses out of context and twisting the meaning and intention of God's Word. They tell us, "God doesn't want you to be poor. He wants you to be rich and enjoy the more abundant life that this world has to offer you."

Many of God's "Servants of Prosperity" often quote Jesus' words in

John 10:10: "*I have come that they may have life, and that they may have it more abundantly.*" They use this verse of scripture to support their "Message of Prosperity." They claim that Jesus died on Calvary's Cross to provide not only salvation for us but also a more abundant and prosperous life of worldly treasures, while we're alive on earth.

Using this scripture as a teaching of prosperity is an outright lie. **Eternal Life, is the abundance of Life that Jesus is talking about in the entire tenth Chapter of John**. The Prosperity Message is a twisted distortion of Jesus' holy teachings!

Their "Message of Prosperity" is comparable to Satan's message to Eve in the Garden of Eden, in that it deceives us and causes us to lose our focus on God. It shifts our focus from pleasing God to pleasing ourselves.

Instead of soaring on the wings of eagles doing spiritual kingdom work and pleasing God, our spiritual eyes shift to focusing on the pleasures of this world, looking for angle worms and night crawlers to appease the pleasures of our flesh. We act like turkeys strutting around on earth seeking earthly food, clothing, and shelter, and everything else that this world has to offer us.

The Bible says, there were rich and poor people before Jesus who died and God's Holy Spirit brought Him back to life. **Jesus didn't die so we could be rich on earth, that's a lie**.

Jesus did not die, so people could be physically healed by his stripes, that's a lie. People were physically healed and brought back to life before Jesus was born as a human.

Jesus came and died in our place, He is our scapegoat, for our death sentence so that we can be saved from spending eternity in Hell **if** we choose to believe in Jesus as the Messiah, and make him the Lord of our life.

Jesus died to confer the blessing that God had promised Abraham in Genesis 12:3 and 18:18 — that *"all peoples and all nations on earth will be blessed through you."* This blessing is not a

CHAPTER 19 - THE CONDITION OF TODAY'S CHURCH

promise of a more abundant life of worldly possessions. Abraham was rich with possessions. Before Jesus came to Earth, peoples of all nations were separated from God, enemies of God, and dead to God.

"But Christ has rescued us from the curse pronounced by the law. When he was hung on the cross, he took upon himself the curse for our wrongdoing. For it is written in the Scriptures, *"Cursed is everyone who is hung on a tree." Through Christ Jesus, God has blessed the Gentiles with the same blessing he promised to Abraham, so that we who are believers might receive the promised Holy Spirit through faith."* (Galatians 3:13-14)

Jesus told us, *"I am the gate; whoever enters through me will be saved. They will come in and go out, and find pasture. The thief comes only to steal and kill and destroy; I have come that they may have life, and have it to the full."* (John 10: 9-10).

The abundant life Jesus promised is **Eternal Life**. *"That they may know You, the only true God, and Jesus Christ whom You have sent."* (John 17:3)

Eternal Life occurs when we believe in Jesus. Our believing opens the gate to our having a loving and obedient relationship with our heavenly Father. This is why Jesus died. This is the Gospel Message of Jesus Salvation and the kingdom of heaven that we must preach to all peoples of all nations.

Jesus died to remove sin's power and penalty, so when we trust Christ Jesus for our salvation and repent, Father God removes the penalty of sin from us, sprinkles the blood of Christ Jesus on our heart, cleaning us from our sins, and gives us the power to overcome sin in our lives with the Holy Spirit indwelling in our body.

The difference between today's Church and the First-Century Church is the **attitude of repentance** and the **attitude of worship**. The First-Century Church came together in the name of Jesus, to give thanks, praise, and worship to God. They were a house of prayer. Their ministry and mission was, and still is, to save souls and make disciples of all peoples and nations.

Today many Christians Churches have lost their way. The purpose, vision, and focus, of making disciples of Jesus is no longer their number one mission. Hope and expectation in the First-Century Church were alive. They waited, looked, longed, and hoped for Jesus to return.

Today's Church must seek and find the attitude of worship that the First-Century Church had. We must preach the uncompromised Good News Gospel of Jesus and the Kingdom of Heaven, just the way Jesus taught the First-Century Saints to preach it.

True revival and fire will return to the Church of today," <u>when we fall back in love with Jesus</u>. It is the Father's will that we seek and establish a real loving and obedient relationship with Him, through His Son, Jesus.

In order for us to love, obey, and do the Father's will, we need to believe that Jesus is who He says he is; the only Begotten Son of God. We must turn away from the altars of this world and face God, as we repent confessing our sins and renewing our covenant with God. By faith we rebuild our relationship through Jesus, with the Father. Now we must lay down on the altar of God as a living sacrifice unto Him.

Salvation is a day by day life of walking with God in a loving obedient relationship. God is not onto affairs, He wants a relationship with you

MY PRAYER FOR THIS BOOK

Heavenly Father, in the Name of Messiah Jesus, I ask you to use this book for your glory so that millions of souls may be saved and brought to a greater understanding of you and a closer relationship with you.

May a fresh anointing fall on those who read this book; may they never be the same. I pray that millions of people will be filled with a deep compassion to accomplish the mission of reconciliation that Jesus assigned all of us Christians to do.

Father, I also ask that you grant us the wisdom to understand the authority and power to use the Name of Jesus to accomplish our mission.

May This Book be translated into many different languages and the Co-Authors and editors that perform the translation be blessed and able to teach their culture of the **Good News about Jesus Christ** all over the world, making disciples of Christ our Savior.

Thank You Father God for Your grace, mercy, love, forgiveness, and for hearing and answering our prayer. In the mighty name that is above all names, in the name of Your Only Begotten Son, **Jesus**, we pray. Amen!

ABOUT THE AUTHOR

I was born in Lincoln, Maine, in 1950 and raised in a poor God-fearing Christian family who loved and respected God. Like many teenagers, I rebelled against my parents during my early teens. By the time I began my junior year in high school, I was ready to trade my relationship with God for popularity, pride, recognition, and worldly friends. I turned away from God and left Him behind, thinking I didn't need Him.

Smoking cigarettes, drinking, swearing, and disobeying my parents and God's instructions became my new habits. My relationship I had with God, as a child and young teenager with a desire to become an evangelist preaching the Good News about Jesus, was gone.

After I graduated from high school, I enlisted in the US Army and volunteered to go to Vietnam. I spent one year with the 75th Ranger battalion's November Company, attached to the 173rd airborne division at L Z English in Bong Son Vietnam . I volunteered for an additional six-month tour with the 2nd Ranger Command located in the western central highlands in Pleiku, Vietnam.

During my 18 months at war in Vietnam, whenever I got into bad situations that I couldn't control or get out of, I would turn to God, make some promises, and stay with God just long enough for Him to get me out of my trouble or situation. Then, I would turn my back and leave Him again, <u>not keeping the promises that I had made to Him</u>.

I did drugs and drank alcohol, ran with prostitutes, cursed God, and committed many other sinful acts during my time in Vietnam. There were situations during the Vietnam War in which I should have been killed or maimed for life, yet God took care of me. **Why?**

In 1971, at the age of 21, I got out of the US Army and got married. I allowed the corporations, companies, and the worldly systems I worked for to define my success and my purpose in life. The moral, ethical, and spiritual teachings that I'd received in my early years of life were altered, twisted, and replaced by what appeared to be a more lucrative lifestyle that affected my belief and behavior. I was accepted by the world. I was somebody, or so I thought. To sum it up, I was an ideal sinner, one of Satan's best. **Prideful** of what I had accomplished, what I been through, what I had become, and who I was.

After 40 years of living a life in a worldly structure of lust, selfishness, and pleasing myself, I had hit rock bottom. In the fall of 2002, at the age of 52, I had just gone through a divorce, ending a marriage of thirty-one years. <u>I'd broken all the promises and vows I'd made to God during my entire life.</u>

My word, my integrity, my value, and my purpose for living was gone. I was drinking, smoking, and heading out into the world looking for more sin and destruction. I was a broken man in spirit and in finances, and humbled before God.

I began to read the Bible and meditate on what I read. The Holy Spirit began convicting me of the past 40 years of sin and running away from God. I heard a voice inside me say, "***Come back to me.*** *I love you. No matter how many drugs, no matter how many prostitutes, no matter how much whiskey and beer you drank, in spite of you instigating your divorce, no matter what …* <u>*I love you just as you are*</u>. *I died for you and all the sins you have committed. If you turn away from this sinful, evil life-style,* **I will change you.** *Just repent and surrender to me*, and I'll extract you out from the thick jungle canopy of slavery and sin that Satan has you chained and addicted to. *I'll cleanse you with the purifying blood of Jesus and teach you what to do and say*".

On a cold winter night in February of 2003, I gave up. I surrendered my life in exchange for what God had offered me. I went **all in** for Jesus. I entered through the Narrow Gate and prayed, "God, I know you're real, and I believe in you. I'm a terrible sinner and have lived a life of sin against you. I was ashamed of you and turned my back on you when I was a teenager. I chose my school friends and the lifestyle of the world over what you offered. And now, I am ashamed of all the sins I committed against you and what I did to you all during my life. I am unworthy of your love. I failed you!"

ABOUT THE AUTHOR

So I began to search the Bible to see what God said about such a sinful person. I read that Jesus loved me so much that He came to Earth as God in the flesh and died for me, so that my sins would be forgiven if I confessed them to God.

Jesus said that no matter what sin I had committed; stealing, lying, adultery, homosexuality, pornography, divorce, hating and mistreating people, God would forgive me. All I needed to do was to **_turn from my wicked ways_**, _repent from my heart, believe in Jesus as the Son of God_, and _obey His teachings_. If I did this, He would forgive me.

On a Cold February night in 2003, with a heart full of remorse, shame, and sorrow, I knelt down on my rented apartment floor in Sanford, Maine. I put my cigarette out and pushed my glass of scotch and water away, and <u>without knowing how to pray</u>, I began to talk to Jesus. I asked God to forgive all my sins that I could remember, as well as all those that I couldn't remember, and accept me just the way I was. I pleaded with God not to turn me away because I had been in the pig-pen of life. I asked Him to wash me in the blood of Jesus, so that I would be clean to serve Him.

I pledged to do anything as long as He would allow me to become His son. I began to tell God that I was not worthy to be a son in His kingdom, **but before I could say anything else, I felt this big, strong, warm arm slide around me.**

I asked God for His Holy Spirit to come into me and give me the strength to live and do His will. I had never felt that kind of warmth before. God's Holy Spirit was all over me. Before I could complete the sentence "I am not worthy," **I felt Satan's chains of addictions and bondage, all of them, break away from me.** <u>I was free of sin</u> it was like lying on the back of eagle, soaring into the sun.

After all the sins I had committed against God, He forgave me. **He saved my soul from Hell**. He gave me His Holy Spirit to live inside me.

Then, I asked God if I could have an anointing to serve Him and tell others of the Good News of Jesus and what He has done for them. I asked

God if my hands could touch others and pray for them to be made whole spiritually and physically, displaying His glory in signs, wonders, and miracles.

The first miracle He performed was that He healed me from the inside out. I became a new man as the Holy Spirit convicted me of many sinful acts and attitudes. As I read the Bible, the Holy Spirit created a desire within me to seek God in a closer relationship.

God said, "*I have washed you and cleansed you in the blood of Jesus. I put clean clothes on you and have shod your feet.* **You are My son.** *I am with you.*

I have sealed you with the seal of the Holy Spirit, who will always be with you and will teach you all things. You must love Me, obey Me, and always walk in My ways. I'll never hurt you, and I'll never leave you. You will become a disciple and teach others the Good News about Me and how to become disciples. I will be with you *until the end of time.*"

Jesus gave me a purpose and a mission for life. He has allowed me to see a nineteen-year-old young man in Trinidad who couldn't walk – get up out of the wheelchair and walk.

God has used my hands to touch and pray for a boy in Tanzania as God removed a tumor from his head. He allowed me to be used in Tanzania to pray for a woman who was possessed by an evil spirit. We prayed and commanded the evil spirit to come out of her body and leave her. She was delivered and set free, and she gave her life to Jesus.

God has allowed me today to introduce to you His Only Begotten Son, Jesus, the undisputed Savior of the World and King of Heaven and Earth. He loves you and wants to establish a loving relationship with you. The time has come to fall into a deep, loving relationship with Jesus. He told us: "*Behold, I am coming soon! My reward is with me, and I will give to everyone according to what he has done.*" (Revelations 22:12).

Author;

Danny Clifford

ABOUT THE AUTHOR

If this book has blessed you, tell others, get one for your friends.

I have written two other books;

1. ***Lost Behind Enemy Lines***: available in Paperback, Audio, and E book.

2. ***Who Do You say I Am***: available in Paperback, Audio, and E-book.

If you're a Church group and want my Pastor and spiritual mentor, Prophet Daniel Senga or I, to come and share with you about Jesus and reviving today's Church, contact us at: **http://www.jarme.org**

Thank you!

May God bless and keep you in His care.

Author and Pastor

Danny Clifford

www.ingramcontent.com/pod-product-compliance
Lightning Source LLC
Chambersburg PA
CBHW070730020526
44118CB00035B/1130